Power & Security

Power & Security

Critical Choices for Americans

Volume IV

Edward Teller

Hans Mark

John S. Foster, Jr.

Lexington Books
D.C. Heath and Company
Lexington, Massachusetts
Toronto   London

Library of Congress Cataloging in Publication Data

Teller, Edward, 1908-
   Power & security.

   (Critical choices for Americans; v. 4)
   Prepared for the Commission on Critical Choices for Americans.
   Includes index.
   1. Energy policy—United States. 2. United States—National security.
3. Technology—United States. I. Mark, Hans Michael, 1929-   joint
author. II. Foster, John S., 1922-   joint author. III. Commission on
Critical Choices for Americans. IV. Title. V. Series.

HD9502.U52T44   333.7   75-44722
ISBN 0-669-00416-2

International Standard Book Number: 0-669-00416-2

Library of Congress Catalog Card Number: 75-44722

Foreword

The Commission on Critical Choices for Americans, a nationally representative, bipartisan group of forty-two prominent Americans, was brought together on a voluntary basis by Nelson A. Rockefeller. After assuming the Vice Presidency of the United States, Mr. Rockefeller, the chairman of the Commission, became an ex officio member. The Commission's assignment was to develop information and insights which would bring about a better understanding of the problems confronting America. The Commission sought to identify the critical choices that must be made if these problems are to be met.

The Commission on Critical Choices grew out of a New York State study of the Role of a Modern State in a Changing World. This was initiated by Mr. Rockefeller, who was then Governor of New York, to review the major changes taking place in federal-state relationships. It became evident, however, that the problems confronting New York State went beyond state boundaries and had national and international implications.

In bringing the Commission on Critical Choices together, Mr. Rockefeller said:

As we approach the 200th Anniversary of the founding of our Nation, it has become clear that institutions and values which have accounted for our astounding progress during the past two centuries are straining to cope with the massive problems of the current era. The increase in the tempo of change and the vastness and complexity of the wholly new situations which are evolving with accelerated change, create a widespread sense that our political and social system has serious inadequacies.

We can no longer continue to operate on the basis of reacting to crises, counting on crash programs and the expenditure of huge sums of money to solve our problems. We have got to understand and project present trends, to take command of the forces that are emerging, to extend our freedom and wellbeing as citizens and the future of other nations and peoples in the world.

Because of the complexity and interdependence of issues facing America and the world today, the Commission has organized its work into six panels, which emphasize the interrelationships of critical choices rather than treating each one in isolation.

The six panels are:

Panel I: Energy and its Relationship to Ecology, Economics and World Stability;

Panel II: Food, Health, World Population and Quality of Life;

Panel III: Raw Materials, Industrial Development, Capital Formation, Employment and World Trade;

Panel IV: International Trade and Monetary Systems, Inflation and the Relationships Among Differing Economic Systems;

Panel V: Change, National Security and Peace;

Panel VI: Quality of Life of Individuals and Communities in the U.S.A.

The Commission assigned, in these areas, more than 100 authorities to prepare expert studies in their fields of special competence. The Commission's work has been financed by The Third Century Corporation, a New York not-for-profit organization. The corporation has received contributions from individuals and foundations to advance the Commission's activities.

The Commission is determined to make available to the public these background studies and the reports of those panels which have completed their deliberations. The background studies are the work of the authors and do not necessarily represent the views of the Commission or its members.

This volume is one of the series of volumes the Commission will publish in the belief that it will contribute to the basic thought and foresight America will need in the future.

WILLIAM J. RONAN
Acting Chairman
Commission on Critical Choices
for Americans

Members of the Commission

EDWARD TELLER
Senior Research Fellow, Hoover Institution
on War, Revolution and Peace,
Stanford University

ARTHUR K. WATSON*
Former Ambassador to France

MARINA VON NEUMANN WHITMAN
Distinguished Public Service Professor
of Economics, University of Pittsburgh

CARROLL L. WILSON
Professor, Alfred P. Sloan
School of Management,
Massachusetts Institute of Technology

GEORGE D. WOODS
Former President, World Bank

Members of the Commission served on the panels. In addition, others assisted
the panels.

BERNARD BERELSON
Senior Fellow
President Emeritus
The Population Council

C. FRED BERGSTEN
Senior Fellow
The Brookings Institution

ORVILLE G. BRIM, JR.
President
Foundation for Child Development

LESTER BROWN
President
Worldwatch Institute

LLOYD A. FREE
President
Institute for International Social Research

*Deceased

J. GEORGE HARRAR
Former President
Rockefeller Foundation

WALTER LEVY
Economic Consultant

PETER G. PETERSON
Chairman of the Board
Lehman Brothers

ELSPETH ROSTOW
Dean, Division of General and Comparative Studies
University of Texas

WALTER W. ROSTOW
Professor of Economics and History
University of Texas

SYLVESTER L. WEAVER
Communications Consultant

JOHN G. WINGER
Vice President
Energy Economics Division
Chase Manhattan Bank

Preface

America's greatness has been influenced by its leadership in energy and technology development and its strong commitment to national security. Yet, in contemporary America, all three are being looked at anew and are being re-examined in terms of their mission and contribution to the national purpose.

To help in the development of policy options, and to assist in bringing the wide spectrum of materials and proposals into sharper focus, the Commission on Critical Choices for Americans asked authorities in the areas under study to prepare reports to the Panels in their fields of special expertise. Three of these reports appear in this volume.

Dr. Edward Teller was requested to develop a pragmatic program for meeting the United States energy needs by the year 2000 for the Commission's Panel I study of "Energy and Its Relationship to Ecology, Economics and World Stability." He was asked to set forth an action plan with as much specificity as possible, including additional United States energy production, conservation measures, national security and financial consideration. Dr. Teller's report is an important contribution to the energy field. Uniquely, it proposes how the United States can meet its own needs and even become an exporter of oil and coal by 1985.

Dr. Hans Mark was asked to examine America's role in technology development. Although its world leadership position in a number of areas is no longer as certain as it once was, the United States still retains unchallenged leadership in the vital area of technology development. Dr. Mark suggests that it is time Americans explicitly recognize their historical as well as present strength in this field and build this into new definitions of our national purpose.

Dr. John S. Foster, Jr. was asked to discuss the trends in the military balance between the United States and the Soviet Union in a report to the Commission's Panel V, "Change, National Security and Peace." In its study of the United States role in the world, the Panel would not have had time to examine in detail the polarized opinion regarding this nation's military preparedness. Dr. Foster's report provided the Panel an opportunity to examine all the elements of the United States' relationship with the rest of the world. He offers alternative national choices on the needed military posture for our national security and suggests basic objectives for United States military policy.

W.J.R.

Contents

List of Figures

List of Tables

Introduction

Energy, the force behind America's economic and industrial greatness; technology, the American genius behind that force; defense, the strength that enables us as a nation and people to live our lives in freedom. Together, these three contribute even more powerfully to America's greatness.

Today, many debates are stirring the national conscience. For example, in energy, "Does the United States want to be self-sufficient in energy? Must we continue to rely on imports from the OPEC exporting nations?" In technology, "In what areas should we concentrate priorities? How is it best funded?" In defense, "How much spending is necessary to assure continued national security? How should the Soviet Union's military buildup be viewed—or matched?"

To help define the facts and clarify the issues of the debate—and to outline the choices confronting us—the Commission invited Dr. Edward Teller—(Energy), Dr. Hans Mark—(Technology), and Dr. John S. Foster, Jr.—(Defense) to write the authoritative reports that follow. Their work—and their insights—themselves are a notable public service and a contribution to America's view of a secure and noble future.

I Energy—A Plan for Action

Edward Teller

1. Introduction

Early in 1942, President Roosevelt made a decision that changed the course of history. He called on American industry to build 60,000 planes which would win World War II. The first reaction to the plan was incredulity from friend and foe.

In January 1975, President Ford, in his State of the Union message, reminded us of that great episode of World War II. He had good reason to do so. Today, we are rapidly approaching troubles that may well become as great as the Second World War. There is no blood—yet. There is no hatred—yet. If we take the right course, violence and hatred may be averted.

It is a great privilege to participate in the work of the Commission on Critical Choices for Americans. My thanks go to those members of Panel I, "Energy and Its Relationship to Ecology, Economics and World Stability," who participated in our several meetings and provided many illuminating and constructive comments. I am particularly grateful to the intellectual stimulation and the breadth of vision coming from Vice President Nelson A. Rockefeller.

It was the devoted work of my associates, Martha L. Golar, Ann D. Fogle, and Tom G. Berliner, and most particularly, Raymond A. Gilbert, who made it possible to pull together our results into a coherent form.

My associates at the Lawrence Livermore Laboratory, Olivette A. Chinn, Gary H. Higgins, and Stuart D. Winter made important contributions.

Valuable advice was given by Hans Mark, director of the NASA Ames Research Center and George A. Lincoln, professor of economics and International Studies, University of Denver, and former director of the Officof Emergency Preparedness.

The topics discussed in this report are so broad and expertise is so widely distributed that a claim to completeness would make no sense. I am grateful to many friends for suggestions, objections, and discussions which helped us to fill in some obvious gaps.

But the right course must certainly not be business as usual. If we allow historic trends to continue, energy shortage will turn into energy crisis and finally into fatal energy disease. Neither will it do to continue to dream. The bucolic ideas of "limits to growth" will lead to disaster as surely as simple continuation of past patterns of action. We cannot go forward or backward along simplistic, straight lines. We must find new directions.

This proposal may shock the reader. It is analogous to Roosevelt's 60,000 planes. Without those planes, we would live in a terrible world today. The American genius could do what was necessary to win the war a third of a century ago. It can do now what is required to prevent conflict over energy and to start the work that will satisfy the needs of all people.

There are some requirements which are novel: foresight and patience.Four years sufficed to win World War II. It may take the rest of the twentieth century before a realistic solution will have been found to the problem whose parts are ample energy, clean environment, satisfaction of economic needs, and world stability.

2. Measuring Energy

Most people think of energy in terms of fuel, that is, gallons of gasoline, barrels of oil, cubic feet of gas, and tons of coal. They also think of energy in terms of everyday usage like kilowatt-hours of electricity. However, it is possible to measure energy in its own terms. In this report we shall use a unit accepted by technical people but not widely known to the public: the quad. (In 1973, the State of Iowa [population about 2.8 million people] used about one quad of energy for all purposes.)

The reason for using this unit is that it is precisely defined (it is based on the British thermal unit or Btu, which is defined as the amount of energy required to raise the temperature of one pound of water one degree Fahrenheit) and it is a convenient size for measuring national needs. A quad is short for one quadrillion Btu (1,000,000,000,000,000 Btu or 10^{15} Btu).

Table I-1 gives some useful conversion factors.

3. Summary and Objectives

Before giving the details of our plan, some general points will be summarized.

Our objective is to have sufficient energy that is inexpensive, clean and secure.

In the 1950s and 1960s, energy was inexpensive and its price was falling. Postwar recovery and the prosperity of the industrialized nations depended on the availability of energy. The sources of energy were secure and we imagined that they would remain secure.

Table I-1

Measuring Energy in Quads: Some Useful Conversion Factors

1 quad per year	= 0.472 million barrels of oil per day*
	= 1 trillion cubic feet of gas per year
	= 44.4 million tons of coal per year**
	= 33.4 million kilowatts of electricity
	= 293 billion kilowatt-hours of electricity per year at 100% efficiency
	= 95.2 billion kilowatt-hours of electricity per year at 32.5% efficiency

Note: Because of the inherent inefficiency in generating electricity from conventional heat sources, about 3.0 to 3.3 quads of energy from oil, gas, coal or nuclear are required to produce one quad of electricity.

*1 barrel = 42 gallons.

**For medium heating value coal at 11,250 Btu/1b or 22.5 million Btu/ton.

During the first half of this period little thought was given to the question of pollution. In the 1960s, pollution became an obvious problem. Steps were taken to legislate cleanliness. At that time the availability of energy was taken for granted.

Today, the law of the land recognizes that the time of neglect of the ecosphere is gone and industry can no longer ignore environmental concerns. On the other hand, the United States can no longer count on ample, dependable supplies of inexpensive and clean fuels. Appropriate trade-offs must be made, for example, between limiting emissions and the availability of reliable power, so that our domestic economy and essential services are not compromised. However, any change of existing strict environmental statutes must be fully justified. Wherever possible these changes should be temporary.

At the same time, we must maintain our commitment to an improvement of our environment, including urgent elimination of health hazards. Further improvements must be made with the help of research to establish necessary and realistic standards and to develop methods of pollution abatement which can keep the environment as clean as possible at a price we can afford.

In addressing the relationship between energy and the environment, the key concept is balance. We suggest that it is necessary and urgent to review current federal, state, and local environmental legislation to establish an appropriate balance between a clean environment and adequate energy production and use. Ambient air standards essential to protect health (primary air standards) must be maintained, but it may be prudent to defer temporarily requirements to meet more stringent standards (secondary air standards), at least in some regions. To protect air quality some state and local governments have imposed general restrictions on the quality of the fuels that may be burned. These restrictions, aimed at ensuring that air quality standards are not exceeded, may be unnecessarily strict. Fuels which exceed these state or local quality standards can frequently be burned in plants, if stacks are high or if weather conditions are favorable, without violating the primary standards which are essential to human health.

The Threat

For some years exhaustion of our energy supplies has caused worries among a few. Then the oil embargo and the precipitous rise in the price of oil in the fall of 1973 brought into focus for the whole world the painful and critical energy shortage.

The functioning of the advanced industrial countries has been tied to oil. Other energy sources can and will be developed. But this will take years, even decades. Oil produced in new areas (like Alaska and the North Sea) will give some relief in a few years; a thorough exploitation of even the known basins in the United States will take more time. The worldwide energy shortage will be with us for a long period. The shortage has severe consequences which will become more critical in the next few years.

Within the United States, we are threatened by acute shortages which may be caused by a new oil embargo or by an interruption of sea traffic. The energy shortage will cause a further slowdown of our economy and could lead to its collapse. Cold homes, a gasoline shortage, increase of unemployment, and troubles with foreign exchange are some of the possible consequences. An epidemic of bankruptcies similar to those that occurred in the 1930s cannot be excluded.

Month by month, the outlook has become darker. The winter embargo of 1973-1974 found us in a relatively strong position. A new shortage may do much more damage. Increasing inflation may wipe out all savings. Unemployment may easily exceed the ten million figure. The postwar generation—which has never experienced real hardship—may find out what deprivation and hunger mean.

Domestic disturbances may become severe, but the situation abroad is worse. Payment of $100 billion per year to the Organization of Petroleum Exporting Countries (OPEC) members and formation of surplus capital in the Arab OPEC countries ($60 billion in 1974) are danger signals. Italy and England are on the verge of insolvency. The almost complete dependence of Japan on imported energy will cause profound damage. The tripling of fertilizer prices may bring about the starvation of millions more on the subcontinent of India and elsewhere. Trouble and despair abroad are bound to react on our own country. Our interdependence with other countries was demonstrated when the October War of 1973 triggered the oil crisis. Similar and more dangerous situations affecting wide regions or even the whole world may well occur in the near future.

The Response

It is urgent to take radical but realistic measures to resolve the interrelated problems of energy, ecology, economics, and world stability. The United States has responded successfully to other challenges. The mobilization of our industry during World War II, including a plan to build 60,000 planes, is one example. Actually, more than 125,000 planes were built in a single year. Our success in landing a man on the moon impressed the world. Our reaction to the oil embargo was, by comparison, insufficient. When the embargo was lifted and President Nixon declared that the crisis was over, even the little progress in energy conservation and public awareness that had been made began to disappear.

Within the next year, progress can be made by implementing a national conservation ethic, by introducing available energy-saving devices, by removing barriers to increased energy production, and by establishing better cooperation among energy-consuming nations. Necessary action to achieve these aims will be outlined in this report.

While we recognize the desirability of planning jointly with other advanced nations—and this is being done—the United States must also set its own house in order. Accordingly, our plan is primarily for the United States, but it also takes the needs of our allies into account. Indeed, many of our proposals are either for joint action or can be implemented, with suitable modifications, by other oil importing nations.

1985 Target

The main thrust of our proposal is to establish badly needed and realistic objectives and a plan for achieving them by the year 1985. The existence of a plan and public understanding of its objectives will make it easier to accept temporary difficulties and to avert dangerous developments. The elements of the plan include:

1. Economic and effective use of energy.
2. Substantially increased oil and gas production in known domestic basins.
3. Much greater use of coal.
4. Public acceptance of and greater use of nuclear energy.

Our purpose is to establish by 1985 a strong energy position that can serve as a basis for healthy development of our economy and that can provide badly needed help to our allies by exporting coal and oil from the United States. We propose to increase production of energy sources not requiring great innovative research. These are oil, gas, coal, and nuclear energy. As early as 1980, our oil imports and coal exports may balance if we pursue this program vigorously.[a]

Our target[b] is a domestic production of energy by 1985 that is 83 percent above the level of 1973, that is, an increase of 5.0 percent per year. This is generally more ambitious than plans proposed by others since the embargo. U.S. domestic demand for energy would increase only by 36 percent, that is, by 2.6 percent per year or by 1.8 percent per person per year.[c] This compares to an annual growth of 3.2 percent per person per year during the last ten years. Of the difference between 3.2 percent and 1.8 percent, approximately one-half is due to reduction in demand and one-half to more efficient and effective utilization of energy.

If our target is reached by 1985, the United States could export 13 percent of the energy produced domestically. This would include the export of a little less than three million barrels of oil per day, an amount which may be almost 10 percent of the expected oil requirements of our allies. In addition, we would export about a million tons of coal per day. These exports should have a moderating influence in the oil market and would suffice to protect any one country among our allies from the effects of an oil blackmail. Even the expectation of a modest U.S. oil export capability could deter the OPEC countries from limiting oil production to conserve oil underground instead of increasing production for export.

Conservation

Consumption can be influenced more rapidly than production. It is both necessary and possible to reduce U.S. energy consumption immediately. This can be done in a manner compatible with a healthy economy. The first step is the development of a national conservation ethic. A substantial and lasting contribution can also be made by the use of energy-conserving technology in our industry and our homes. The influence of these measures can be felt immediately and can increase with time.

Security of Supplies

The security of a substantial fraction of our oil imports will remain in jeopardy in the near future. Announcement of a plan for energy self-sufficiency may tend

---

[a]See Section 7 for our 1980 targets.

[b]See Section 7.

[c]We assume the following population estimates for the United States: 210.4 million in 1973, 230.9 million in 1985 and 250.7 million in 2000. The average annual exponential growths are thus 0.78 percent for 1973 to 1985 and 0.55 percent for 1985 to 2000. These figures are based on the U.S. Bureau of Census Series F Projections.

to discourage an oil embargo. It is necessary, however, to establish emergency measures, such as the legal and administrative bases for emergency allocation, rationing, and distribution systems, to be taken in case a new energy shortage should develop for whatever reason. These plans will reduce the impact of any shortage. Measures which are adopted jointly by the oil-consuming countries might be particularly effective.

Cost

The cumulative capital expenditures required to carry out this program up through 1985 are approximately $840 billion.[d] This amounts to a yearly investment of almost $80 billion in energy alone, which is about four times what we have spent for this purpose in the past. We believe that this is the most difficult condition that needs to be fulfilled if our plan is to be realized although heavy expenditures will be required in any case during the next decade. In order to finance this plan, other capital intensive programs may have to be cut back and capital formation must be stimulated both by direct and indirect government action. It may be necessary to increase the fraction of the gross national product going into private investment. How we do this and what we are willing to sacrifice for this purpose are critical choices connected with any energy plan.

Of the $840 billion, approximately $200 billion is to be spent on electric plants, including transmission and distribution systems. We believe that without continuing expansion of our electric utilities, our economy will not be healthy.

The capital investment to be spent on coal is considerably smaller, approximately $40 billion. Coal is our largest domestic source of fossil fuel and is a relatively inexpensive form of energy. We plan to expand its production most vigorously.

Oil and gas account for a capital investment of $300 billion. About $270 billion of this amount will have to be spent to meet increased domestic requirements while eliminating imports.

Approximately $50 billion of capital investment is to be spent on environmental improvements. Considering the justified public demand for a clean environment, this expenditure is not excessive.

Approximately $100 billion in capital investments will be needed to introduce energy-saving devices. We assume that funds would be spent on better utilization of energy rather than on the production of more energy wherever this is economically feasible. Added advantages of this approach are decreased pollution and conservation of resources.

In the period through the year 1985, $150 billion will be needed for investments which will produce energy after 1985. This gives a total of $840 billion. The distribution of these investment needs is summarized in Figure I-1.

---

[d]This figure and the following figures are given in 1973 dollars.

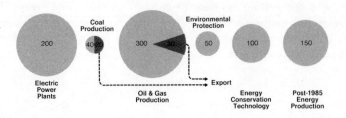

TOTAL $840 billion

Figure I-1. Investment Through 1985. Public and private (millions of 1973 dollars).

Of this $840 billion, approximately $50 billion is to develop the capability to export 9 quads per year or about a million tons per day of coal and 6 quads per year or nearly three million barrels per day of oil. We estimate that $20 billion in coal and $30 billion in oil are required to meet these export targets. This investment to change the status of the United States from a self-sufficient nation to an energy exporting nation, would put us into a position to influence the world energy market in an active way. The decision to become an energy exporter could be reversed as late as the early 1980s if international developments should take an unexpected turn which makes exports inadvisable.

Some of the $840 billion will produce revenue by the end of 1985. Offsetting these revenues, however, will be a comparable figure representing the cost of energy imports minus the payments received from energy exports.

For the sake of comparison (using a similar kind of accounting), we estimate that continued dependence on foreign oil could reduce the expenditure of $840 billion through 1985 by about $100 to $200 billion. The lesser expenditure would be due to a considerable reduction of capital investment which would be offset, in part, by a greater deficit in our balance of payments. In making a decision, one should consider that, according to our proposal, we would spend money at home which creates jobs. According to a more conventional approach, we would spend money abroad. Although this would be a lesser amount, it would not contribute to the U.S. economy in a similar manner.

Beyond the $840 billion of capital expenditures, about $40 billion will be required for research and development. (This includes private sector funding and is about twice the currently planned federal expenditures.) This corresponds to an annual research and development expenditure of about $4 billion—an amount not very different from the present practice if spending by government and by industry is included. The present research and development expenditures are not in an ideal balance. Industry emphasizes developments that are to bear fruit within the next couple of years. Government research, on the other hand, is oriented toward the next century. More should be done to take care of the next ten years. If we emphasize better exploitation of fossil fuels (better drilling equipment and advanced methods of fuel recovery) and short-term development of nuclear reactors (greater safety and a switch to abundant thorium as the main fuel), together with other medium-term developments, the cumulative expenditure of $40 billion for research and development will be an excellent investment. The results of research and development are uncertain; they may fall short or exceed expectations. In either event, the results may also be quite beneficial in fields other than energy.

In addition to the sums given above, about $20 billion will be required through 1985 for pilot, demonstration, and initial production plants to make sure of the technical and economic feasibility of new fuel production processes. Figure I-2 compares the funds needed for research and development and for pilot, demonstration and initial production plants on the same scale as Figure I-1.

Manpower

A problem, less conspicuous but possibly no less difficult, is the availability of properly trained manpower. A new technical problem requires new skills. The difficulty is that this general area did not receive proper emphasis in recent years.[e]

The Year 2000

While the next section contains our targets for 1985 and a plan for achieving them,[f] in the longer term we face different and less defined problems. By the year 2000, more abundant resources must be used in place of oil and gas. The proposed target for 1985 may result in the depletion of known domestic oil and gas resources by the end of the century. By the year 2000, we should, and we can, develop additional resources which are clean, available in sufficient quantity and not too expensive.

Our objective for the year 2000 is a healthy, global energy economy with ample, clean, and secure energy for everyone. One explicit goal is that the energy-poor, developing nations should not be put at a disadvantage because of energy, as they now are with the current high OPEC prices of oil.

[e]See Section 11.

[f]Section 6 contains recommendations for those actions which are urgently needed, in the large, to meet our targets for 1985.

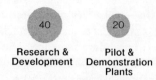

Research &   Pilot &
Development   Demonstration
Plants

Figure I-2. Other Costs Through 1985. Public and private (billions of 1973 dollars). Note that, through 1985, costs of research and development and of pilot and demonstration plants are small compared to investment.

For 2000, alternative policy options have to be considered. Potential energy resources are ample, but it is impossible to predict at this time which ones will be the cheapest, most plentiful, and compatible with environmental requirements. An example of how the U.S. energy demand and supply may evolve by 2000 is given in the last section. Figure I-3 compares demand and supply for 1973 with our 1985 target and our 2000 example.[g]

Research and Development[h]

In all phases of our program, special emphasis must be placed on research and development. This is needed in the next decade to increase efficiency in the production and utilization of energy. It is also needed to provide access to new energy sources and to remove uncertainties about the availability of these sources. The latter points are particularly important for the period beyond 1985. In some essential cases, like in situ coal gasification and shale oil production, we must move through research and pilot operations to small scale production by 1985. Only then will it be possible to plan realistically for the remainder of the century.

Conclusion

The proposal which we present here differs from other recent studies in two important points. One is that with respect to the international situation we have taken a positive stance of achieving not merely independence, but interdependence, whereby the United States will be in the position to make a positive contribution to the world economy.

The other difference is that we are emphasizing some technical possibilities which have not, as yet, received general acceptance. One of these is to

[g]See also Section 7.

[h]See Sections 9 and 10.

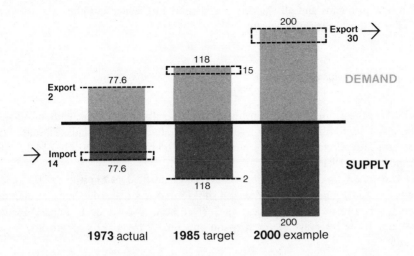

Note: Supply equals demand. Imports make up the difference between domestic production and supply, exports make up the difference between domestic consumption and demand.

Figure I-3. U.S. Energy Demand and Supply (in quads).

incorporate thorium in present nuclear reactor designs to produce uranium-233 as a readily available substitute for other nuclear fuels. Used in this manner, thorium, which is much more abundant and available worldwide, can solve the nuclear fuel shortage problem without a lengthy and expensive development program. The other is the use of in situ processes which, after a relatively brief research and development effort, may well make oil from shale and gas from deep coal deposits available sooner and at much less expense, either in dollars or in environmental damage, than equivalent surface processes.

Past discussions of the energy problem have either been confined to completely known technologies or have emphasized the longer range technologies that are, hopefully, ideal solutions, but which, in fact, are quite uncertain both technically and economically. We stress a strong technical development program which can produce significant results before 1985 and can provide the basis for further substantial progress through 2000 and beyond.

We believe that our target figures for 1985 are realistic and our plan for 2000 is illustrative of an open-ended, but determined and well-directed development effort.

One objective we do not address in this proposal: To solve the energy problem forever. Human ingenuity is great, but it is not possible to anticipate all the new problems and all the new possibilities with which our children will have to live in the twenty-first century.

4. Targets for the Year 1985

In 1973, the United States consumed domestically about 75.6 quads of oil and exported an additional 2.0 for a total demand of about 77.6 quads. To meet this demand, the United States produced about 63.5 quads and imported 14.1. (Net imports were 12.1 quads.)

Our target for 1985 is to constrain U.S. domestic consumption to 103 quads and to export 15 for a total demand of 118. To meet this demand, we plan on producing 116 quads and importing 2. (Net exports are to be 13 quads.) Figure I-4 and Table I-2 show energy demand and supply for 1973 and our targets for 1985.

To meet these targets, we will have to slow the rate of growth of domestic consumption. This can be done without lowering our standard of living or affecting, in any major way, our continued economic development. The key is conservation.

The increase in total domestic energy consumption from 75.6 quads in 1973 to 103 in 1985, would be at a slightly lower average annual growth rate than for the past decade. This increase, combined with a vigorous conservation program, should be sufficient for the strong, continued development of American industry.

We also must increase substantially our domestic production of oil, gas, coal, and nuclear power. In doing so, we will have to protect public health and safety and strive for a better, cleaner environment. The critical problem is the appropriate balance.

Conservation

We must begin at once a serious and continuing effort to conserve energy—particularly oil and gas. At the same time, our economy must remain vigorous if our targets for 1985 are to be reached.

The most serious problem is petroleum and this is exceedingly hard to resolve. Continued imports of oil on a large scale would hurt our trade balance, would deprive us of capital badly needed in other areas and would antagonize our allies who would consider us as an unwelcome competitor in the oil market. Import of gas is both expensive and dangerous. Therefore, we must find ways to live with less petroleum.

Reduced oil consumption will have the greatest impact on the transportation sector. The availability of oil and gas also affects electricity generation.

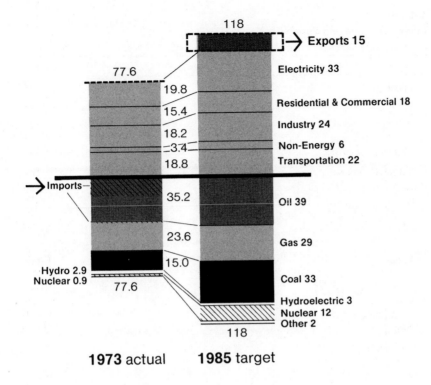

1973 actual   **1985** target

One quad per year = 0.472 million barrels of oil per day = 1 trillion cubic feet of gas per year = 44.4 million tons of coal per year. Also, one quad produces about 95.2 billion kilowatt hours of electricity at normal generating efficiencies. (See also Section 6, fig. 1-9.)

Figure I-4. U.S. Energy Demand and Supply (in quads).

In the transportation sector, where the United States has been extravagant, we plan a slight decrease in petroleum products consumed per person, per year, between now and 1980.[i] To accomplish this, the following measures should be implemented:

1. Strict enforcement of the 55-mile per hour speed limit.
2. A conservation ethic for private automobiles, which includes a drastic reduction in short trips and pleasure-driving and a substantial increase in car pools.
3. Cars with better gasoline mileage must be introduced. One straightforward way to do this may be to discourage the use of heavy cars by imposing a substantial annual federal license fee based on weight.

---

[i]See Section 7, Table I-6 for a breakout of the types of energy consumed in each demand sector.

Table I-2
Energy Demand and Supply
(All figures in quads per year = 10^{15} BTU's per year)

Demand		1973 Actual		1985 Target
Electricity[1]		19.8		33
Residential & Commercial[2]		15.4		18
Industry[2]		18.2		24
Non-Energy[3]		3.4		6
Transportation[2]		18.8		22
Subtotal—Domestic		**75.6**		**103**
Export		2.0		15
Liquids	0.5		6	
Gas	0.1		0	
Coal	1.4		9	
Totals		**77.6**		**118**
Supply				
Liquids		35.2		39
Conventional	22.2		35	
Shale	0.0		2	
Synthetic	0.0		1	
Imports	13.0		1	
Gas		23.6		29
Conventional	22.5		28	
Synthetic	0.0		2	
Imports	1.1		1	
Converted[4]	0.0		−2	
Coal		15.0		33
Nuclear		0.9		12
Hydroelectric		2.9		3
Other		0.0		2
Totals		**77.6**		**118**

1. Primary fuel demands—energy consumed by the electric utilities to produce electricity.
2. End-use sector totals exclude electricity consumed.
3. Includes 0.3 quads of liquids not accounted for in 1973. The item "non-energy" is the production of materials such as fertilizer and plastics which use coal or hydrocarbons for their substance rather than as a source of energy.
4. Gas which is converted to synthetic liquids (methanol).

4. Vehicles which have a relatively short lifetime and which are driven largely in metropolitan areas (taxis, small trucks) should be powered by diesel engines.
5. Increased support of public transportation systems.

In the case of electricity, savings are also essential, particularly in the residential and industrial sectors. To achieve these savings, the following means are available:

1. Practicing a conservation ethic.
2. Permitting electric rates to rise, not only to give the utilities a fair return, but also to accumulate capital for investment in new plant and to discourage waste of electricity.
3. Changing the electric utility rate structure to discourage excessive use of electricity, particularly during peak hours.
4. Replacing bulk metering of electricity in apartment houses with the metering of the consumption of individual tenants.
5. Encouraging the use of "bottoming cycles," that is, using a part of the exhaust heat, which at present causes thermal pollution, to drive additional generators using a low-boiling working fluid. This may be accomplished by taxing reject heat above a certain temperature. (It should be noted that the technology at low temperatures is more advanced than that at high temperatures.)

Among conservation measures in the residential and commercial sector, it is particularly important to use less fuel for heating, for air-conditioning, and for heating water. The proposed measures are:

1. Requirements for good insulation in new dwellings if a government loan is to be available.
2. Loans, or a tax rebate, for improving insulation in old dwellings, particularly in ceilings.
3. Research, regulations and incentives for better insulated mobile homes. (At present, they make up 40 percent of the market for single dwellings and are poorly insulated.)
4. Use of sunlight for hot water production, and for space heating and air-conditioning. (This source of available energy does not appear in Table I-2 since it goes hand-in-hand with insulation.)

Indirect as well as direct measures of conservation are needed. Reprocessing of discarded goods must be encouraged. It is even more important to cause manufactured goods to last longer by appropriate fabrication and by maintaining spare parts and repair facilities. The economics of rapid obsolescence is out of date. All of this is so important as to demand action by the government. Such actions may take the form of tax incentives and penalties, mandatory labeling of goods or other regulations.[j]

Altogether, we propose to invest, by 1985, $100 billion to save from 5 to 10

---

[j]See Section 6.

quads per year. This corresponds to an investment of more than $20,000 on the average to save a barrel of oil per day in the favorable case and twice that amount in the unfavorable case.[k] Another 5 to 10 quads per year would be saved by vigorously exercising a conservation ethic and by other means which are not capital-intensive.

Efforts to reduce consumption by applying new energy-saving technology will take time. Some companies, however, have found that they can reduce fuel consumption by about 30 percent with the help of energy-saving equipment now available and can amortize the capital investment within a year by reduced fuel consumption.

More than half of the capital expenditures on energy-saving devices should be spent before 1980. The public must participate in an effective drive to use less energy. The conservation ethic should be taught in schools; publicity and government initiatives are indispensable.

At the same time, the proposed moderate increase of per capita energy consumption is essential for the following reasons:

1. To maintain a reasonable quality of life for all Americans.
2. To assist the underprivileged whose energy consumption is largely for heating, cooking and travel to and from work.
3. To provide growth of industries sufficient to provide employment for all, including the underprivileged.

Target Demand[1]

In the electricity sector, our target is to increase the input from 19.8 quads in 1973 to 33 in 1985. We propose to accomplish this objective largely by increasing the use of coal and nuclear power, even while decreasing the use of oil and gas. Reduced oil and gas consumption may be offset by increased consumption of other energy sources such as solid waste and geothermal.

The residential and commercial sector, which consumed 19.1 quads in 1973 (15.4 of primary fuels and 3.7 of electricity), should increase to 24 quads in 1985 (18 of primary fuels and 6 of electricity). The figures on electricity may look low, but it should be remembered that about 3 quads of energy are needed to produce each quad of electricity. Thus, in 1985 generating the electricity for the residential and commercial sector will consume about as much primary energy as this sector will use directly. The increase, in addition to electricity, is to come largely from gas. We propose a decrease in the use of heating oil.

[k]We are actually proposing to spend more capital on saving a barrel per day of oil than on finding a barrel per day. This is justified both by a decrease of subsequent operating cost and by environmental considerations.

[1]See Section 7.

The industrial sector is to increase from 20.9 quads in 1973 (18.2 of primary fuels and 2.7 of electricity) to 29 quads in 1985 (24 of primary fuel and 5 of electricity). Again, the fuel consumption in generating electricity is three times greater than the figures given. We are proposing a slight decrease in oil consumption, offset by a similar increase in gas demand. The major increase is to be in the use of coal along with greater use of electricity. The actual availability of energy for industrial production will be even higher than indicated by these figures, since in the next eleven years we will introduce more efficient ways to utilize energy. A large expenditure of capital is justified for energy conservation purposes in the industrial sector.

The non-energy sector uses include fertilizers, plastics, and other petrochemicals, as well as asphalt, waxes, lubricants, and commercial solvents. In 1973, this portion of industry consumed 3.4 quads, of which 2.5 were of oil, 0.7 of gas, and 0.2 of coal. We are proposing that in 1985, we should consume 6 quads—2 of oil, 1 of gas, and 3 of coal. This suggestion represents a radical change from the past. Gas could be used in Alaska for non-energy purposes, but the equipment for its use there is presently nonexistent. Coal could be used by the petrochemical industries in the United States, as it was in earlier decades.

The transportation sector, aside from the gas used in pumping gas through interstate pipelines, is almost entirely dependent on oil. In 1973, the transportation sector consumed 18.8 quads (oil accounted for 18.0 quads or 8.5 million barrels per day); in 1985 we expect this figure to increase only to 22 quads (oil would account for 21 quads or nearly 10 million barrels per day).

We are also planning for the United States to become an exporting nation. Our target is to increase exports from 2.0 quads in 1973 to 15 in 1985 (6 quads or nearly three million barrels per day of oil and 9 quads or about a million tons per day of coal).

Table I-3 compares our 1985 target demand figures with estimates taken from other energy reports published since the 1973 embargo was lifted. (The table should be read column by column to compare the various approaches.)

Target Supplies

Increased domestic supplies of fossil fuels and nuclear power are essential to meet our targets. Some aspects of increased production are treated more fully in Section 7.

Electrical Energy.[m] The production of 6.4 quads of electricity in 1973 con-

---

[m]Our estimates of the energy required to produce electricity from non-fossil fuel sources (such as geothermal, hydroelectric and nuclear) are given as the equivalent fossil fuel energy which would be required. This equivalence is based on converting 10,500 Btu of heat to one kilowatt-hour of electricity or at an efficiency of 32.5 percent.

Table I-3
Estimates of Domestic Energy Demand
(Rounded to nearest 0.1 quad per year)

	Electricity	Residential & Commercial	Industry*	Transportation	Gross	Net**
FEA[1] – Accelerated Supply with Conservation						
Oil at $7 per barrel						
Primary Energy Sources	37.7	16.7	25.0	20.4 ·	99.7	
Including Electricity		23.7	29.3	20.4		73.4
Oil at $11 per barrel						
Primary Energy Sources	35.6	16.0	24.4	20.0	96.0	
Including Electricity		23.1	28.2	20.0		71.3
Ford Foundation[2]						
Historical Growth						
Primary Energy Sources	37.5	18.1	34.5	26.0	116.1	
Including Electricity		24.9	40.6	26.0		91.5
Technical Fix						
Primary Energy Sources	23.2	17.8	30.7	19.6	91.3	
Including Electricity		22.6	33.9	19.6		76.1
CED[3]						
Primary Energy Sources	31.0	15.5	33.5	25.0	105.0	

This Report

Primary Energy Sources	33	18	30	22	103
Including Electricity		24	35	22	81

*Includes non-energy.

**The figures in this column represent the energy *used*. They differ from the previous column by the energy wasted in generating electricity. The difference is substantial, but it must be realized that other energy-uses also are connected with some waste – a fact not evident in the table.

Sources:
1. Federal Energy Administration, *Project Independence Report*, November 1974.
2. Ford Foundation Energy Police Project, *A Time to Choose*, 1974.
3. Committee for Economic Development, *Achieving Energy Independence*, December 1974.

sumed somewhat under 20 quads (see Figure I-5). Our target for 1985 is to consume 33 quads in order to produce 11 quads of electricity. This corresponds to an annual increase of slightly less than 4.3 percent in the consumption of energy for the generation of electricity, which is well below the 6.7 percent average rate of increase during the 1960s. To achieve even this lower average rate of growth, it is necessary to establish a fair return to the utilities so that they can expand and improve their plants.

Actually, the amount of electricity produced should rise somewhat faster with the introduction of more efficient generating equipment, unless improved efficiencies are entirely offset by "losses" in environmental protection equipment (stack gas scrubbers, cooling towers). Savings should be achieved by eliminating current incentives to waste electricity, such as lower rates for high consumption. The recent general increases in electric rates may provide a significant incentive for savings, particularly for industrial and commercial concerns.

In order to better utilize electrical generating capacity, energy storage will be needed. This may be pumped storage reservoirs or advanced devices such as chemical storage, improved electric batteries or flywheels. If the storage is properly distributed, savings can be realized in the construction of transmission lines, as well as in central generating plants.

Specifically we project the 33 quads consumed by the electric utilities in 1985 will come from the following primary energy sources:

1. Nuclear plants will consume 12 quads. This could be accomplished by 1985 if nuclear plants are standardized, if their safety is improved and if nuclear

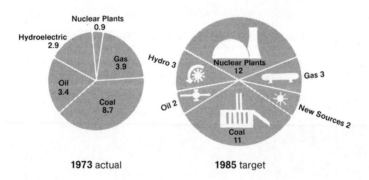

1973 actual   **1985** target

One quad of heat or hydro energy will produce 95.2 billion kilowatt-hours of electricity at a generating efficiency of 32.5 percent.

Figure I-5. Energy Required to Produce Electricity (in quads).

power gains public acceptance, and if, as a result, licensing and siting become easier. We recommended special attention be given to determining the feasibility of siting nuclear reactors underground.

2. Hydroelectric plants will account for 3 quads, which represents a very small increase over 1973 figures.
3. Coal will account for 11 quads. In the case of coal-burning plants, it will be necessary to improve the control of stack gases. Still, regulations requiring inflexible nationwide controls on sulfur must be temporarily modified in order to avoid a sharp increase in oil consumption and to encourage the orderly development of the coal industry.
4. Gas will account for 3 quads, which is less than was burned in 1973.
5. Oil consumption should be decreased to 2 quads or about one million barrels per day.
6. Two quads may be supplied from geothermal sources, from urban wastes, and possibly from other unconventional sources.

The total investment of $200 billion in electric plants and distribution systems corresponds to $25,000 per barrel of oil per day used in the generation of electricity. If the efficiency of electric generation can be increased to between 35 percent and 40 percent, the energy delivered as electricity would cost the equivalent of $70,000 per barrel of oil per day in capital. Although this is a high cost, one must realize that the use of electricity is flexible and in many respects is irreplaceable.

Oil. We propose to increase the domestic production of crude oil from 22.2 quads or 10.5 million barrels per day in 1973 to 35 quads or about 16.5 million barrels per day in 1985, as indicated in Figure I-6.[n] This sizable increase[o] requires immediate and thorough exploitation of known reservoirs and includes more complete recovery from existing and abandoned oil wells. It also requires vigorous development of and production from resources on the Northern Slope of Alaska, including Naval Petroleum Reserve Number 4, and the continental shelf, including the Santa Barbara Channel and the west coast of Florida. These programs require public acceptance which may be forthcoming if proper precautions are taken to avoid oil spills and if methods are perfected to clean up an oil spill, should it occur.

Because new oil discoveries require time to develop, it may not be the lack of oil deposits that will plague us, but a shortage of the means of producing oil. The previous low prices and easy accessibility to Middle East oil led to a drop in demand for oil rigs and drilling equipment which, in turn, led to the production curtailment of oil drilling platforms and rigs. Some manufacturing facilities here in the United States were converted to make other products. It will take

[n]These figures include liquids associated with gas.
[o]The justification for the feasibility of such an increase, which some may find surprising, is given in Section 8.

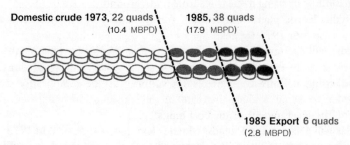

Domestic crude 1973, 22 quads   1985, 38 quads
(10.4 MBPD)   (17.9 MBPD)

1985 Export 6 quads
(2.8 MBPD)

One quad per year = 0.472 million barrels of oil per day. MBPD = million barrels of oil per day.

Figure I-6. U.S. Oil Production Target, 1985.

considerable time and money to build or rebuild the plants needed to provide the additional drilling equipment to meet the target.

To reach our target, we will have to improve our existing procedure for leasing public lands, placing emphasis on production performance rather than on revenue to the U.S. Treasury. For instance, it might be appropriate to commit an agreed level of funds to the development of the property, in lieu of a large lease payment. The government could obtain additional revenue through royalties.

An additional incentive for exploration might take the form of a government guarantee that the price for oil will not be allowed to drop below a "floor," which is appropriately indexed and which might be set initially at $7 per barrel in 1973 dollars. This price floor should be coupled with an excess profits tax which would apply to all earnings not used for appropriate reinvestments in energy, such as exploration, development, research, and environmental improvement.

To the 35 quads or about 16.5 million barrels per day of domestic crude production in 1985, we would add:

1. One quad or about one-half million barrels per day in the form of methanol (which, in addition to other uses, might be introduced as a valuable additive to gasoline). Methanol can be obtained from natural gas or coal. One possible location for production might be at the southern end of an Alaskan natural gas pipeline near Anchorage or Valdez.
2. Another 2 quads or about one million barrels per day produced from oil shale by in situ retorting methods. This is an ambitious target which can probably be reached if early priority is given to appropriate developments.

The proposed rate of oil production may well result in a great reduction of our oil reserves by the end of this century. The development of a method of producing oil from shale could compensate for the gap in oil reserves. It is necessary to push the development of oil shale beyond the pilot plant stage to moderate scale production as early as 1985.

We deliberately omit coal liquefaction above ground from our target for oil production. We consider existing methods for liquefaction of coal expensive, requiring too much water in arid regions, and necessitating relocation of hundreds of thousands of workers if western deposits are utilized. Therefore, we do not advocate this method for production, but only for research and development as insurance (to the extent of a demonstration plant to produce perhaps one-quarter quad per year) if other developments fail.

In addition to the production of oil estimated above, we recommend an import by pipeline of:

1. At least 1 quad per year or a half million barrels per day from Canada into the northern part of the Midwest.
2. One or 2 quads (one-half to one million barrels per day) from Mexico into the U.S. Southwest and California. This last item is not contained in our tables and may be considered as insurance.

We would thus have a total of 39 quads per year or about 18.4 million barrels per day of oil (without the Mexican supply) by 1985, from which we could export in oil tankers as much as 6 quads per year or three million barrels per day. This capability to export oil could have a profound effect on the OPEC and may well blunt the oil weapon.

Unfortunately, the development of new oil fields takes five to ten years. In fact, our target cannot be reached unless we sharply increase production of oil rigs, platforms, and other equipment as indicated above.

Our projected domestic supply of 38 quads per year of oil is smaller than the FEA maximum production of 42.4 quads per year under an "Accelerated Supply" scenario with oil at $11 per barrel.

Gas. President Ford took an important step toward increasing domestic production of gas by proposing decontrolling the prices of natural gas moving interstate. If gas prices are indeed decontrolled, or if the price ceilings are raised to levels approaching the prices of petroleum products, we expect domestic production of natural gas to increase from 22.5 quads in 1973 to 28 in 1985 as shown in Figure I-7. A considerable portion of this increase is expected to be associated with increased production of oil.

The measures needed to increase domestic gas production parallel those for increasing domestic oil production. They include new procedures for the leasing

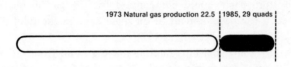

One quad = 1 trillion cubic feet of natural gas.

Figure I-7. U.S. Gas Production Target, 1985.

of public lands, increased production of necessary drilling equipment, and appropriate incentives to drill and develop marginal gas wells that are not sufficiently profitable under present interstate price ceilings for gas.

In addition to these 28 quads, we recommend the production of 2 quads from in situ gasification of coal. Just as the vigorous production of oil may result in the depletion of our oil reserves, justifying the accelerated development of shale oil, the danger of depleting our gas reserves through sharply stepped-up production of natural gas should be compensated by the development of in situ gasification of coal. By this technique, we could exploit deep, thick coal veins which are hardly accessible or are inaccessible with present methods.

We subtract 2 quads of gas from our totals to produce 1 quad of methanol. Although this process has a conversion efficiency of little more than 50 percent, the methanol is needed as an additive to gasoline. Also, it has the quality of a refined product and is easily transported.

Adding 1 quad of imports to the net domestic production contemplated in our scenario would bring the 1985 total to 29 quads per year.

Surface coal gasification plants run into many of the difficulties of surface shale oil production plants, but we recommend the development of a demonstration surface coal gasification plant as insurance against unforeseen difficulties in bringing in situ processes on line.

In 1973, we imported a little more than 1 quad of natural gas. To import liquified natural gas in ships is quite expensive and dangerous. We, therefore, advocate no imports of liquified natural gas. Gas might, however, be brought by pipeline, Trans-Canada, to the lower forty-eight states, probably as part of a joint energy policy between the United States and Canada,[p] or possibly from Mexico.

The capital expenditures for producing, refining, and distributing petroleum (oil and gas) is estimated to require a cumulative capital investment of $300 billion. Since practically all present oil wells and gas wells in the lower forty-eight states will be exhausted (or will require advanced recovery methods) by 1985, the $300 billion must be considered as the capital needed to produce

[p]A Trans-Canada pipeline may be necessary in order to meet our gas target for 1985.

domestically about 66 quads of petroleum and to construct the additional pipelines and refineries which will be required. To establish the production and distribution capability of one barrel per day, or its equivalent in gas, we propose to invest between $9,000 and $10,000 of capital or about one-half the capital estimated to conserve a barrel per day in better equipment.

Our capability to export 6 quads of oil per year (little less than three million barrels per day) can be established at a capital cost of about $30 billion.

Coal. It is proposed to increase coal production from 15 quads in 1973 to 33 in 1985, as indicated in Figure I-8. Coal is amply available, but mining equipment, means of transportation, capital, and environmental considerations may be serious constraints.

Most of the additional coal will probably come from surface mining in the western states. Expansion of coal production will require additional equipment (drag lines, drilling equipment, coal movers, tractors, and gondola cars), as well as incentives and possibly subsidies which might cover partial costs for some items, such as transportation and coal parks near utility boilers.

The number of miners engaged in surface mining in the West is quite limited; it need not exceed 20,000 men by 1985. Nevertheless, surface mining per se raises environmental objections. In most places, these objections can be met by careful restoration or improvement of the sites, although the shortage of water presents problems in arid areas. The value of the coal in Montana, Wyoming, and Alaska is several hundred thousand dollars per acre. This is enough to permit the necessary investment for site improvement. Indeed, such improvements are being made at present by some mining companies.

In addition to technical problems and environmental questions, it is not obvious how coal operators can acquire the land which is appropriate for surface

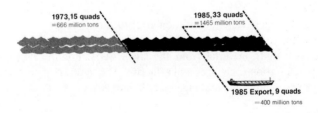

1973,15 quads
=666 million tons

1985,33 quads
=1465 million tons

1985 Export, 9 quads
=400 million tons

One quad is equal to 44.4 million tons of coal of medium heating value (11,250 Btu per pound).

Figure I-8. U.S. Coal Production Target, 1985.

mining. Leasing or sale of public land and appropriate arrangements for privately owned real estate must be worked out.

Of the 33 quads per year anticipated for 1985, we could export 9. At present, we are exporting coal mostly for metallurgical purposes. The additional exports discussed here should help to relieve the energy shortage in other parts of the world. Many developing countries can use coal almost as easily as oil. If we appear in the world market as a seller of 9 quads per year of coal, as well as 6 quads per year of oil, we will make a profound impression. If other strengths in our economy are maintained (in the fields of high technology and food) we could have the potential to act as a stabilizing factor in the world economy for many years to come. The capital investment (including environmental expenditures) needed for the export of 9 quads of coal will be about $20 billion.

Table I-4 compares our 1985 supply figures with estimates taken from other energy reports published since the 1973 embargo was lifted.

Environment, Health, and Safety

The plan we are discussing is compatible with an environment which is greatly improved compared to the present situation. To accomplish this, realistic steps must be taken to improve air quality at an acceptable cost. At the same time, the oceans must be protected against oil spills and the land against abuses which are connected with mining. Finally, serious hazards, which have caused a great deal of worry, must be eliminated.

In order to satisfy the requirements of improved environment and safety, we are proposing a capital investment of $50 billion to be spent by 1985. (The major part of this amount would be spent by the private sector and would influence the price of the final product, that is, the environmental costs would be "internalized.") Approximately one-half of the $50 billion would be spent in connection with the production and use of coal. Funds are needed to:

1. Restore land to an excellent condition after surface mining.
2. Remove sulfur from coal and oil before, during or after actual combustion.
3. Remove particulate material from the stack gases. For the larger particles, electric precipitation is cheaper and effective. The removal of smaller particles is yet to be accomplished and appears to be necessary.

The enforcement of environmental regulations must be timed, and possibly delayed, so as to make it possible to introduce adequately demonstrated, appropriate technological improvements, such as a practical means for ensuring clean stack emissions, in order to comply with the regulations. The initial developments are, to a considerable extent, jobs which may be carried out using government funds. The larger costs associated with purchasing and installing the necessary equipment would, of course, have to be borne by industry.

Table I-4
1985 Estimates of Domestic Energy Supplies
(Rounded to nearest 0.1 quad per year)

	Oil	Natural Gas	Coal	Nuclear	Other*	Totals
FEA[1] Maximum Production Levels						
Oil at $11 per barrel						
Business as Usual	31.8	23.4	24.8	7.0	4.6	
Accelerated Development	42.4	29.3	47.3	8.2	8.7	
Ford Foundation[2]						
Historical Growth						
High Domestic Oil and Gas	32	29	25	10	9	105
High Nuclear	32	29	23	12	9	105
Technical Fix						
Self-Sufficiency	30	27	16	8	4	85
Environmental Protection	29	26	14	5	4	78
CED[3]	28.5	26.5	21.5	10	8.5	95
NAE[4]	28.8	33.1	21.2	17.6	3.6	104.3
This Report	35	28	33	12	8	116

*Includes shale oil, synthetic oil and gas, hydroelectric, geothermal, solid waste, solar, etc.

Sources:

1. Federal Energy Administration, *Project Independence Report*, November 1974.
2. Ford Foundation Energy Policy Project, *A Time to Choose*, 1974.
3. Committee for Economic Development, *Achieving Energy Independence*, December 1974.
4. National Academy of Engineering, *U.S. Energy Prospects: An Engineering Viewpoint*, 1974.

Stack Gases. A standard for air quality has been legislated without sufficient knowledge of the harmful ingredients emitted into the air. One particularly interesting and important case is that of the sulfur oxides. The presence of more than 1 percent sulfur in much Eastern coal limits the use of that commodity.

Evidence is accumulating that the direct product of combustion, which is sulfur dioxide, is essentially not harmful. Further oxidation to sulfur trioxide, however, and the conversion of that substance into sulfuric acid and sulfates appears to produce a health hazard. The hazard is made more acute when the sulfates become absorbed by small, micron-sized particulates which deposit the dangerous sulfur compounds in the lungs. The conversion of the innocuous sulfur dioxide into harmful products may occur by the action of these small particulates.

We encounter here an important problem. Is it sufficient to eliminate the small particulates from the stack gases to avoid the danger that the harmful forms of sulfur will occur in the air? If so, the removal of the small particulates would be easier and less expensive than the avoidance or removal of the sulfur. Or do we have to assume that the dangerous sulfates will occur even if the small particulates are removed from the stack gas? The Environmental Protection Agency believes the answer to the latter question is yes. They do not have a convincing proof as yet. In view of a residual uncertainty the question merits detailed investigation.

It would, of course, be particularly worthwhile if simple, inexpensive methods were found to remove the sulfur from coal or oil before it is burned. In the sulfur-rich coals, however, half of the sulfur is usually not contained in the coal itself but in pyrites which can be separated out after the coal has been pulverized. To develop this technology appears worthwhile; the process probably will not be very expensive. Alternative processes consist in the removal of sulfur oxides during or after combustion. Both of these processes are available in principle, but they have not been thoroughly tested in practice. The disposal of the removed sulfur or sulfates is not a trivial question.

Automobiles. Another considerable part of the needed expenditures will have to be dedicated to cleaning up automobile emissions. Too little progress has been made in improving the engines in our automobiles to make them compatible with environmental standards or to improve fuel economy. One of the most difficult problems is how to induce the automobile manufacturers to perform the necessary research and development to be able to produce viable alternative modes of personal transportation. Automobiles which will consume less than half the energy of current medium-sized automobiles per vehicle-mile traveled, particularly in the "stop and go" traffic of metropolitan areas, are needed. Reducing the fuel consumed by one-half would also decrease pollution. In case electrical energy is used, the fuel needed to produce the electricity must, of course, be counted.

In the case of automobile emissions, nitrogen oxides, unburned hydrocarbons, and carbon monoxide play important roles. (Nitrogen oxides also occur in the stack gases of fossil fuel burning powerplants.) All these ingredients are harmful, but more detailed study of their effects needs to be undertaken. Novel proposals such as the stratified charge engine may bring about a great reduction in, but not an elimination of, some undesired by-products. It might be easier to control the formation of the contaminants in steadily burning, external combustion, or "steam engines" which, instead of steam, use an appropriate organic compound as the working fluid. Some simpler process such as mixing a little methyl alcohol and possibly water droplets with the gasoline might produce cleaner and more efficient burning in the internal combustion engine. Altogether, improvements of the automobile engine is a wide-open field.

The introduction of electric or hybrid cars (using a gasoline engine and batteries) is another possibility. Hybrid cars will be more expensive but would help considerably to decrease fuel consumption and pollution. It is particularly regrettable that in the last half-century, technically oriented research was not strongly supported in the automobile industry. A change in the "life style" of the Detroit factories is overdue. The present slump may act as a badly needed incentive.

Surface Mining. Elimination of the damage caused by surface mining has made great progress. It has been pointed out that revegetation will be difficult in the arid regions of Montana and Wyoming. It should also be noted that in these regions we find coal seams with thicknesses of 50 feet or more at shallow depths. The value of this coal is so great as to make it possible to improve the land far beyond the state in which it was found prior to the mining operation.

Oil Shale. If oil shale is to be used in surface operations and if this should account for a sizable fraction of our liquid fuel needs, each day millions of tons of shale will have to be brought to the surface. Only about 60 percent of this material can be returned to the original volume. The resulting environmental problem may be too great to handle. In situ operations using high explosives could reduce to about 20 percent the amount of shale that has to be brought to the surface. If, in the end, nuclear explosives are used (which are apt to be more economical and which create underground cavities without extensive mining operations) the environmental damage due to spent shale could be avoided altogether. Most environmentalists have not yet realized this advantage in the use of nuclear explosives.

Oil Spills. General discussions have ignored the fact that oil spills from underwater drilling are exceedingly rare. The well-publicized occurrence in the Santa Barbara Channel resulted from a waiver of the requirement to case the well along its whole length. This mistake certainly will not be committed again.

In addition to strict enforcement of proper precautions, we need research to reduce the consequences of an oil spill should it occur. It is possible to corral an oil spill within a short time of its occurrence unless the sea is quite rough. If the operation succeeds, the oil spill can be promptly cleaned up. If, on the other hand, the oil spill has spread extensively, disposal by oil-consuming bacteria may be an appropriate technique. These bacteria are present in nature, but there are few of them. They dispose of natural or man-made oil spills; dropping appropriate bacterial cultures (which are quite harmless) on a contaminated region can greatly accelerate the disposal of oil.

Safety. The construction of nuclear reactors has been opposed because of dangers which, in some cases, are imaginary and, in others, real, but exaggerated. It must be emphasized that the only real danger is connected with the massive escape of radioactivity in a major accident. There is no danger whatsoever that a nuclear reactor will explode like a nuclear bomb; even in the worst possible case, the total energy released will be unimportant in its direct effect.

Questions of hazards are prominent in the thinking of environmentalists. We find the remarkable situation of environmentalists opposing the construction of nuclear plants, which in themselves do not contribute to pollution. The problem here is the question of what would happen in the case of a severe accident. In order to preserve a sense of balance, we should compare the dangers from nuclear plants with other dangers connected with the generation of energy. One may consider, for instance, the case of dams needed for the generation of hydroelectric power. Collapse of such dams have killed thousands of people and made many more homeless. No industrial nuclear reactor in the United States has damaged the health of any individual due to the effects of radioactivity, which is the only specific danger connected with such plants. This record should indeed be maintained.

Another appropriate object for safety investigation is liquified natural gas (LNG). In particular, large ships carrying LNG need special attention. Because of its low boiling point, this gas can readily mix with air and remain close to the ground. A spark, or open flame, may ignite the mixture and the flame can spread back to the LNG ship. Careful investigation in a few special cases showed that, in those cases, the LNG ship did not explode. The energy available, however, in such a ship is greater than that of the Hiroshima bomb. In contrast with nuclear reactors, an explosion of an LNG ship cannot be ruled out by simple arguments in a general and convincing manner. On the basis of conventional criteria LNG ships appear to be safe, but we are dealing here with one of those situations where not a single explosion can be tolerated in a populated area. The possibility exists of a combination of circumstances that may lead to an explosion. While careful consideration has been given to the problem, the thoroughness of these investigations seems less than that connected with the possibility of a nuclear accident. It is a remarkable fact that nuclear reactors cannot be insured, but private companies can insure LNG ships. When Lloyd's insures an LNG ship, however, the insurance covers only the ship. It does not cover the damage that may result from the explosion of the ship in a harbor.

The above examples make it clear that danger is a relative thing. What is needed is a careful reappraisal and a more rational basis for comparing hazards. The public should be made aware of these considerations and comparisons.

In the case of nuclear reactors, the present situation may be acceptable, although further safety improvements remain a worthwhile objective. An improvement which appears to be particularly useful is to build additional nuclear reactors in appropriate underground locations. A depth of about 200 feet should suffice. The protection of the earth cover added to other safety measures should practically eliminate any danger to an innocent bystander.

Costs. All the environmental, health, and safety objectives mentioned above can be accomplished for the approximate sum of $50 billion. The present stance—to postpone development of energy sources on account of environmental restraints—will be incomparably more expensive in the long-run to the national economy than proceeding, prudently but expeditiously, with the development of nuclear power. We believe it is much more reasonable to put the greatest emphasis in our environmental efforts on the development and improvement of appropriate technical solutions, rather than to rush into enforcement of regulations (which may be overly conservative or even wrong, because adequate data are not available) without regard to the effects on the national economy. In the long run, the appropriate balance will lead to a cleaner and better environment for all, including the underprivileged who may be the first to suffer in a critical shortage of energy.

Balance. We cannot claim that producing energy will not result in any pollution whatsoever, nor that it will be completely free of risk. A proper and balanced evaluation, together with the required actions, can reduce both pollution and risk to levels considerably lower than those which have been accepted up to the present time.

5. An Example of Our Position in the Year 2000

In the 1990s, new energy sources[q] such as gas from in situ coal gasification, shale oil, oil from the deep ocean, geothermal energy, new forms of nuclear energy, solar energy, and possibly energy developed from non-fossil organic materials, wind energy, and tidal energy will be indispensable in the United States and abroad. Fortunately, a number of these alternatives could provide appropriate substitutes for the primary energy sources upon which we now rely. None of these new sources by itself can "solve" our energy problem, but by a well-chosen mix, we can reach our objective of ample, clean, and reasonably priced energy for the United States, while providing a truly impressive level of exports to help our allies and the developing nations.

Long-term predictions are inherently uncertain. Some may doubt the wisdom of "squandering" our oil and natural gas in the near future. But in the absence of a vigorous program for the near term, we may not be in charge of our destiny after 1985. We do advocate the taking of risks. In view of the several alternatives that remain open and in view of our past record of overcoming difficulties, these risks do not appear excessive.

Industry has been reluctant to make substantial investments in developments which may not begin to pay off until more than ten years in the future. The

[q]See Sections 8, 9, and 10.

years up to 1985 should be used to develop and demonstrate the technical and economic feasibility of alternative energy sources, so that we may select the most advantageous energy supplies to be exploited during the remainder of this century.

The extensive research and development efforts[r] that should yield results by the year 1985, or even earlier, require financing by the federal government. In most cases, this financing should take the form of contracts with private companies. This may well be the most effective plan since it utilizes the skills of private industry, while it gives the government the opportunity to accelerate the research and development in order to satisfy the needs of the country. In some cases, the federal government might support the research and development directly or jointly with industry, while in other cases, inducements offered by the government to industry might be more useful.

Rather than attempt to predict what could or should happen in the year 2000, we include in Table I-5 an example of energy demand and supply for the year 2000, as an illustration of what might be developed. We also should point out that starting with our 1985 target as the base, we are predicting an average increase in the total domestic energy production of a little more than 3.6 percent per year and an average increase in the domestic consumption of energy per person of about 2.8 percent per year. This latter figure will be augmented in its effects by using energy more efficiently.

The very substantial increase in the use of nuclear energy should be particularly noted. The main problems connected with the large-scale development of nuclear energy are public acceptance and the availability of fuel.

We also continue to increase our potential exports to 11 quads or more than five million barrels per day of oil and 19 quads of coal for the impressive total of 30 quads in 2000. In this way, we may make a great contribution toward the improvement of the conditions in resource-poor developing countries.

All this should be considered not as a target, but as an example of what might happen. The following discussion is to show that what we plan to accomplish by 1985 will not necessarily lead into difficulties beyond that date.

Conservation and Energy Demand

It may be noted in Table I-5 that the only demand[s] (according to our example) which is to decrease between 1985 and 2000 is in the transportation sector (from 22 quads to 20; demand for oil would decrease from 21 quads or about 9.9 million barrels per day to 19 quads or to 8.7 million barrels per day). We hope to accomplish this by a radical improvement in the propulsion of automobiles. Today we burn gasoline in our cars with an efficiency in the neighborhood of 15 percent. It is vital to find ways to raise this figure; a value as high as 30 percent may be reached.

---

[r]See Sections 9 and 10.
[s]See Section 7, Table I-6 for a breakout of the types of energy consumed in each demand sector.

Table I-5
Energy Demand and Supply
(All figures in quads per year = 10^{15} BTU's per year)

Demand	1973 Actual	1985 Target	2000 Example
Electricity[1]	19.8	33	85
Residential & Commercial[2]	15.4	18	20
Industry[2]	18.2	24	30
Non-Energy[3]	3.4	6	15
Transportation[2]	18.8	22	20
Subtotal–Domestic	**75.6**	**103**	**170**
Export	2.0	15	30
Liquids	0.5	6	11
Gas	0.1	0	0
Coal	1.4	9	19
Totals	**77.6**	**118**	**200**
Supply			
Liquids	35.2	39	50
Conventional	22.2	35	30
Shale	0.0	2	15
Synthetic	0.0	1	5
Imports	13.0	1	0
Gas	23.6	29	25
Conventional	22.5	28	20
Synthetic	0.0	2	15
Imports	1.1	1	0
Converted[4]	0.0	−2	−10
Coal	15.0	33	50
Nuclear	0.9	12	60
Hydroelectric	2.9	3	5
Other	0.0	2	10
Totals	**77.6**	**118**	**200**

1. Primary fuel demands–energy consumed by the electric utilities to produce electricity.
2. End-use sector totals exclude electricity consumed.
3. Includes 0.3 quads of liquids not accounted for in 1973. The item "non-energy" is the production of materials such as fertilizer and plastics which use coal or hydrocarbons for their substance rather than as a source of energy.
4. Gas which is converted to synthetic liquids (methanol).

One way of doing this might be the hybrid car burning gasoline and also running on batteries. The gasoline engine would insure a long cruising range. The batteries, to be used in city traffic, could supply extra energy for acceleration so that the gasoline engine would always run at optimum efficiency. A new type of battery (still to be developed) might also be partially recharged when the brake is applied converting most of the kinetic energy of the car back into stored electricity.

This is only one example of a possible improvement, but it assumes that the automobile industry will make more technical progress than was the case in past decades. Other conservation measures include an increase in the efficiency of generating electricity to a figure exceeding 50 percent in some advanced plants. We also hope to eliminate most of the transmission losses.

The electric utilities, as well as the automobile industry, have not supported research and development in an adequate manner. This situation must change— hopefully by inducements.

By the year 2000, most of the heating of houses should be by heat pumps[t] which do not generate heat from fuel, but only transfer heat from a lower temperature to a higher temperature using much less energy. Also, by that time, industries can install more advanced energy saving equipment which, in some cases, can reduce fuel requirements by as much as 50 percent and, in a few cases, by as much as 90 percent.

Nuclear Energy[u]

It is reasonable to increase the fraction of energy used in the form of electricity. Improved generating efficiency, flexibility of usage, and good environmental controls at generating plants lead to this conclusion.

Clean nuclear energy will probably become the main source of electric power generation. Consideration of fuel availability and environmental impact favor such a development. Public acceptance and safety raise problems which can and must be solved. Many foreign countries lack other primary sources of energy and will have to rely on nuclear reactors.

Low cost uranium mineral deposits may be exhausted in the process of fueling reactors of the present types. Relatively small changes in current reactor designs will permit the use of abundant and inexpensive thorium as an auxiliary fuel. We recommend an early introduction of the use of thorium as a solution to the fuel problem.

Equitable and mutually profitable international cooperation should be encouraged in perfecting nuclear reactors. This is particularly desirable in the case of the Canadian heavy water reactor (CANDU) which is readily adaptable to the use of thorium. International cooperation may also be profitable in the field of

---

[t]Heat pumps use electricity and can be loosely described as airconditioners running in reverse. (Air-conditioning cools the inside and heats the outside. Heat pumps heat the inside of the house but cool the outside. Conventional heating heats the inside and the outside and is much less efficient.)

[u]See also Section 8.

fast breeder reactors which are not likely to contribute before 1990 and in which there is considerable international interests, for example, in France and Germany.

According to our example, most of the expansion in electrical power between 1985 and 2000 will be in nuclear reactors. In fact, our tables show an increase of 48 quads, which is the greatest projected increment. The capital expenditure for this item alone is estimated at $600 billion (in 1973 dollars).

From the technical point of view, fission reactors are available now and will remain available in the foreseeable future as a substantial energy source. In fact, nuclear fuels are so abundant that they approximate what some call an inexhaustible, if not renewable, energy source.

Oil

It will be necessary to pursue beyond 1985 the proposed vigorous production of oil. However, unless big, new reservoirs are discovered, oil production will decline before the end of the century. This danger will be less if we discover oil and gas at greater depths and, particularly, on the continental rise[v] (where ocean depth is a mile or more). Organic material deposited on the continents and the continental shelves have been carried down in geologic times over the precipitous continental slope to the more gentle continental rise to form sedimentary layers which may be oil and gas bearing.

Exploitation of these suspected rich deposits of oil on the continental rise will require truly novel production methods. We recommend that:

1. Exploration of the continental rise and development of remote-control methods to produce oil and gas from these deposits should be undertaken before 1985.
2. Thought should be given as to whether and to what extent this exploration and development should proceed jointly with other nations.

Many people consider the riches of the oceans common property of mankind, not subject to national sovereignty. If the exploitation of these riches is to proceed on some international basis, or at any rate under the control of more than one nation, then the research and development leading to such exploitation may also have to be carried out on a similar broad basis.

---

[v]The continental rise is the region of gradually decreasing depth when we approach a continent from the abyss which has a depth of several miles. The continental rise, which forms the outer base of the continents, is generally tens of miles away, or even farther, from the shore.

In Situ Processes

In situ processes offer a further promising solution to the exhaustion of conventional fuels. In situ processes (to derive oil from oil shale and gas from coal) are predicted to yield 4 quads by 1985. In comparison to production of synthetics on the surface, in situ production is expected to be less expensive, to require less capital, and to bypass many social, environmental, and economic obstacles. By proceeding beyond the pilot plants to moderate production by 1985, we will obtain the reliable cost figures that are needed for future planning.

If in situ processes reach their target figures in 1985, expansion to 15 quads of shale oil and 15 quads of gas from coal is realistic for the year 2000. The supply should then suffice throughout the twenty-first century.

Other Energy Sources[w]

Many other energy sources (geothermal, solar, fusion, wind and tidal) can contribute by the year 2000. Geothermal energy, particularly in the West and near the Gulf Coast will meet some of our future electrical energy demands if research and development are aggressively conducted. Currently, technologies are not available to extend the use of geothermal energy (except for dry, high temperature steam) to major power plants and large industrial applications. More research and development is essential. International cooperation (for example, with the Japanese, who have studied geothermal deposits associated with volcanoes and who could greatly benefit by the development) is recommended.

The burning of urban wastes is another supplementary domestic source of energy. Indirect energy savings may also be achieved by recovering, from the wastes prior to combustion, materials such as steel and aluminum, which require substantial amounts of energy to refine initially but considerably less to reprocess. Economic incentives to change current waste disposal methods are: less land will be needed for sanitary landfills; pollution caused by open dumps or combustion of refuse will be reduced, and the generation of heat or electricity will partly defray the costs of refuse disposal. Worldwide trends toward urbanization will enhance the heating value of wastes as we approach 2000.

Solar energy is abundant, inexhaustible and nonpolluting. At present, it can be used to produce hot water, heat and cool buildings, and produce low grade steam for industry.[x] More remote objectives are: using sunlight to produce steam and then generating electricity in conventional power plants; conversion of sunlight directly into electricity; the use of trees, algae, and other organisms as energy crops and the derivation of methanol from these crops. Further

[w]See also Section 9.

[x]This latter item, while not mentioned explicitly in the previous section, was included together with improved insulation in the energy-saving procedures.

research efforts on solar energy are necessary. Eventually one of these possibilities, or some other solar application, might become economically competitive with other energy sources.

Wind energy is economical today wherever steady winds of 25 miles per hour are available.[y] (This is the case on the windward hills of Oahu, Hawaii.) Better engineering may lead to the exploitation of winds at a lower velocity. Thus, wind energy sources may become more readily available in many parts of the world, particularly in remote areas where small powerplants are needed. Economical energy storage would be an extremely useful complement.

Tidal energy may be employed in special localities like the Bay of Fundy. The total contribution, however, will remain small.

Temperature gradients in the oceans might be exploited, but the needed capital expenditures are high and will probably remain high. Cold water from the deep ocean may become useful as a coolant for plants located near the seacoasts which, in turn, could lead to better utilization of other energy sources.

Controlled fusion research should be supported in spite of the uncertain eventual capital costs. We are already investing more than $100 million per year in this area. Success in research and engineering may lead to the availability of a clean and safe energy source, with unlimited fuel. International cooperation, including Russia's, was introduced in 1958 and is working satisfactorily.

There is much talk about a future hydrogen economy, utilizing hydrogen in a liquid form, in the expectation that oil will be exhausted eventually and that we shall therefore need a new, compact energy package. Hydrogen appears to be the most obvious since it is clean-burning, easily transportable, and readily storable. Research on production, distribution, and use of hydrogen should indeed be investigated. At the same time, the question remains whether there may be other energy packages with more desirable properties than hydrogen.

In the long run, a hydrogen economy (or an economy based on other energy packages) may be required unless electrical energy should assume a truly dominant position (much more than 50 percent) in our energy production. At present, electric energy has the drawback of being particularly capital-intensive. In the long run, this may be less important and, due to technical innovations, may not even be true.

6. Recommendations for Urgent Action

This section contains recommendations for actions which should be undertaken by the federal government at the earliest practicable time. Those set forth in italics are recommended for immediate action. The recommendations are separated into six sections:

---

[y]Winds at 25 miles per hour are almost twice as effective as wind at 20 miles per hour.

1. Conservation
2. Environment
3. Production
4. Oil Supply Security
5. Research and Development
6. General and Institutional

These or similar types of recommendations need to be acted on quickly and decisively to deal with the energy crisis which will be with us for the next decade at least. The actions recommended here, or equivalent actions, are essential to meet our 1985 targets. Other actions, particularly relating to research on and development of other energy sources, are recommended in Section 9. A discussion of research and development priorities can be found in Section 10.

Conservation

Reduced consumption is the quickest way to alleviate energy shortages.

Recommendation. The federal government should take aggressive steps to restrain the U.S. demand for energy by:

a. Providing industry inducements (for example, tax credits or loans) for installing equipment which will improve the utilization of fuels (improved insulation, more efficient processes, use of waste heat).

b. Funding research on methods, processes and systems for making better use of available fuels.

c. *Revising FHA, VA and other appropriate regulations to require better insulation in new construction and providing investment tax credits to commercial enterprises or tax deductions for private dwelling owners to induce upgrading the insulation of present structures.*

d. *Requiring the labeling of equipment and appliances to indicate average annual cost to operate under normal use.*

e. *Prescribing that equipment and appliances will have minimum lifetimes under normal use, that they will be capable of being easily maintained and repaired, and that spare parts will be available for a minimum period of time after sale. All this is needed to counter rapid obsolescence.*

f. Obtaining information from industry on the comparative capital costs for developing new energy sources and for saving an equivalent amount of energy.

g. Restricting, where feasible, the under boiler use of oil and gas by electric utilities, except for peaking generators, and restricting the use of oil by industry for process steam raising after appropriate transition periods.

h. *Penalizing the owners of large automobiles with gasoline engines by imposing stiff taxes which increase with time, for example, annual federal license* *fees on passenger cars ranging the first year from $300 for cars weighing 3,000 pounds to $600 for cars weighing 5,000 pounds. In the second year, these fees should be doubled and in the third and succeeding, these fees would be tripled.*

i. Requiring, after a suitable transition period, taxis and trucks to use diesel engines.

j. Maintaining and enforcing a national 55-mile per hour speed limit.

k. Encouraging, through incentives, such as favorable freight rates or federal funding of local waste disposal projects, the recycling of materials (for example, aluminum) whose production from ore requires large amounts of energy.

l. Encouraging conversion to other energy sources as developed elsewhere in this section.

m. Requiring the establishment of flat rates for each kilowatt-hour of electricity (energy) purchased, regardless of time of day, customer or amount used, but permitting reduced demand (power) rates to industrial customers using electricity during off-peak hours.

n. Requiring public utilities to purchase surplus electricity generated in connection with industrial processes, provided that electricity meets electric utility voltage and frequency standards.

Environment

Recommendation. The federal government should take additional steps to protect the environment by:

a. Prohibiting the import of liquified natural gas (LNG) until the risks associated with LNG ships are reduced to the levels commensurate with, say, nuclear electric generating plants. Remote off-loading locations may be considered to relieve acute shortages of gas.

b. Reducing the chance of spills in harbors, rivers, and bays by establishing and enforcing strict rules on control of traffic, use of pilots, and foul weather procedures.

c. Reducing the chance of oil leaks from offshore drilling by setting and enforcing minimum standards on procedures and equipment.

d. Imposing a levy on surface-mined coal which is invested in a trust to ensure that funds will be available to rehabilitate or improve surface-mined areas.

Recommendation. The federal government should also take steps to improve confidence of the public in the safety of nuclear reactors and in the security of nuclear materials by:

a. Requiring that nuclear reactors be constructed underground, underwater or in nuclear power parks.

b. Requiring the immediate reporting of all incidents, failures, shutdowns, and accidents to a central government office which will, in turn, immediately distribute the information to the appropriate reactor operators and design companies.

c. *Requiring better safeguards against sabotage and unauthorized diversion or use of fissionable materials or radioactive wastes derived from spent fuel rods. This should include improved reliable procedures at the reactor sites and for the transportation of nuclear materials; and also secure and safe sites for the long-term storage of radioactive wastes.*

d. Continuing an aggressive hazards analysis, evaluation and safeguards program aimed at further reducing potential nuclear reactor accidents.

Recommendation. The federal government, in cooperation with the states and industries concerned, should make appropriate plans for the necessary influx of people into the sparsely populated lands where low sulfur coal and high grade oil are currently found.

Recommendation. *In attempting to strike an appropriate balance between environment and energy demands, the federal government should reevaluate ambient clean air standards and environmental regulations to determine whether they should be tailored to specific regions of the country, based on a better understanding of sulfur chemistry in the atmosphere and whether they should permit different levels of emitted pollutants under varying weather conditions or different stack heights. Early action on a temporary change of regulations is necessary.*

Production

Oil and Gas. The current worldwide energy crisis is closely connected to the shortage of indigenous supplies of oil and gas in many countries and the high prices of imported oil and gas. Increasing domestic supplies of oil in the United States will help relieve worldwide shortages and will have an impact sooner than substitutions of the other energy sources.

Recommendation. The federal government should stimulate the production of domestic supplies of gas and oil by:

a. Expediting the submission and processing of environmental impact statements and the leasing of federal lands to facilitate the exploration of new areas, particularly in Alaska and on the outer continental shelf.

b. Undertaking a federal exploratory drilling program within the conterminous states, giving priority to areas where oil and gas are most likely to be found to arrive at a better estimate of available oil and gas reserves, especially before leasing federal lands.

c. *Making public lands available under federal leases which require little or no front-end money and which are awarded on the basis of guaranteed exploration efforts within specified time limits. This should include appropriate incentives for production or penalties, including loss of lease in case of inadequate performance.*

d. Permitting industry profits adequate to raise, internally or in the market, the necessary capital for needed additional exploration and development and to provide the industry incentives to develop new fields or processes. This might be accomplished in part by eliminating the price differential between "old" and "new" oil and gas and by establishing suitably indexed price floors for oil and gas production. At the same time, the consumer should be protected by taxing excess and windfall profits which are not reinvested in exploration or research and development connected with the availability of energy (including the question of environmental impact).

e. Establishing a joint federal government industry committee to work with the oil and related manufacturing industries to ensure the availability and appropriate allocation of scarce rigs and materials.

f. Encouraging greater use of tertiary oil recovery by eliminating the two-price structure of oil and permitting oil companies to jointly apply tertiary recovery procedures to common pools and to share costs and output.

g. Supporting exploration (possibly on an international basis) and later, production of oil and gas from the continental rise (in the oceans at the depth of several thousand feet).

Coal. Coal comprises the most abundant fossil fuel reserve in the United States and can be substituted for oil and gas in many non-transportation uses.

Recommendation. The federal government should implement an aggressive program to utilize our abundant deposits of coal in lieu of natural gas and oil by:

a. Resolving pending legislation regarding surface mining.

b. Making available public lands containing low sulfur coal under federal leases which require little or no front-end money and which are awarded on the basis of guaranteed production within specified time limits with appropriate incentives for production or penalties, including loss of lease for lack of performance.

c. Providing guarantees for long-term loans of needed capital to coal producing and consuming companies.

d. Ensuring the adequate production of coal mining and transportation equipment (such as drag lines, hopper cars, diesel engines, barges, freighters, pipelines) and the improvement of railroad roadbeds, harbors, docks, and canals needed for the transportation of coal by setting appropriate interstate rate structures and by guaranteeing loans, if required.

Nuclear Reactors. Nuclear reactors can provide an important alternative to fossil fuels as the heat source for electric power generation.

Recommendation. The federal government should take aggressive action to increase quickly and substantially the use of nuclear electric generating plants in the United States by:

a. Establishing with industry, standardized reactor designs and, with states and local governments, standardized reactor siting criteria, which will be used as criteria for licensing new reactors and approving current reactor proposals which have not been approved; and by establishing federal quality control and inspection procedures and acceptance criteria, including adequate instrumentation which reactors must meet before operations are approved.

b. Streamlining licensing procedures by establishing federal guidelines and taking appeals out of courts, delegating them instead to a quasi-judicial, administrative agency.

c. Assisting in the training of engineers and technicians who will be employed in the design, construction and operation of nuclear reactors for electric power generation, and sponsoring special courses on nuclear safety.

Recommendation. The federal government should eliminate potential future bottlenecks in the expanded use of nuclear reactors by:

a. Increasing the price offered for uranium oxide or yellow cake to encourage more exploration and mining.

b. Permitting the import of uranium oxide.

c. Contracting for additional facilities to process spent fuel rods and nuclear waste.

d. Providing incentives to encourage the installation of new fuel cycles utilizing abundant thorium.

Electricity.

Recommendation. The federal government should take steps to ensure the continued availability of electricity for necessary uses by:

a. Guaranteeing long-term loans for electric utilities, if needed.

b. Requiring the upgrading of interties among the electric utility generating plants to improve load sharing.

Oil Supply Security.

Recommendation. The federal government should take steps to assure that continued supplies of oil are available by:

a. Deterring future embargoes through political negotiations with oil exporting countries and joint agreements with oil importing countries.

b. Providing the president with standby emergency allocation, distribution, and rationing powers to be used should oil supplies be interrupted.

Research and Development

New Technology.

Recommendation. The federal government should fund, partially fund or encourage through appropriate tax incentives, research on and development of improved methods for:

a. Discovering new gas and oil deposits in the United States and offshore.

b. Faster and more economical drilling.

c. Cleaning up oil spills on water, especially under adverse conditions. Use of certain bacteria is one technique.

d. Tertiary recovery of oil.

e. Recovering gas from tight formations using hydrofracturing, high explosive or nuclear techniques.

f. Burning petroleum products more efficiently in motive power plants, such as the stratified charge engine, a lighter weight diesel engine, a Sterling cycle engine.

g. Removing sulfur from coal before, during or after burning.

h. Mining underground to improve the percentage of coal removed, to increase the productivity of miners, to improve mine health and safety, and to minimize environmental effects of subsidence or acid ground waters.

i. Making high Btu gas, methanol, and synthetic petroleum from coal emphasizing in situ processes.

j. Rehabilitating arid land areas which have been surface-mined.

k. Incorporating thorium into reactor designs (for example, CANDU, HTGR, Rickover light water) to produce uranium-233.

l. Processing uranium-233.

m. Using uranium-233 in lieu of uranium-235 in nuclear power reactors.

n. Other breeder reactors including alternatives to the liquid metal fast breeder reactor (LMFBR).

o. High temperature fuel elements and better heat transfer technologies to improve reactor/power plant efficiencies.

p. Improving the efficiency of electrical generating plants through the use of topping and bottoming cycles.

q. Decreasing the losses in electric transmission by using direct current, cryogenic or superconducting transmission lines.

r. Storing energy in batteries, flywheels, and chemical systems.

s. Utilizing fuel cells to provide peak load electricity.

t. Removing in situ oil (and possibly minerals, such as alumina) from high grade (greater than 15 gallons of oil per ton) western shale employing high explosives and, later, where appropriate to scale up to larger production rates, using nuclear explosives to rubblize the shale.

u. Recovering economically in situ oil (and possibly minerals, such as uranium) from low grade (less than 10 gallons of oil per ton) shales which are found in many parts of the world as well as in the United States, for example, the Chattanooga shales.

v. Removing nitrogen and sulfur economically from shale oil to make it an acceptable refinery feedstock.

Demonstration Plants.

Recommendation. The federal government should partially fund a few each of the following types of demonstration scale plants to determine the technical and economic factors related to large scale production by private industry;

a. In situ coal gasification.

b. In situ shale oil production.

c. Methanol from gas.

d. Synthetic crude oil from coal (to provide insurance against unforeseen difficulties in extracting oil from shale).

e. Surface retorting and recovery of oil and minerals, such as alumina, from high grade (greater than 25 gallons of oil per ton) oil shales to provide insurance against unforeseen difficulties in or costs associated with in situ recovery and to determine environmental feasibility.

Underground Nuclear Plants.

Recommendation. The federal government should encourage the investigation of the engineering, design, and maintenance problems and costs of siting reactors underground to improve safety and security by sharing in costs of designing and constructing a large nuclear power reactor underground.

International Cooperation.

Recommendation. The federal government should encourage other nations to participate in joint research and development and should share the results with all nations directed toward:

a. Making gas, methanol, and synthetic oil from coal, sharing the results freely with all nations.

b. Safer and more efficient reactor designs including breeder reactors.

c. Recovering oil and minerals from low grade (less than 15 gallons oil per ton) shale.

General and Institutional

Recommendation. The federal government should establish an agency (which might be called the National Resource Mobilization Corporation) to make guaranteed loans and to purchase products above market price to encourage the development of new energy sources by the private sector or provide subsidies for these products. The financial resources for this agency might come from a tax on energy production or use.

Recommendation. Through an appropriate federal agency (such as National Resources Mobilization Corporation referred to above) the federal government should contract to purchase from each of five different companies, for example, 10 million barrels of oil produced from shale at $20 per barrel and another 40 million barrels from each of five companies at $12 to $14 per barrel. Perhaps 10 million barrels of this shale oil should be reserved for demonstration scale production plants designed to remove the nitrogen from this shale oil and to make the oil suitable for processing by current refineries. The remaining 240 million barrels could be sold for heating oil to help defer the expenses of this program.

Similarly, the federal government should contract to purchase from each of six different companies, for example, 5 billion cubic feet of pipeline quality gas made from coal gasification at $3 per thousand cubic feet and another 20 billion cubic feet from each of six companies at $1.50 per thousand cubic feet. Perhaps 50 billion cubic feet of this gas should be reserved for demonstration scale plants designed to produce methanol. The remaining gas could be sold to the highest bidder (assuming the Congress has removed the ceiling on interstate gas) to help defer the expenses of this program.

Recommendation. *The federal government should develop and put into law standards relating to the siting of appropriate component facilities of various energy production and distribution systems such as: refineries and storage tanks for petroleum and synthetic petroleum liquids and gas (including liquified natural and synthetic gas); electrical generating plants to be owned or operated by utilities (including plants using oil, gas, coal, water under a head, nuclear reactors and solid waste), and electrical transmission lines. Such standards must strike a proper economic and social balance between protecting the environment and providing for the energy needs of the nation and should permit the intervention by the federal government in the event the proposed facilities meet federal standards and undue delays arise from state or local proceedings.*

Recommendation. The federal government should enact legislation establishing an Energy Trust Fund with provisions controlling the expenditure of funds in a manner similar to the Highway Trust Fund. All taxes, fees, and tariffs levied after January 1, 1976 against energy supplies or the companies or individuals producing or using them should be put into the Energy Trust Fund. Disbursements from this fund should be made only to increase the supply or the availability of energy.

7. U.S. Energy Demand and Supply

This section contains the following tables and charts:

Table I-6, Energy Demand and Supply—This table displays the energy demand and supply figures which are contained in the body of the report. In addition, it contains Target figures for 1980 and a breakdown of the demand sectors (Residential and Commercial, Industry, Non-Energy and Transportation) by primary energy sources (oil, gas, coal, nuclear, hydro and other).

The electrical energy consumed by the various sectors appears in parentheses. These parenthetical figures are not part of those sector totals (for instance, under Industry) because these figures have already been included under Electricity. It should be noted that, using 1973 as an example, the electrical energy consumed, 6.4 quads (3.7 quads for Residential and Commercial and 2.7 quads for Industry), is much less than the 19.8 quads given as the total for Electricity. This total represents the energy expended in generating and distributing 6.4 quads of electricity at an average efficiency of 32 percent.

The Totals represent the total primary energy demands including those needed to produce electricity. The Net figures exclude the energy dissipated as useless heat in the production of electricity (see also Table I-7).

The Non-Energy sector comprises petrochemical feedstocks, lubricants, asphalt, waxes, and commercial solvents.

The gas figures under the Transportation sector are for transporting gas in pipelines.

The 1980 Target assumes an immediate and continuing aggressive national energy conservation and production program. With an effective program the United States might be able to reduce its net imports to approximately 1 quad in 1980.

The 2000 Example assumes the 1985 Target is substantially achieved.

Figure I-9, Energy Demand and Supply—This chart shows the information from Table I-6 in a graphic form. The heights of the rectangles represent percentages and the widths represent the energy demand or supply. Thus, the respective areas of the rectangles give a measure of the energy demand in each end-use sector and of the energy supply of each primary energy source.

The primary energy used to generate electricity is distributed to the end-use demand sectors in proportion to the electricity consumed by those sectors. This method of accounting for the fossil fuel or equivalent heat energy lost in producing electricity permits us to represent more realistically the total primary energy demands of the various sectors.

Table I-7, Net Energy Demand—The table gives the energy consumed by the end-use sectors and includes a breakdown by primary energy sources and electricity. Contrary to Figure I-9, in this table the primary energy sources used to produce electricity are not charged to the end-use sectors; only the electricity actually consumed is shown.

Table I-6
Energy Demand and Supply
(All figures in quads per year = 10^{15} BTU's per year)

Demand	1973 Actual	1980 Target	1985 Target	2000 Example
Electricity[1]	19.8	25	33	85
Liquids	3.4	3	2	0
Gas	3.9	3	3	0
Coal	8.7	10	11	10
Nuclear	0.9	6	12	60
Hydro	2.9	3	3	5
Other	0.0	0	2	10
Residential & Commercial[2]	15.4	15	18	20
Liquids	7.0	5	5	7
Gas	8.0	10	13	13
Coal	0.4	0	0	0
Electricity[3]	(3.7)	(5)	(6)	(10)
Industry[2]	18.2	20	24	30
Liquids	3.8	3	3	5
Gas	10.1	11	11	8
Coal	4.3	6	10	17
Electricity[3]	(2.7)	(3)	(5)	(15)
Non-Energy[4]	3.4	4	6	15
Liquids[4]	2.5	2	2	8
Gas	0.7	1	1	3
Coal	0.2	1	3	4
Transportation	18.8	20	22	20
Liquids	18.0	19	21	19
Gas	0.8	1	1	1
Electricity[3]	0.0	0	0	(5)
Domestic Demand	**75.6**	**84**	**103**	**170**
Export	2.0	7	15	30
Liquids	0.5	2	6	11
Gas	0.1	0	0	0
Coal	1.4	5	9	19
Totals	77.6	91	118	200
Net	64.2	74	96	145
Supply				
Liquids	35.2	34	39	50
Conventional	22.2	27	35	30

Table I-6 (cont.)

Supply	1973 Actual	1980 Target	1985 Target	2000 Example
Shale	0.0	0	2	15
Synthetic	0.0	0	1	5
Imports	13.0	7	1	0
Gas	23.6	26	29	25
Conventional	22.5	25	28	20
Synthetic	0.0	0	2	15
Imports	1.1	1	1	0
Converted[6]	0.0	0	−2	−10
Coal	15.0	22	33	50
Nuclear	0.9	6	12	60
Hydroelectric	2.9	3	3	5
Other	0.0	0	2	10
Totals	77.6	91	118	200

1. Primary energy demands—energy consumed by the electric utilities to produce electricity. For non-fossil fuel sources (such as geothermal, hydroelectric, and nuclear), energy consumed is the equivalent fossil fuel energy which would be required. This equivalence is based on converting 10,500 Btu of heat to one kilowatt-hour of electricity or at an efficiency of 32.5 percent.
2. End-use sector totals exclude electricity consumed (see Note 3).
3. Electricity consumed in this end-use sector which is produced by the electric utilities. Not included in sector totals.
4. In the Bureau of Mines News Release of May 13, 1973, from which the 1973 figures were taken, 0.3 quad of liquids was not accounted for; this 0.3 quad was arbitrarily included in this table under non-energy.
5. Net equals total energy consumed less the energy lost in producing electricity. In this table it can be checked by taking the total plus electricity consumed in the end-use sectors (see Note 3) minus energy consumed by the electric utilities (see Note 1).
6. Gas which is converted to synthetic liquids.

Also shown are the average annual percentage rates of change assuming continuous growth. According to our targets, the rate of growth will be slow during the latter 1970s (Net Domestic Demand would grow at an average annual rate of 1.1 percent) because only by saving energy can our deficits be remedied in the near future. Efforts to increase our energy production, which must be undertaken now, will produce a vigorous growth in available energy in the early 1980s (Net Domestic Demand would grow at an average annual rate of 3.8 percent).

8. Aspects of Increased Production

Discussions on energy have created the impression that our energy resources are rapidly diminishing and that use of new resources is needed to satisfy our needs

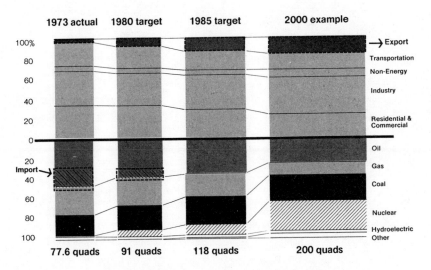

Figure I-9. U.S. Energy Demand and Supply.

even for the next few decades. Exclusive emphasis on resources is somewhat misleading. In the following pages, we shall attempt to show that real limitations are due to need of capital investment and the requirement to satisfy constraints imposed by considerations of the environment and of safety.

Actually, in different areas which we shall discuss (petroleum, extractive processes, coal from the West, nuclear reactors, and electric systems), a different set of technical, economic, and environmental problems arises. But, in all areas discussed in this section, we can expect reasonable solutions of our problems within a decade.

Petroleum

In the case of petroleum, that is, oil and gas, there is almost unanimous opinion that our domestic supplies are in a rapid and unavoidable decline. Among the quantitative predictions of exhaustion of domestic oil and gas, two have received wide publicity. These two are a U.S. Bureau of Mines report[1] and a study by M. King Hubbert.[2] In the following discussion, it will be shown that both of these lead to projections on petroleum recovery which are too low.

The U.S. Bureau of Mines report is a straightforward projection of annual oil reserve additions as reported by the American Petroleum Institute. The API reports are conservative. They also are misleading in that they overestimate the rate at which we are depleting our oil reserves. This is due to a peculiar method of bookkeeping.

Table I-7
Net Energy Demand
(Demand figures in quads per year for years indicated; % per year figures are average growth rates between the years indicated)

	1960	% Per Year	1970	% Per Year	1973	% Per Year	1980	% Per Year	1985	% Per Year	2000
Residential & Commercial	10.6	4.2	16.1	5.7	19.1	0.7	20	3.6	24	1.5	30
Primary	9.3		12.9		15.4		15		18		20
Electricity	1.3		3.2		3.7		5		6		10
Industry	14.2	3.4	19.9	1.6	20.9	1.4	23	4.6	29	2.9	45
Primary	12.9		17.7		18.2		20		24		30
Electricity	1.3		2.2		2.7		3		5		15
Non-Energy	2.2	6.0	4.0	−5.4	3.4	2.3	4	8.1	6	6.1	15
Transportation	10.8	4.1	16.3	4.8	18.8	0.9	20	1.9	22	0.9	25
Primary	10.8		16.3		18.8		20		22		20
Electricity											5
Net Domestic	**37.8**	4.0	**56.3**	3.3	**62.2**	1.1	**67**	3.8	**81**	2.3	**115**
Export	**1.4**	3.6	**2.0**	–	**2.0**	17.9	**7**	15.2	**15**	4.6	**30**
Net	**39.2**	4.0	**58.3**	3.2	**64.2**	2.0	**74**	5.2	**96**	2.7	**145**

If a discovery of oil is made in 1968 in a new oil field, a conservative estimate is entered in 1968 as addition to our reserves in that year. If in 1974 it is found that this same field will produce more than had been estimated, then in 1974 an additional amount is entered with the date of 1968. Thus, discoveries carrying an early date accumulate while discoveries of recent date look meager. If one looks at such a curve at any time, one is led to the conclusion that discoveries will disappear in ten years or less. Actually, the same situation existed ten years ago and we see, with hindsight, that the discoveries of the 1960s are much greater than estimated at that time.

The realistic way to make a projection would be to consider the far past when all revisions have been added. Studies of Canadian field histories, provided by the Alberta Energy Resources Conservation Board, show that the ultimate production from a field is about nine times the reserve estimate made in the year of discovery. When the far past was examined, annual reserves added remained constant per well drilled.

Dr. Hubbert states that oil is a depletable resource and he argues with considerable plausibility that, for a given effort, less oil or gas will be found this year than was found last year. As evidence, he shows that oil found per foot of exploration drilling has declined ever since the discovery of oil in 1859. An analytical equation purported to describe the decline was published in 1958. Using this equation, Dr. Hubbert deduced that as of 1972, there were only 166 quads or 28.6 billion barrels of oil yet to be found in the lower forty-eight states and adjacent continental shelves. Using the same logic, he predicted that reserves would decline every year after 1970. The oil reserves added in 1971, 1972, and 1973 did decline, but in 1974, they increased. In fact, using Dr. Hubbert's data up through 1960, his equations predict that less oil would ever be produced in the lower forty-eight states than his data show were actually produced through 1972.

Actually, exploration has focused on ever deeper strata. The first well drilled in the United States, in 1859, was 70 feet deep; in 1970 the average exploratory well was a little less than 6,000 feet deep. It is obvious that oil found per foot of exploratory drilling has declined and to this extent Dr. Hubbert is correct.

A different way to look at the history of oil exploration is to consider the oil found per well drilled. Though wells are becoming deeper and should be therefore more expensive to complete, this is in part offset by faster and better drilling methods. Figure I-10 shows for the lower forty-eight states the number of oil wells drilled (including dry wells), the number of drill rigs operating, and the reserves added each year. This figure clearly shows a decline in the reserve additions, but it also shows a decline of oil wells drilled, and an even sharper decline in the number of drill rigs. Therefore, one may claim that we are really not suffering from a shortage of oil but only from a shortage of drill rigs. This shortage of rigs was caused by the circumstances that in the Persian Gulf and elsewhere, oil rigs could be employed more profitably. It will take time to replace them.

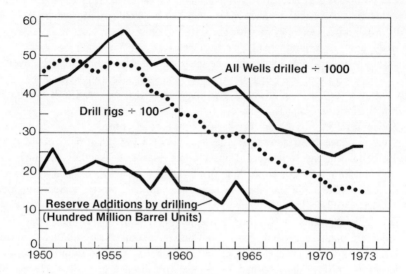

Figure I-10. Oil Well Activity (Lower 48 states)

In Figure I-11, we show the oil found per well. The figure clearly shows that the oil found per well fluctuates around a constant value.

There must be, of course, a limit to the depth of wells at which additional oil can be found. According to the Geological Survey and other expert opinions, there is no reason to believe that radical changes will occur before we reach a depth of 18,000 feet. Furthermore, there is a known amount of oil amounting to 1,200 quads or 207 billion barrels in fields already discovered. Most of this oil cannot be produced but, with advanced methods of recovery, a total production of 660 quads or 103 billion barrels can be expected assuming a price of $11 per barrel of new production. Adding present reserves and expected new discoveries to these figures, the data of the Geological Survey lead to a reasonable minimum of 1,600 quads or 276 billion barrels[z] which still can be produced within

[z]These figures are essentially those given in the COMRATE Report of February1975 (Report by the National Research Council and the National Academy of Sciences on Mineral Resources and the Environment). They give 330 quads or 57 billion barrels corresponding to known reserves, 655 quads or 113 billion barrels as undiscovered recoverable resources (this 113 billion barrels is the only figure mentioned in the Executive Summary of the COMRATE Report under the heading, "Reserves and Resources") and up to 610 quads or 105 billion barrels possibly available from new tertiary recovery techniques, which total 1595 quads or 275 billion barrels (these totals do not appear in the COMRATE Report).

A strong energy supply position in the United States is played down in the COMRATE Report. This is due, in part, to conservatism on advanced processes such as in situ coal gasification and shale oil production (which are not mentioned) and new tertiary recovery techniques (which are included with some caution).

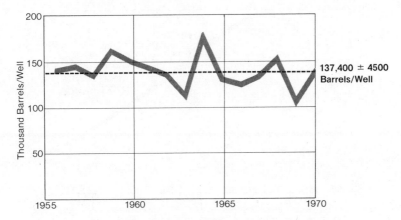

Figure I-11. Oil Found Per Well (Including dry holes).

territory controlled by the United States. On this basis, Figure I-12 gives a projection where a present production (1974) is shown together with an expected production[aa] of 37 quads per year or 17 million barrels per day by 1985 and 33 quads per year or 16 million barrels per day by the year 2000 with production continuing to decline thereafter.

A somewhat more optimistic estimate is that the total recoverable oil in the United States will exceed 3,000 quads or 517 billion barrels, possibly not by a great amount. A realistic, upper limit cannot be easily stated.

The domestic gas supply potential is very large, just as that of liquid petroleum. Its production has been impeded, even more than oil, by economic factors. Gas prices have been regulated at levels far below those which would represent its value as a fuel. This has limited efforts to drill for gas until very recently when intrastate gas sales, which command prices from three to ten times interstate regulated prices, began to be an important stimulant of the gas market. With prices from $1.00 to $2.00 per thousand cubic feet (which compares with $5.80 to $11.60 per barrel of oil for the same energy), it is estimated that recoverable reserves of gas range from 1,200 to 2,000 trillion cubic feet, which is 1,200 to 2,000 quads. Present consumption is about 22 quads per year and our projected figures are 29 quads and 25 quads per year for the years 1985 and 2000, respectively. The life of the conventional natural gas resources, then, is approximately half a century.

Eighty percent of the estimated remaining gas is less than 15,000 feet deep. In the past, a large portion, up to 50 percent, has been associated with oil,

[aa]These estimates are somewhat higher than the figures given in the body of the report. Actual limitation of production may be due more to shortage of funds rather than shortage of oil.

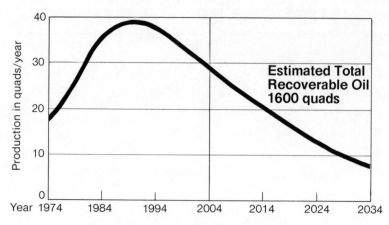

Figure I-12. Life of Domestic Oil Supply.

so that in the future it is expected that a significant amount of gas production will accompany increased oil well drilling.

While development activities in future years will tend to be focused on offshore production and on Naval Petroleum Reserves which are opened up, the present ratio of onshore to offshore production will prevail through 1985. This is because it takes about eight years to develop a new area and because, in any year, production results from the aggregate of reserves added during approximately the past twenty-five years.

In order to reach our target, we assume that there will be two Alaskan oil pipelines and one Trans-Canadian gas pipeline, that "new" oil prices will remain above $10 per barrel, and that interstate gas prices will rise to and remain above $1.50 or more per thousand cubic feet of gas. With these constraints, we estimate the quantities given in Table I-8. These quantities are more than adequate to reach our 1985 targets.

Actually, the figures given in Table I-8 may even be exceeded in an accelerated program. The 1.3 million barrels per day production rate offshore is the expected figure for the known oil deposits in the Gulf of Mexico and off the coast of California. The geological formations along the eastern seaboard will probably also yield oil. Some oil has been found off New Brunswick, but no oil drilling has been conducted as yet along the U.S. portion of the shore.

In an accelerated program we might obtain from Alaska the following production rates in millions of barrels per day for the years indicated; two in 1978, four in 1980, and seven in 1985. A third, somewhat larger, oil pipeline from Alaska would be needed in addition to the two mentioned above.

Table I-8
1985 Production Estimates

	Oil				
	Domestic				
	Onshore*	Offshore**	Natural Gas Liquids***	Alaska	Total
In quads per year	24.7	2.7	3.0	8.5	38.9
In millions of barrels per day	11.7	1.3	1.4	4.0	18.4

	Gas			
	Non-Associated****		Associated****	Alaska	Total
In quads per year	17.3		10.1	2.1	29.5

*Of the 24.7 quads per year or 11.7 million barrels per day of on-shore oil production about 20 percent is expected from novel recovery methods.
**Development of oil fields off-shore takes more time. This is the reason for the limited amount in 1985.
***Liquids from gas wells.
****Non-associated gas is from gas wells; associated gas is from oil wells.

Extractive Processes. The processes covered are general, in situ, fracturing or rubblization, thermal, and chemical.

General. Fossil fuel deposits are plentiful in the aggregate amount and conventional means of obtaining gas, oil, and coal from the earth are straightforward. Wells are drilled into fuel-bearing sands and the pressure within the deposit forces some of the gas and oil to flow to the wells and then to the surface with the aid of pumps. In some cases, extraction is aided by forcing water through the deposit (water flooding) which washes out additional oil. The extraction of coal is also a straightforward endeavor, whether by surface mining or underground mining. But even though these extraction techniques may be straightforward, they often require highly sophisticated, expensive equipment. This is the case in coal mining and also when drilling either at sea or at great depths. These conventional means of extraction have been able to meet the nation's needs in the past, but may not be adequate for the future beyond the year 1985.

The amount of oil that can be extracted in the conventional way averages about 30 percent of the total resource in place. Much more oil and gas can be obtained through the use of new extraction techniques. Similarly, fuels may be extracted from solid deposits (coal, oil shale) using novel approaches.

One may consider techniques of two types. One category includes technologies in which the resource is mined and then processed in a surface plant; these are called surface processes. The other technologies, which require little or no mining, are called in situ processes.

Surface processes can be used to extract oil from tar sands or oil shale and to convert coal either to gas or liquids. While technological progress continues to be made, estimates of the costs for the surface processes have increased significantly. Capital requirements, operating expenses, and the costs of meeting environmental standards have caused most of the processes to appear uncompetitive, even with increased oil and gas prices. Therefore, we do not expect that surface processes will be important and we turn our attention to the in situ processes.

In Situ Processes. The distinctive feature of any in situ process is that the resource is converted, underground, into a form from which usable fuel can be extracted, while leaving unnecessary or harmful ingredients underground.

In situ processes can tap many of the same resources that surface processes can, and a number of others. These in situ processes can be used to obtain additional oil from old oil fields. They can extract heavy oil too viscous for conventional techniques. They can tap gas deposits in which the pores in the rock are too small to allow the extraction of gas by conventional means.

The advantages of the in situ process are numerous. They appear to be less expensive because they require less capital equipment, less physical equipment, and fewer people. They also need less water and are less disruptive to the land. The fact that fewer people are required is of major importance since the locations in the West, where most of the resources exist, are sparsely populated. A threat to the environment in those regions is connected with a rapid influx of people.

With two exceptions, in situ processes have not yet been proven on a large scale. One exception is the extraction of residual oil using thermal processes. Steam injection has been in use for almost a decade and produces a sizable percentage of the oil in California. In situ combustion, in which a fire is ignited in the oil deposits, has also undergone a decade of development and is technically and commercially successful in many fields. The success of in situ combustion in this application is encouraging for other in situ combustion applications.

In situ processes on which much more research and development is required are:

1. Stimulation of tight gas formations.
2. Conversion of oil shale into shale oil.
3. Extraction of oil from tar sands
4. In situ coal gasification.

In many gas-bearing rocks, the pore sizes are so small that the gas cannot be pumped out. We must fracture or rubblize the formation. This can be done by water injection, by use of conventional chemical explosives or, since the deposits often have a thickness of hundreds of feet, by nuclear explosives.

Oil shale frequently is found in even thicker layers (up to 2,000 feet) and nuclear explosives may be used. Thorough rubblization is necessary. This is followed by underground retorting (similar to a well-known surface process). Part of the rubblized material is burned and much of the rest of the hydrocarbon is driven out by the heat and condensed as shale oil.

Tar sands require less heating. Injection of hot water may suffice. The major known North American deposits are in Alberta. If research is to proceed, it should be done jointly with the Canadians.

In situ coal gasification was tried and it failed. This was due to low gas prices, to the circumstances that the coal deposits were at shallow depths where the required high pressures could not be maintained and to the use of thin coal seams in which the gasification proceeded horizontally and bypassed most of the coal. There are thick (between 50 and 200 feet) and deep coal seams in Montana and Wyoming. If these are rubblized with chemical explosives (the thickness is not great enough to justify the use of nuclear explosives) and then burned in the presence of high pressure steam, a product similar to natural gas is obtained. For pipeline-quality gas, oxygen rather than air has to be injected to avoid the presence of useless nitrogen in the product.

Fracturing or Rubblization. The fracturing and rubblization that may be required can be achieved in three ways. Chemical explosives can be used, nuclear explosives can be used or water can be injected under high pressure to cause the deposits to crack.

When a nuclear explosion is detonated deep underground, it first creates a cavity about 200 feet across. The roof of this cavity collapses and a continuing collapse extends upward several hundred feet, thus forming a rubble chimney of high porosity. Cracks and fractures extend outward to a comparable distance from the center of the explosion. Experiments of this kind proved the feasibility of gas stimulation, but higher quality deposits will have to be stimulated if the process is to produce gas at $1 per thousand cubic feet.

The nuclear explosion causes an earthquake of moderate and predictable intensity. This, of course, excludes the use of nuclear explosives in populated areas. Safety requires evacuation of people within a few miles. In case of low population density, this amounts to a few dozen people. The cost of the repair of the material damage to homes by the shock should not exceed 2 percent of the cost of the operation.

If nuclear explosives are used, some radioactive materials are generated. Most of these remain bound in the rock. Hundreds of nuclear explosions in Nevada have given us experience. On the basis of this experience, augmented by careful, stepwise procedures, one can ensure that no amount of radioactivity that is deposited in the rocks will enter the biosphere. Some radioactivity, particularly tritium (which is not deposited in the rocks), will enter the gas or oil we produce. This will cause exposures to the public which, in the worst case, amounts to less than 1 percent of the natural radiation which is, indeed, universally present.

In any case, nuclear explosions in oil shale should be delayed and we should proceed with chemical explosives. This can be done on a smaller scale and is certainly appropriate for pilot operations.

Chemical explosives can be used to fracture a deposit of tight gas, oil shale or coal. A number of wells are needed. When high porosity in the rubble is required and chemical explosives are to be used, it is necessary to mine out a cavity and then load the ceiling of the cavity with explosives. When detonated, a rubblized chimney, similar but smaller than that formed by the nuclear explosions, is created. When working at a shallow depth, chemical explosives are undoubtedly preferable, but at great depths nuclear explosives are better because no mining is required and the number of wells needed is greatly reduced.

Creating a large crack in a deposit by using water under high pressure is called "massive hydraulic fracturing." This approach may be used to produce gas from a tight formation. First, a well is drilled into the deposit. The well is cased and perforations are then made in the casing where the fracturing is to occur. Fluid is pumped into the well at pressures high enough to cause the rock near the perforations to crack. When a crack occurs, fluid flows into the crack causing a drop in pressure; more fluid is added, bringing the pressure back up and the process is repeated over and over, making the crack longer and longer. Usually, a single crack is formed extending outward from the well in opposite directions.

Massive hydraulic fracturing involves no explosives and since it is supposed to induce a long crack, it would require fewer deep wells than would be needed using chemical explosives to fracture tight gas deposits. But since it produces a single planar crack extending outward in opposite directions from the well, it is limited in its applications. It is not suitable when a thorough fracturing or rubblization is required.

Thermal Processes. Sometimes, the subsequent process may simply be heating, as in the case of the thermal tertiary oil recovery techniques. Or the process can be more complicated, as in coal gasification in which a series of chemical reactions take place simultaneously. For in situ oil shale recovery and coal conversion, and for some forms of tertiary oil recovery, the fire supplies heat and creates steam and carbon dioxide. These reduce the viscosity of the oil and make it possible to pump the oil out of the deposit. In the oil shale process, the fire (fed by the less volatile components of the hydrocarbons) is needed to change the kerogen (the original form of the hydrocarbon) from a solid wax tied in the rock to liquid-free petroleum. The fire should be lit at the top of the rubblized zone in this case, as well as in the case of coal gasification; the fire will then spread downward after it has consumed the fuel of the top layer. This insures more complete utilization of the deposit.

Chemical Processes. In addition to thermal processes, there are a number of chemical processes used in tertiary recovery of oil. Whereas heat is used to reduce the viscosity of oil, certain chemicals are often used both to reduce the surface barriers between water and oil and to reduce the adhesion of oil to the rock deposits. Both of these mechanisms allow large, additional quantities of oil to be recovered after primary production has been completed.

In converting coal into gas, combustion is required to supply heat for the chemical reactions between steam, oxygen, and the coal to proceed at a reasonable rate. (Coal, oxygen, and water react to yield carbon dioxide, carbon monoxide, methane, hydrogen, and small amounts of other products; the carbon dioxide is soluble in water and can be easily removed.) The reaction will best proceed at a relatively high pressure (corresponding to a column of 500 feet of water). Salt water may be used in the process.

Coal from the West

In the case of coal, there is no shortage of resources nor is the needed capital investment high. Problems are connected with environmental objections and with the labor force.

At present, most of our coal comes from the eastern half of the United States. Most of it is obtained from underground mines and we need more than 100,000 miners to produce 15 quads per year. The coal is of high quality (40 million tons give a quad and we mine approximately 600 million tons per year). Mining is hard, dangerous, and is connected with health hazards (black lung disease). Therefore, there is a real labor problem and one may wonder whether we can count on domestic coal with much greater certainty than on Arab oil. Furthermore, much of the eastern coal is rich in sulfur (3 percent to 6 percent sulfur content) and this raises environmental problems.

In the western half of the United States, there are great coal deposits, which have different advantages and disadvantages compared to the eastern deposits. The advantages seem to predominate and we recommend that we obtain 18 additional quads per year from the West and Alaska to give a total figure of 33 quads. The coal is of lower quality and 50 million tons are needed to give 1 quad. Thus, the additional production (by 1985) would have to amount to 900 million tons per year. The coal is low in sulfur. In Wyoming and Montana, deposits with sulfur content as low as 0.3 percent are available. In Alaska, in fields quite near to the Cook Inlet, we have coal of less than 0.2 percent sulfur content. The coal is highly suitable for surface mining. In Wyoming, 70-foot veins with 70 feet of overburden are frequently encountered. Near the Cook Inlet, 120 feet of overburden above a 50-foot deposit are more appropriate figures.

Highly mechanized surface mining requires a relatively small labor force.

Though we want to mine an additional 900 million tons per year (compared to our present production of 600 million tons), we would have to increase our present labor force of more than 100,000 by less than 20,000 workers. Furthermore, the work is not difficult, hazardous or injurious to health. In the West, the labor force could probably be recruited from the local population. Only in Alaska does it appear necessary to bring in workers.

Surface or strip mining is opposed by environmentalists. This opposition is justified as long as the mined surface is neglected after the operation is completed. Today, such a procedure is no longer legal. In the West, there is an additional objection due to doubt whether vegetation, once uprooted, can be replaced in an arid climate. Two feet of water per acre mined should suffice to compensate for the sparse precipitation. If income from 70 feet of coal is available, there should be no economic difficulty in providing two feet of water, but legal and political problems will remain.

Another question is connected with the transportation of coal. Transportation from the West to the Midwest is feasible by ship, by rail or by slurry-pipeline. The slurry-pipeline is relatively inexpensive, but it requires much more water than the reconstitution of the land. If subsurface salt is available and compatible with the pipeline this may be a satisfactory solution. Disposal of the salt water could present a problem at the output terminals.

Coal could be burned near the mines to generate electricity. Instead of transporting coal, one can transmit the electric power. It is planned to burn coal in Utah to generate power for Los Angeles.

The Cook Inlet is most fortunately located for sea transportation. The coal is a few miles from the coast. The Pacific Basin, including California and Japan may benefit.

Full development of the new coal fields for 1985 may take as much as ten years with more than half of the increased production coming in during the latter part of the period. Availability of the equipment will probably pace the development.

Nuclear Reactors

Public Acceptance. The chief problem concerning nuclear reactors is public acceptance. We discuss below the items that have raised doubts and objections in the minds of many. But, beyond certain concrete objections, the acceptance of reactors runs into a psychological barrier. This barrier may be due to the fear of the unknown, to the memory of Hiroshima, and to exaggerated statements about the danger of the atom.

In order to overcome this psychological barrier, the concrete objections must be discussed in a careful manner. An outline of each argument is given below. In the end, a thorough educational campaign is needed. Without this, the mass employment of nuclear reactors will not be accepted.

State of the Art. Light Water Reactors (Pressurized Water Reactor and Boiling Water Reactor) have been developed, particularly in the United States, into relatively inexpensive and safe sources of energy. A heavy water reactor, CANDU, has been developed in Canada; it is very safe and is competitive except for the requirement for large amounts of expensive heavy water (which may be less expensively produced by novel methods if adequate research is devoted to the purpose). The High Temperature Gas Cooled Reactor (HTGR) has been developed in the United States and abroad (Germany). It is, likewise, competitive.

Existing reactors could play a major role in solving the energy problem except for a number of problems which will be discussed below. We believe that these problems can be solved.

Safety. Safety is a problem because a nuclear reactor, after it has operated for a while, contains great amounts of radioactivity which might escape in case of a violent accident and cause considerable damage to life and health. The psychological impact would be even greater. It should be stressed that an accident, no matter how violent, will cause little or no damage which is due to an explosion of the reactor. The idea which lurks in the public mind that a nuclear reactor can become an atomic bomb has no basis whatsoever.

The fear of radioactivity, however, has a foundation, even if it is exaggerated. If a big nuclear accident ever occurred, thousands of people could be killed and the health of thousands of additional people could be damaged. But many millions of people will wrongly imagine that they are in danger. It is this last unreasonable fear which should be dispelled. It is not generally realized that all of us are exposed to natural radiation and the number of people who will get a much greater dose than the natural radiation will be quite limited, even in the worst possible case.

U.S. individual reactors have, so far, a perfect record. The health of no individual has been damaged in the slightest by radiation from any of these reactors. This record must be maintained by strictly enforced standards and by further improvements.

One of these improvements may well be the location of reactors below 200 feet of earth or 200 feet of water (possibly in a submarine hull). If this could be done at an acceptable cost, safety may well be increased to such an extent that insurance through normal channels (which at present is not available) would become feasible. This would be a great convenience and would also have a badly needed positive influence by reassuring the public.

Environmental Impact. Reactors have been criticized because of the small amount of radiation emitted by them and because of the thermal pollution they cause. The former is negligible compared to the natural background. The main problem is one of public understanding which will permit people to see the effects of radiation in proper perspective.

Thermal pollution may have an effect on the biological environment in rivers and lakes. To the extent that an effect exists, the effect may indeed be harmful or helpful, and it is possible to make adjustments in the aquatic flora and fauna so that the positive aspects of environmental changes will predominate. To call the effect "thermal pollution" is a usage of words which prejudges a straight-forward evaluation.

In any case, the need for energy is more urgent and more vital than a shift in the animal and plant population of a river or a lake, particularly if the shift is performed in a way to moderate the effects.

Nuclear Waste Disposal. The accumulation of nuclear wastes has caused public concern. The fact that some radioactive species have long lives and, therefore, will remain a hazard for many years has caused considerable public concern. Actually, the long-lived radioactive species emit less intensive radiation and to that extent are less dangerous. (This does not hold for alpha emitters, which can be quite dangerous at low intensities. These, and in particular plutonium, are highly usable and will be kept under control for economic reasons as well as for reasons of safety.)

Several methods of safe disposal have been worked out. One is to incorporate the radioactive wastes (after a cooling period of a few months) into solid rods which are hard to break and will not pulverize if broken. These, in turn, are kept in strong bunkers. The radioactive substance can be recovered if and when needed. If a bunker happens to be destroyed, we are faced with a nuisance, not a catastrophe. Another method is to place the radioactive wastes in salt domes at locations whereno earthquake has occurred for a million years. The substance then would be effectively isolated from the biosphere.

The worry about disposal of radioactive wastes is much greater than would seem to be justified and the two solutions mentioned (and possibly other alternatives) should be adequate. Most methods of waste disposal are inexpensive; therefore, cost does not play a major factor in making the selection.

Delays in Reactor Construction. At present, the time needed to build a reactor is approximately ten years. Much of this time is spent in procedures connected with licensing. It would be highly desirable to standardize both reactor designs and the criteria of reactor siting. A speed-up in procedures may lead to reactor construction in five rather than ten years. At the same time, standardization may lead to greater reliability of components and fewer reactor shutdowns. Finally, appropriate standards could be an important factor in the continuation of the unbroken safety record of U.S. industrial reactors.

Sabotage and Theft of Nuclear Explosives. Information on nuclear reactors is available. A well-informed person, with the help of an armed group, could take over a reactor and cause a reactor malfunction with most serious consequences.

Alternatively, reactor-material (for instance, plutonium), could be stolen and used to produce an atomic explosion of high (but probably not of the highest) power. While information on nuclear explosives is secret, there is no insurance against the use of nuclear materials as has been pointed out in the public press.

For these reasons, it is necessary to safeguard reactors with utmost care. (If this has been possible in connection with skyjacking of airplanes, it should be possible in safeguarding reactors.) Locating reactors in reactor farms, underground or underwater may be a sufficient measure to permit effective and complete safety against sabotage. At the same time, transportation of nuclear material must, of course, be controlled in the strictest manner.

Availability of Nuclear Fuel. Reactors of the present type consume the easily utilized portion of uranium available in the rich deposits which are mined today. The expectation that the rich uranium deposits will be depleted has led to the demand for construction of new types of reactors, particularly the Liquid Metal Fast Breeder Reactor (LMFBR) which would utilize approximately a hundred times more of the mined uranium than is utilized today. Unfortunately, the construction of these reactors has run into considerable difficulty and no one expects that they will contribute to our energy supply before 1990. Additional objections have been raised against the LMFBRs on account of safety and accumulation of great amounts of plutonium. These latter objections are probably not justified.

To construct fast breeders will take a big research and development effort. The capital investment that will be needed per plant is quite uncertain and success will certainly be delayed beyond previous schedules. These factors make it necessary to look for alternative solutions. Fortunately, such alternative solutions are available.

One is the use of poorer uranium ores. While the use of such ores will increase the cost of electricity from nuclear reactors, the cost of mined uranium contributes at present only 5 percent to the cost of electricity (not counting costs of isotope separation). Thus, increased fuel costs are not particularly important in this case.

An even better possibility is the use of a substitute fuel, namely, thorium. In consuming a certain amount of uranium, one may produce 80 percent, 90 percent or more new fissionable material (uranium-233) from thorium. If appropriate reactors are used and if thorium is added in appropriate places (for instance, in the blanket of the reactor), the net amount of uranium consumed will be diminished to 20 percent, 10 percent or even less, compared to the amount that would be needed without the thorium. Fortunately, thorium is abundant and widely available. Some reactors, particularly the CANDU reactor and the HTGR, can be easily adapted to the use of thorium. The light water reactors would need more modification, but the cost is small compared to that needed to develop an LMFBR.

The thorium economy could be introduced step by step in such a manner as to couple the appropriate development with the actual deployment of reactors. Thus, the thorium economy can be introduced smoothly and at an early time.

In summary, one may state that shortage of nuclear fuel need not hold up the development of nuclear reactors for the generation of electricity. It is possible that in the end, the LMFBR will become the most useful reactor. But claims to the effect that sooner or later the LMFBR will become unavoidable are unproven.

Reactors Abroad. Due to the availability of oil, gas, coal, and oil shale in the United States, the use of nuclear reactors is, for us, a good option rather than an absolute necessity. In some foreign countries (like Italy or Taiwan) there may be no alternative to nuclear energy. (Since nuclear fuel is cheap and can remain cheap, dependence on a foreign nuclear fuel source need raise no problem in the long run.)

It is necessary to give careful thought to the question of whether the international proliferation of nuclear reactors is compatible with a limitation of the availability of nuclear weapons. It is also important to raise the question of whether it is more hopeful to limit the proliferation of nuclear weapons or to eliminate causes for international conflict. In neither case can we expect an easy solution. It is certain that by encouraging the international use of nuclear reactors, a great contribution can be made toward a worldwide alleviation of the shortage of energy. It is improbable that the United States will succeed in stopping the spread of nuclear reactors even if we were determined to do so.

Electrical Systems

Power shortage is more than just a part of the energy shortage. Due to the present position of the utilities, we are facing a deficiency in generating capacity. This means that the system will be overstrained. Brownouts and even widespread blackouts may result. It is, therefore, essential to relieve the power shortage and to do so in a manner which is not too demanding on capital. We shall discuss four methods (other than the necessary expansion of our generating plants) which will alleviate the situation. These are:

1. Efficient use of fuels in electric generating plants.
2. Energy storage.
3. Improved electrical transmission.
4. Use of computers.

Efficient Use of Fuels in Electric Generating Plants. One of the obvious drawbacks of using electricity is that the efficiency with which energy of fuels is converted into electricity is at present little more than 30 percent. There are a variety of ways in which this efficiency can be improved, some available, some in the stage of research.

One reason for the low efficiency is the heat discharged in the exhaust. This becomes "thermal pollution." Whenever the temperature of the discharge exceeds 600° F., an additional electric generator can be added, raising the efficiency by approximately 10 percentage points (for example, from 32 percent to 42 percent). This can be accomplished by boiling and condensing, within a closed system, an appropriate working fluid similar to the fluids utilized in our refrigerators. A technology which can deliver more generating capacity at a cost in the neighborhood of $300 per installed kilowatt (depending on the exhaust temperature) is available. This development is particularly desirable because the added energy comes from greater efficiency and does not consume additional fuel. Such "bottoming cycles" are, therefore, ready for widespread application.

A further step in utilizing the energy of the fuel is the utilization of lower temperature exhaust gases for applications like space heating. In Germany it has been proposed that the steam exhausts may be distributed over wide areas for the purpose of heating dwellings.

A further improvement in efficiency can be brought about by utilization of high initial temperatures which are available in most fossil plants and in some nuclear plants. This is a more difficult undertaking due to the incompatibility of materials with the high temperature. Gas turbines using exotic materials are being developed. Another possibility is to couple partly ionized high temperature streaming gases with electromagnetic fields and produce electric currents without the employment of moving solid parts. Stationary structures can generally be designed to withstand higher temperatures.

These "topping cycles" could increase the efficiency of power plants by another 10 percent. Total efficiency of more than 50 percent is in sight provided that research and development is carried forward in a vigorous manner.

Energy Storage. Figure I-13 is an often presented figure showing the demand for power. The actual capacity has to be higher than the maximal demand by an appropriate safety margin to take care of possible outages. By inexpensive storage, we could reduce the number of needed plants to a level which satisfies the average need with an appropriate safety margin.

The present method to store energy in a form available as electric power is pumped storage. Artificial lakes are filled and then emptied. This, of course, is possible at present only in limited geographic locations. The cost for the equipment for the storage is approximately $100 per kilowatt and the cost for storage space may be estimated at $15 per kilowatt-hour. If one wants to store for eight hours, one will have to spend $220 per kilowatt. One also should recognize that in the process of storing the energy by filling up the lakes and later generating electricity, one loses approximately one-third of the original electrical energy.

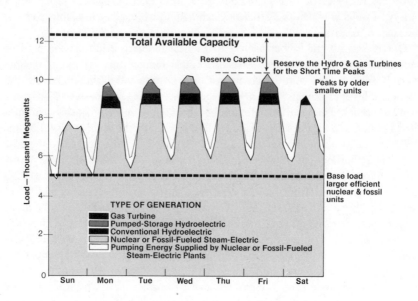

Figure I-13. Typical U.S. Weekly Electricity Demand.

There are several novel methods of storage. One of these is the use of improved batteries; another is the use of flywheels. Both of these methods can store energy in small amounts and therefore in locations near to the consumer. This helps to eliminate transmission costs and transmission losses.

In the case of storage batteries, the conversion equipment will cost $50 per installed kilowatt to which one has to add the cost of storage capacity at $30 or more per kilowatt-hour stored. The energy losses are only slightly less than in the case of pumped storage. At present, there is a disadvantage in that the lifetime of batteries is quite limited and new capital investment will be needed after short periods. Advanced batteries will have lifetimes of five years or more.

The use of flywheels has been limited in the past. They have great promise particularly if the flywheels will be made of inexpensive fiber compositions (for instance, E-glass) whose mechanical properties are much superior to steel (high tensile strength around the periphery and relatively easy compression in the radial direction). The conversion costs are low (approximately $20 per kilowatt). The cost for stored energy is estimated to be $40 per kilowatt-hour stored. (This amounts to $340 per stored kilowatt for an eight-hour period, but the flywheels are much more economic if storage is needed for shorter periods.) The advantages of the flywheels are longer lifetimes (probably thirty years or longer) and the small losses in that at least 90 percent of the original electrical energy can be recovered.

If energy is to be stored over long periods, a low cost per stored kilowatt-hour is required. This is best accomplished by storage in a chemical form such as hydrogen obtained from electrolysis. In this case, the cost per stored kilowatt-hour could become less than $10 and might become as little as $2. On the other hand, the costs of conversion are as high as $250 per kilowatt. This means an investment which approaches that of the original generating plant. Also, in some of these systems, two-thirds of the electrical energy, or even more, may be lost. Fuel cells could perform a most important function here.

Electrical Transmission. Improved electrical transmission would offer another great advantage. Inexpensive transmission which involves less loss in electricity per mile would give us greater freedom in locating power plants. At the same time, better transmission would allow greater freedom in establishing interties between power plants. Such interties have a great advantage; they permit the use of electricity at any one time from the cheapest available source. They also serve as an insurance against blackouts and brownouts although it has to be noted that when the interties fail, very widespread blackouts can occur, as was the case in the big blackout in the Northeast in November, 1965.

Better transmission can be obtained by applying a higher voltage. Indeed, high voltage lines (up to one million volts) are being installed. Some of these high voltage lines can be placed underground, protected by a tube of pressurized insulating gas such as SF_6.

Another possibility is to transmit electricity at low temperatures at which resistance of metals becomes quite small. These low temperature transmission lines would have to be installed underground.

Still another solution might be to use exceedingly low temperatures at which some metals become "super conductors." A "super conductor" is a strange state of a metal in which it has no resistance whatsoever. Thus, electricity losses would be eliminated. Known super conductors require cooling by liquid helium, which is difficult; they will take a long period of development. It is not clear whether they will be more economical than other low-temperature systems.

Use of Computers. Computers have been introduced in central control stations to control interties for the purpose of optimizing the use of energy by drawing at any time on the cheapest available source of electricity. These computers are also beginning to be used to store and display data about the state of the major components of the generating plants and transmission lines. This will help the dispatcher to make the right decisions, for instance, by accepting a local and temporary brownout, or even blackout, rather than permitting an overstrained system to break down.

9. Other Energy Sources

A considerable number of other energy sources have been proposed. Some of them have widespread support. Quite a few of them could make moderate contributions in the near future and some have the promise of becoming important by the year 2000.

Geothermal Energy

Geothermal energy is often called a "renewable" resource. This claim is not valid. There is a steady supply of energy flowing from the deep interior of the earth, but the rate at which this supply becomes available is not very large. If all of it could be utilized under ideal conditions (and this situation cannot be even approached), geothermal energy would barely suffice to supply our needs for electricity in the 1980s in the conterminous forty-eight states.

Actual geothermal possibilities depend on the heat energy already present in the few miles near the surface of the earth. This "fossil heat" is comparable in magnitude with the energy contained in our coal deposits. It is, however, more difficult to utilize.

The simplest use occurs where intrusion of hot magma near water-bearing layers generates dry steam at high temperatures. Inexpensive electric power in San Francisco is obtained in this way. The availability of such heat is limited. Where it is available, it may well be depleted in a few decades.

Wet steam at lower temperatures is more abundant, but cannot be used unless materials are developed which can resist corrosion, erosion, and scaling (deposition of materials).

One may use high-temperature dry rock by fracturing it and adding water. This may become a rather ample resource but the needed research, development and engineering will take many years. The eventual cost is uncertain. One must bear in mind that coal and hydrocarbons are more concentrated in energy and prol ably more lucrative. If one has to take such difficult steps as breaking rock, it may be better done in oil and gas deposits.

Recommendations. The United States research efforts should be threefold.

a. Conduct exploration for sources of geothermal energy of the present type (dry steam) in the Western United States.

b. Conduct research to use other types of geothermal sources such as wet steam, dry hot rock (the rock must be cracked and water added) and other variations.

c. Share our research effort with other countries, particularly with Japan, which has an excellent geothermal research program on volcanism.

Solar Energy

It seems obvious to many that solar energy, a source which is widely distributed, constantly renewed, and plentiful, should be the eventual solution to the energy problem. Unfortunately, to collect solar energy for the generation of electricity is expensive. Capital expenditures, maintenance and replacement costs, and the need to utilize large areas make it impractical to exploit solar energy on a large scale in the near future.

The very fact that solar energy is dispersed makes it appropriate for local use in water heating, space heating, and air conditioning. For space heating, necessary energy storage can take the form of hot water reservoirs or other materials which can retain a lot of energy. It is a little more surprising that solar energy can also be used for air conditioning. This can be done using a principle similar to that used in refrigeration, a process employing hot water and another sealed working fluid (for example, ammonia) which can extract heat from the interior of a house and deliver it on the outside.

For buildings which are not higher than three stories, one can collect enough solar energy on the roof to serve the heating and cooling purposes which have been described above. The collection of solar energy is a relatively simple matter, using the "green house" effect. This permits the entry of solar energy, but impedes the reradiation of the invisible longer waves, which is the general mechanism by which heat is lost from the earth. Collection does not require expensive focusing or even glass; water can be heated over a black surface if a plastic cover is provided. This procedure is on the verge of becoming quite economical at present due to the development of cheap and durable plastics. In the body of the report, we have recommended this method of employing solar energy.

A much more ambitious plan is to use solar energy for large-scale electricity generation. There are two main possibilities. One is to focus the sunlight, boil water (or some other fluid), and use a steam engine. Even though the technology is well-established, this possibility is uneconomical because the capital requirements are too high by about a factor of ten.

The second method is to use sunlight to move electrons in solids. The technology was used in our spacecraft. The current capital investment is too high by approximately a factor of one thousand. The field is new, however, and great improvements can, and are, being made. Even so, an improvement by a factor of one thousand will be difficult, perhaps impossible, to achieve.

Recommendations. There should be two major areas of United States involvement.

a. Encourage the development and mass production of solar devices to produce warm water with application to heating and cooling of houses and to mobile homes. An approach through state governments is appropriate since conditions in various states are widely different.

b. Fund, or subsidize and encourage research on conversion of solar radiation into electricity. Economically feasible solutions are not probable before the year 2000.

Energy from Crops

Plants transform solar energy into fuel. Therefore, energy from crops may be considered as a variant of solar energy. Carbon dioxide from fossil fuel plants can be collected under plastic covers over ponds growing algae. This speeds up the growth of the algae and enhances the utilization of sunlight.

Recommendation. Encourage research and development on the production of fuels (like methyl alcohol) from algae, wood, corn stalks, and other vegetable products.

Energy from Urban Wastes

A number of cities are currently operating, or have under consideration, electric generating plants which use solid waste as fuel. Among these are Norfolk, Virginia; St. Louis, Missouri; Miami, Florida; Nashville, Tennessee; and Saugus, Massachusetts. The State of Connecticut has under construction or has announced plans for twelve regional plants. A number of other cities and states have also announced plans for such plants.

Recommendation. Improve or develop methods to generate electricity by burning urban waste. Even current plants appear to be economically sound investments when one considers the need to dispose of the urban waste. The execution should remain in the hands of state and municipal authorities with research and other help made available by the federal government.

Wind Energy

Wind energy has been used for centuries. As the wind velocity doubles, the energy output increases by a factor of eight. It is important to raise the rotors well off the surface because surface friction decreases wind velocities close to the ground. Gusts and unusually high winds impose special problems. Some form of energy storage or backup energy supply is necessary for periods of relative calm.

Recommendation. Establish wind-powered generators in locations of high and steady winds. One excellent location is found in the hills of Oahu, which give rise to local intensifications of the trade winds. Since effectiveness of wind power depends sensitively on the strength and steadiness of the wind, the number of places where this power can be used is quite limited.

Energy from Tides

Dams or underwater "windmills" (water wheels) are required to take advantage of tidal energy. The energy output is predictable but not uniform over time.

Recommendation. An engineering study of the exploitation of the strong tides in the Bay of Fundy is justified. A good location in the United States is not available. The project calls for cooperation with Canada.

Heat Energy from the Ocean

Temperature differences in the oceans caused by surface heating of water with cold water at depth appear to offer a "renewable" energy source. The temperature differences, however, are small and, consequently, even theoretical efficiencies are low. To produce electricity commercially at such low efficiencies with present technology requires excessive capital investment.

Recommendation. Continue research on the exploitation of the temperature difference between warm, tropical surface water and cold water at depth on a modest scale. Economic success is not in sight at the present time. Cold water from deep ocean layers might improve the efficiency of electrical generating plants located near the coasts.

Energy from Nuclear Fusion

Nuclear fusion in an explosive form was demonstrated in the early 1950s. Ever since, there has been a sizable effort to bring nuclear fusion under control and make it applicable for steady energy production. The process demands exceedingly high temperatures. At present, two approaches are pursued.

One approach is based on the fact that at high temperatures, atoms are torn apart into charged particles—nuclei and electrons. In the presence of a magnetic field, these particles are forced to spiral around the magnetic field and they can be kept away from the walls of the vessel. Thus, the exceedingly hot gas (which is called plasma) can, in principle, be contained in an arrangement that has been called a "magnetic bottle."

At the exceedingly high temperatures (about 100,000,000°), the density must be low so as to reduce the pressure to a tolerable value. Unfortunately, at the required pressures magnetic bottles turn out to be leaky. For more than two decades work has concentrated on making the containment tight; this work seems to be nearing completion. In the first years, the effort was secret. But, in 1958, at the Second Atoms for Peace Conference, a full disclosure was made and, since that time, a vigorous international effort has been proceeding. In the United States, approximately $100 million are going to be spent each year, according to present plans. The effort in Russia is somewhat larger. The exchange of information is highly satisfactory. In fact, the major attempt toward a first demonstration of a controlled fusion energy generator, Tokamak, is based on Russian experiments.

The realization of an economic power source based on controlled fusion is, however, in the distant future. It has been correctly stated that the fuel source for fusion is practically unlimited and that the radioactive products are so greatly reduced (as compared to a fission reactor) that we can consider the projected fusion reactor both clean and safe. What will determine the economy of fusion power will be the needed capital investment and the maintenance costs. It is obvious, even at the present time, that the system will be exceedingly complex and these costs may be quite high. It is, therefore, premature to assert that fusion power will develop into the ultimate energy source.

Past experience shows that from demonstration to economic feasibility, two decades are needed. While the development may be faster in this case, the engineering difficulties are also greater. One may assume, therefore, that this type of fusion power will not make a major contribution to the energy economy prior to the year 2000.

The other method for the constructive application of fusion is the "nuclear internal combustion engine." In this case, we substitute for steady burning a series of micro-explosions. The explosions are similar to those in a hydrogen bomb except for the fact that less than a millionth of the thermonuclear fuel is involved, giving rise to less than a millionth of the energy released in each explosion (unlike the present internal combustion, the individual "micro-explosions" would still be quite large). All this can be done provided one compresses the thermonuclear fuel more than a thousandfold, a feat which is possible in principle, but exceedingly difficult in practice. To accomplish this, great amounts of energy must be concentrated in less than a billionth of a second in a volume not much greater than a billionth of a cubic inch. The plan is to concentrate this energy with the help of well-focused lasers, which are novel light sources of incredible intensity.

The practical execution runs into the overwhelming difficulties of needed developments in laser technology, of compressing tiny droplets to unprecedented densities (at pressures exceeding the pressure at the center of the sun) and, finally, of being able to repeat such explosions billions of times without the necessity of major adjustments. The scientific parts of the program are both exciting and they are apt to be rewarding in unexpected ways. Practical and economic large-scale energy production for our economy may never be feasible; if it is feasible, it may take half a century to accomplish it.

International cooperation in laser fusion is, unfortunately, not as well established as in the case of the older, magnetic-containment fusion efforts. Due to the difficulty of the job, it is a field where contributions from the best minds should be used according to the traditions of free scientific interchange.

The two fusion concepts discussed above enjoy great popularity in some scientific and political circles. The vigorous research effort should indeed be continued. But, due to the situation described above, there seems to be limited reason to consider energy shortage as a motivation for uncontrolled expenditures on controlled fusion.

Recommendations. United States research efforts should concentrate in two areas.

a. Continue research on magnetically contained controlled thermonuclear fusion on the present scale and under the present rules which encourage broad international cooperation. Commercial success by the year 2000 is possible.

b. Continue recently initiated research on laser fusion (which depends on concentration of high energies in a small volume). Encourage international cooperation on the model of the previous recommendation. Commercial success may be attained in the next century. This research, as well as the research recommended above, may produce interesting applications outside the field of massive energy production.

The Hydrogen Economy

Hydrogen has been recommended as an energy package which could be widely available. The technology is difficult.

Recommendation. Conduct research on the production of hydrogen, the burning of hydrogen in various engines, the distribution and, particularly, the safe handling of hydrogen. In the twenty-first century, the results of such research might pay off.

Other Chemical Fuels

To put the hydrogen economy in proper perspective, other novel chemical fuels should also be explored.

Recommendation. Conduct research on other chemical fuels and on systems of producing, distributing and using these more complex fuels.

Use of Fuel Cells

Fuel cells are not an energy source. They convert fuels, particularly hydrogen, into electrical power with high efficiency. In a fuel cell, a chemical reaction, such as hydrogen and oxygen combining into water, converts chemical energy into direct current electricity. Actually, something entirely similar is happening in the lead acid battery. In this case, however, the chemical reaction that gives rise to the electricity is the oxidation of lead. The problem in the fuel cell is to convert hydrogen into a state where it can enter the fluid in an electric battery. Conventionally, this is done with the help of platinum which takes up hydrogen gas and permits hydrogen ions to enter into an aqueous solution.

In principle, fuel cells work, but because of the use of platinum and the handling of other components, they are expensive. Furthermore, the production and handling of hydrogen itself is expensive and dangerous. In order to make fuel cells economical, it is important to replace platinum by a cheaper substance. In principle, this seems possible.

It would be furthermore highly desirable to have well-working fuel cells in which hydrocarbons (for instance, methane) are used up instead of the hydrogen. The direct conversion of hydrocarbon into electricity at high efficiences would be of great advantage if it could be done at a reasonably low capital cost.

Recommendation. Encourage ongoing industrial efforts to decrease the cost of presently expensive fuel cells and to extend the use of fuel cells to other fuels, for instance, methane.

10. Priorities in Research and Development

Important topics for research and development have been mentioned in the previous sections. We shall summarize the research and development which is needed on energy resources and we shall order the topics according to a rough evaluation of their priorities. The highest priority topics are listed first.

The priorities are judged on three bases:

1. The importance of the project.
2. The expectation of early success.
3. The contribution research can make to the project.

In Situ Technologies

Fossil fuels, particularly oil, gas, coal, and oil shale, will continue to be our most important energy sources for the rest of the century. In the production of these fuels, it will become increasingly important to induce changes underground (that is, in situ) before the product is obtained.

In the case of oil in the United States, only one-third is produced by usual methods, while two-thirds is left underground either because it is too viscous or for other reasons. Methods such as the fire drive, which burns some of the oil underground to produce heat and carbon dioxide to reduce the viscosity of the remaining oil, or the use of surfactants, which reduce the capillary attraction between the oil and the rock, may be applied to get additional oil production.

In the case of coal, the underground burning of coal under appropriate conditions in the presence of high pressure steam might produce gas from the coal in an inexpensive and environmentally acceptable manner.

In the case of oil shale, burning the non-volatile component drives out the volatile hydrocarbons. This process is similar to the usual retorting process employed above ground, but it can proceed underground after the shale has been transformed into rubble.

These three processes have similarities in the technical sense. They may lead to effective exploitation of the resources without heavy capital expenditures, with less human labor and with the use of little or no water. This research and development effort is given the highest priority because in the case of a favorable outcome, oil and gas resources would be greatly increased and because the cost of the produced oil and gas may well be quite moderate (see Section 8).

Inaccessible Oil and Gas

In recent years we have looked for oil and gas at increased depths. This makes drilling equipment with greatly increased drilling rates highly desirable. The same equipment has great advantages in the oil and gas production on the continental shelf where each day of drilling means great expense. Therefore, one of the important research and development projects is the production of better drilling equipment which is, indeed, one of the goals vigorously pursued by private enterprise.

A somewhat similar research and development effort will be needed where we try to use the sedimentary deposits found at depths of several thousand feet under the ocean. Exploitation of oil pools which are suspected in these deposits will require new equipment which can be operated by remote control.

We must rely in the short run on petroleum. Therefore, this research and development is important for the United States and for the world.

Environmental Research

Environmental legislation has been introduced without full knowledge of the effects of pollutants and in the absence of equipment that could be used to reduce pollutants to acceptable levels without seriously restricting the production of energy. In order to reconcile the requirements for energy with the requirements for a clean environment, a number of research projects are needed. The following may serve as examples:

a. Research on the effects of sulfur dioxide emission, the effects of particulate emission, and the effect of interaction of these two emissions.

b. Research and development on apparatus for reducing pollutants in stack gases.

c. Research and development on methods of cleaning up oil spills.

d. Research and development on methods of reducing automobile emissions, while improving engine efficiencies.

The results of investigations and developments of this type will allow us to reduce environmental damage without severe and unnecessary interference with our various needs for energy. Therefore, this environmental research and development activity should have high priority.

Improved Transportation

Most of our scarce oil is used in transportation. Therefore, economizing in the use of energy for transportation is vital. Following the remarkable development of the automobile industry in the beginning of the century, further technical research was not emphasized in Detroit. It is probable that some of the suggestions for producing auto engines which consume less fuel will prove successful.

Replacement of automobiles by other modes of transportation, particularly rapid transit, has received a greater share of our research and development effort. In spite of this, rapid transit is not playing an important role. The reason may be that the conveniences of dispersed housing and transportation available to the individual at the time he chooses, are not given up easily. Even so, research and development in rapid transit and other modes of transportation may be important in reducing expenditures of energy.

Research and development in transportation will probably not succeed without participation by the government or inducements established by the government.

Equipment to Reduce Energy Consumption

The principles by which energy can be saved in industry are known and a considerable amount of the engineering and development of the relevant equipment has been performed. This engineering must be adapted to the many different industrial applications. It seems that this adaptation can be best performed by industry itself. The role of the government may be to encourage this development by appropriate financial incentives We are speaking here of a continuing effort. Some of the payoff may come within a year. But much more can, and should, be done in the next decade.

Nuclear Fission Reactors

Reactors of the present type are satisfactory, but should, of course, be further perfected. Improvements should be made in reactor safety (including the safest place to locate reactors), in reliable waste disposal, in methods of separating isotopes needed in reactor construction, and in methods of mining uranium (particularly uranium minerals of a poorer grade). Finally, thorium should be introduced as a supplementary fuel. This last important item requires limited modifications in existing reactors which, in turn, will amount to a short-term development effort (see also Section 8).

The expensive effort to develop fast breeders cannot pay off before 1990; it should be continued, but with a lower priority.

Transmission and Storage of Energy

Improved transmission of energy would result in savings and would allow greater freedom in locating electric generating plants. Research on this topic is progressing and needs support.

An issue of equal importance is the storage of energy so that electrical power plants may be more fully and more steadily utilized. There are various possibilities to improve pumped storage plants or to supplement them with batteries, flywheels or chemical storage and fuel cells.

As a consequence of the creation of a vigorous research organization that serves the utilities, the Electric Power Research Institute, proper priority may be given to these problems.

Geothermal Energy

Today, geothermal energy accounts for less than 0.1 percent of our energy supply. Research on utilization of various kinds of geothermal energy which, on the basis of today's technology, cannot be used, could raise this contribution to perhaps as high as 3 percent by the year 2000. This would be a welcome addition and such projects should be pursued.

Domestic Use of Solar Energy

The use of solar energy in water heating, in space heating, and in air-conditioning is, in principle, solved. In practice, the available methods are on the margin of becoming cost effective. Solar energy engineering, development and production for these applications is quite worthwhile, but little or no true research effort is needed.

Electricity from Solar Energy

Various schemes to derive electricity from solar energy have been proposed, but capital expenditures must be brought down by a factor of ten or more before any scheme can become practical. Effective imitation of photosynthesis in the test tube might result in a revolutionary change in the utilization of the energy of the sun. There are no immediate prospects for this, and massive expenditure of funds is not likely to make a significant difference. The project should be pursued on moderate priority because in the long run, it might result in a practical, good solution to a part of the energy problem.

Nuclear Fusion

Research on this subject has proceeded for more than two decades and no demonstration of feasibility has yet been accomplished. The topic, as well as a recent modification, laser fusion, has high intrinsic interest and may in the long run give rise to a clean source of energy using a virtually unlimited fuel supply. It is reasonable to maintain present rates of research expenditure (more than $100 million per year), but the energy shortage provides only marginal reason to accelerate this research.

Fuels from Urban Waste and from Crops

A moderate percentage of our electrical energy needs may be supplied from these sources. An effort in engineering and coordination with activities in waste disposal are justified.

Wind Energy

The technology for using the energy of the wind exists. The possibility for use of this energy would look better if appropriately coupled with energy storage. It seems rewarding to undertake these projects only in places where the average wind velocity surpasses 20 mph. This limits the applicability to approximately 1 percent of our electrical needs. Some effort is justified.

Fuel Cells

Recent success in using fuel cells in space exploration has stimulated industrial research on this instrument for energy conversion. The inherent efficiency of fuel cells makes them an attractive possibility if costs can be made competitive at least for specialized applications.

The Hydrogen Economy

The technology lies in the distant future and the research connected with it should have low priority.

Ocean Energy

The tides and temperature differences in the ocean could make a modest contribution to electrical requirements. Because of the limited amount of energy and not too favorable economics, research and development should have a low priority.

11. Manpower Requirements

Research, development and implementation are limited by the availability of technical manpower. The lack of popularity of technical subjects among our young people in the 1960s has resulted in a shortage of appropriately educated manpower.

No matter what popular opinion asks us to believe, technology, and especially the development of new technology, will be crucial for human survival. Contrary to much of our current thinking, technology and its development is not antithetical to human values. Indeed, quite the opposite is true. Tool-making and the social organization it implies are very deeply ingrained in our natures. This is, in fact, the primary attribute that distinguishes man from other animals. We must continue to adapt our technology, which is, in essence, our ability to shape nature more effectively in order to face the problems that the human race faces today.

It is for this reason that the development and expansion of technical education is so important. It is only through the possession of high skills and the development of educational systems for the acquisition of these skills that human prosperity can be insured.

The cutback of scholarships, fellowships, and traineeships has caused serious damage. This damage has been compounded by an antiscientific trend among our young people which has abated, but has hardly been reversed as of yet. Education of scientists takes four to eight years. The deficiencies will not be corrected before 1985.

Apart from appropriate financial aid, the program must be made attractive to the young people. This may be done in connection with ecology. The realization that environmental aspirations can be achieved only by scientific and technical means may help to make scientific studies popular among our students. Furthermore, decisive help may come from economic hardships which cause students to turn to subjects where fellowships are available and where good employment is in prospect. If appropriate information is made available and fellowships are offered, the training of scientists will probably proceed in a satisfactory manner.

The shortage of engineering students is not as severe as the shortage of scientists. The measures recommended above will provide us with an adequate number of engineers.

Training technicians and craftsmen presents a different problem. There is an increasing shortage, which is partly due to the fact that the job of a technician is not an easy one and partly due to the circumstance that the rewards for technicians are not very substantial, either in money or in status. The monetary rewards should be increased. It is difficult to fill the numerous jobs which are considered routine but which, in fact, require considerable skills.

Programs dealing with the education of engineering technicians and paraprofessionals should be centered in the nation's rapidly growing two-year junior and community colleges. As in the case of training craftsmen, the intention here is to bring into the educational process organizations that will ultimately employ the products of the programs. In the junior colleges, programs for the training of engineering technicians are generally laid out as work-study programs where the student spends one quarter in school and the following quarter working in some kind of a job that leads to an increase in his skills as a technician. Four-year programs lead to a degree of Associate in Arts and a paraprofessional certificate. The educational program could either lead to a journeyman's standing in a craft or be counted as work experience if the individual seeks a position as a technician in a non-craft area.

Training in the crafts is done primarily within a well-organized series of apprentice programs. Apprentice programs in this country are operated by individual concerns, construction companies, machine shops, and other organizations of this kind in collaboration with the nation's trade unions. The time taken to achieve a journeyman's rating in a given craft, at the present time, is usually four to six years.

The main problem for education in the crafts is to raise the status of craftsmen in our society. We must be able to attract much better talent into the crafts than is presently drawn into these fields. The best opportunity to encourage young people to pursue careers as craftsmen is presented first in the nation's high schools. The term "vocational education" is usually applied to these programs and they tend to be contrasted unfavorably with the "academic programs" that are operated by the same high schools. Industry and other employers of craftsmen should be brought in to help the high schools run craft programs. Outside groups of this kind are able to make available equipment that high schools generally cannot purchase. The opportunity to work with sophisticated equipment will, in turn, raise the prestige of crafts programs among the students. Part-time programs using industrial equipment available in the neighborhood should be instituted on a large scale. Nominal salaries should be paid to high school students who participate in part-time educational programs in the crafts with local industries. The salaries work to make these programs more attractive than "academic" programs operated by the high schools.

Considering the whole complex of problems, we may take some encouragement from reading the language of the Land Grant Act of 1862:

The leading object shall be, without excluding other scientific and classical studies and including military tactics, to teach such branches of learning as are related to agriculture and the mechanic arts, in such manner as the legislatures of the States may respectively prescribe, in order to promote the liberal and practical education of the industrial classes in the several pursuits and professions of life.

This was, and still is, an excellent charter. The educational institutions that were developed under its provisions, have served the nation well for more than a century. It is not hard to establish the connection between our obvious strength in agriculture and technology and the educational initiative taken by Senator Morrill and his congressional colleagues in 1862. To the extent that the spirit of this charter may gain in influence in our high schools, colleges, institutes of technology, and universities, we shall be on our way to solving the manpower problem.

12. The Contribution of the United States to World Stability

Research on meeting the energy problem for the period after 1985 must be undertaken now. Engineering and scientific breakthroughs require both the development of a supporting technology, and an industrial and economic establishment willing to finance and use the new technology. Public acceptance of new technology on grounds of safety and environmental effects also takes time.

We have referred to the need for international cooperation in energy research. Worldwide interdependence is becoming more necessary and more pronounced with each decade. By the year 2000, it will become unavoidable that the present precarious world order be replaced by an order which is more stable and more just.

Energy is a good case in point. A sound world order requires an equitable solution of the worldwide energy shortage. Our target for 1985 has been set to satisfy U.S. energy needs; this development is under our own control. In addition, we have proposed that we strive for the capability of exporting energy to relieve part of the worldwide energy shortage and to exert an influence in the direction of a more stable world economy.

The long-term action on energy must meet international requirements. We should favor the particular forms of energy that will prove most economical, clean, and easily available. Our objective is to make energy available in a manner that will avoid endangering the stability of the international monetary system and the economy of the world.

The U.S. attempt to achieve energy self-reliance before 1985 should be considered as a necessary first step toward a more difficult eventual objective. The longer range objective is to use U.S. influence—as we did in the period following the Second World War—to establish a viable order in the world and an economic and political climate which is compatible with our ideals, and with the aspirations of the world community.

The sharing of research among nations is the proper introduction to a world energy plan for 2000. In this way, the technical basis will be laid on which proper decisions can be made with inputs from all participants. Furthermore, the organization and progress of research will bring about personal contacts between the technical experts, the economic experts, and the political organizations of the various countries. The formulation of concrete plans may then be carried out by people who consider themselves more as collaborators and less as opponents.

The technological revolution has two consequences. One is to bring about even closer interaction among the peoples of the globe; the world is becoming more crowded and full of danger. The other is the opportunity to discover new resources so that we need not fight for the necessities of life.

The energy crisis is the latest event in this rapid change. If we manage to solve it there will be other—probably bigger—difficulties to solve. But at this moment the name of the danger and of the opportunity is energy. We must surmount the danger—and we must seize the opportunity.

Notes

1. U.S. Bureau of Mines, *Assessment of U.S. Petroleum Supply With Varying Drilling Efforts*, Report No. 1.C. 8634, March, 1974.

2. *U.S. Energy Resources, A Review as of 1972.* Prepared for Committee on Interior and Insular Affairs, U.S. Senate, June, 1974.

II Technology Development and the National Purpose

Hans Mark

1. Introduction

This year, the United States enters its third century of existence as a sovereign nation. We possess the oldest continuous form of republican self-government among the major nations in the world today. This is truly remarkable considering the turbulence and instability of the times encompassed by the last two centuries. The main reason for this stability is the unique adaptability of our Constitution to changing conditions. The nation has been able to change its fundamental goals several times and the system has adapted accordingly. We seem now to be at a point where some fundamental new directions in our national life are evolving, challenging us to define clearly the new directions and to modify our ancient political institutions in an appropriate manner.

The author would like to express his thanks to the many people with whom he discussed the contents of this chapter and who contributed by making substantial comments. Among those are: Sheldon M. Atlas, Michel Bader, John W. Boyd, Loren G. Bright, Arthur E. Bryson, Jr., Alan B. Chambers, Dean R. Chapman, Robert Colvin, Henry Diamond, James C. Fletcher, John S. Foster, Jr., Glen Goodwin, E.Z. Gray, Thomas Gregory, C.W. Harper, Harold Hornby, Roy P. Jackson, Robert T. Jones, Robert M. Jopson, Donald B. Kornreich, George M. Low, Bernard Lubarsky, Bruce T. Lundin, William H. Magruder, Herman F. Mark, Alfred Mascy, Leornard Roberts, Nelson A. Rockefeller, Walt W. Rostow, Oscar Ruebhausen, Joseph Sharp, Frederick Sytles, C.A. Syvertson, Wilson K. Talley, Edward Teller, Theodore Walkowitz, Richard Wood, George D. Woods, and Alfred M. Worden. Special thanks are due to Robert E. Machol, who edited the final draft and who made many important substantive contributions. Finally, the author is grateful to Mrs. Edith W. Watson, who competently handled the mechanics of the numerous drafts of the manuscript, and to Miss Ann Fogle and Mrs. Linda Cox for typing the drafts and the final manuscript.

For the first hundred years of our existence, the national objective was to occupy and develop the vast western frontier. This goal was explicitly formulated in the early years of the nineteenth century under the doctrine of "manifest destiny." The nation's political life revolved around this objective, and it is interesting to remember that our most profound internal crisis, the Civil War, was actually triggered by issues related to the organization of new territories that were being occupied (Missouri Compromise, Kansas-Nebraska Act, etc.).

During our second century, our national goals were less explicit but, nevertheless, a clearly recognizable thread runs through this period; namely, the evolution of the United States as a world power. The establishment of our "influence" in the world began to preoccupy some of the country's leaders in the last years of the nineteenth century. This was a clear departure from George Washington's warning in 1796 against "foreign entanglements."[1] There was no general agreement regarding the nature of the "influence" that we wanted to exert. Some felt that it should be political in that we should attempt to export our political institutions to the rest of the world. Cuba, Mexico, and the Philippines, for example, were to be annexed and become American states with the same institutional arrangements existing in Iowa or Vermont. Others believed that we should become a first-class military power in order to extend our influence. Admiral Alfred Thayer Mahan, the distinguished military historian, was particularly important among the people in this group. His voice influenced the decision to construct a large navy, which became the "big stick" of President Theodore Roosevelt's foreign policy. Others felt that American influence could best be exerted on a moral and spiritual level, and this feeling led to the extensive denominational missionary activities sponsored by Americans in this period.

It was also during this period that the United States became a creditor nation. We began to invest American funds to develop resources in other nations rather than the other way around. This development was due largely to the very active and successful free enterprise system that had evolved in the United States during the nineteenth century. Finally, the United States was drawn into conflicts in other parts of the world by the very existence of our vast resources and our consequent physical power. In many cases, the United States simply expanded into a power vacuum left by the decline of other nations.

All of these diverse activities were more or less successful. In 1945 we stood at the zenith of our influence in moral, political, economic, and military terms. It is important to recognize that our position in 1945 was not the result of a grand design but came about due to a combination of circumstances in the world and the strong general feeling in this country, that U.S. "influence" had to be a permanent feature in world affairs. In that sense, our implicit national goal to exert our influence in the world was achieved.

Since 1945, our position has eroded substantially—our moral leadership is being seriously questioned, our political ideas have not been accepted, our economic position has weakened, and we are no longer the world's leading military power. There is, however, one vital area in which we retain unchallenged leadership and that is in the development and application of technology.

What we have done since 1945, and what we are continuing to do, is to Americanize the world through our technology. For example, 85 percent of all commercial aircraft in the world are of American manufacture. We have a near monopoly in the development and sales of commercial nuclear electric power stations. Our advanced agricultural technology is desperately sought after by nations on all continents. Our communications satellites have added a new dimension to people's ability to talk with others around the globe. Finally, our electronics and computer technology has revolutionized control and management systems of all kinds. While other nations (the Japanese and Germans, in particular) have exceeded us in productive efficiency, none has, as of now, mastered the art of developing new technology as well as we have.

The time has come to recognize explicitly our strength in technology development and to define a national purpose around our abilities in this field as a focus for the third century of our existence as a nation.

At first glance, this suggestion might seem strange. Now, when there is general agreement among influential elements of our population that technology should be curbed and that the effects of technology are bad, why should we concentrate on it? As a matter of fact, the problem is not technology and its applications, the problem is its control. It is now fashionable to say that technology cannot be controlled. This is simply nonsense. Any human activity can be controlled and properly channeled if it is sufficiently well understood. We must learn to understand the effects of the application of technology in much greater detail than we do now and we should do this explicitly and as a national objective. We have, in fact, already made some very important strides in this direction in the last few years. The national debate over the ecological effects of the large-scale applications of technology has led to considerable public enlightenment. For example, we have long known that the use of DDT has some adverse consequences, but we have recently learned that not to use it may be even more damaging (the recent large-scale destruction of certain timber areas in the Pacific Northwest by the tussock moth[2] and the upsurge of malaria in Ceylon are examples). This debate has led to a much broader public understanding of the complex relationship between technology and its impact on the "natural" world.

In a democracy such as ours, there is no way to examine and to settle these issues except by vigorous and informed public debate. This is not a clear or even orderly procedure, nor is it guaranteed to be foolproof or free from error. It is, however, the best method we have, and toward this end the efforts we are now organizing to assess the impact of new technology should be encouraged. It is impossible to say at this time how successful these attempts at assessment will be, but we are surely moving in the right direction. In political terms, our problem is one that is common to all democratic societies: how do we control the "experts"? It is important to recognize that this problem is with us no matter what we elect to do, and that we must learn to control "experts," be they military, legal, economic, or scientific and engineering people. This is not an easy thing to do, but we have generally been more successful at it than other societies, and the healthy skepticism we have as a nation toward anyone who claims to be somehow "special" will stand us in good stead.

In the remainder of this chapter, we shall attempt to show that the United States is uniquely well qualified to undertake the enterprise of technology development to implement our national objectives. There are basic reasons for this that range from the subliminal recognition of phrases such as "American know-how" and "Yankee ingenuity" to concrete events in our history. Furthermore, we already have the institutional structure, the educational system, and the economic resources to remain, in the long term, the world's leader in technology development.

Technology development is, of course, a means to an end rather than an end in itself. This document makes no attempt to propose what our national ends or goals should be or how they should be determined. The two most important processes we have for defining national goals are the adversary process (such as the national debates that led to civil rights or antipollution legislation) and the reaction to a crisis perceived as such by a majority of our people (such as the attack on Pearl Harbor, Sputnik, and the Arab oil embargo). Whatever these goals and ends may be, technology development has been outstanding among the means to attain them.

The focus on technology development suggested here cuts across all lines of human endeavor. There are many critical choices that will have to be made regarding which technologies are the most important ones to highlight in the years ahead. We will show in this chapter that the *basic choice to concentrate on technology development as the primary means for achieving our ends* is so deeply embedded in our history and our social fabric that it has already been implicitly made. It is in this sense that we will advocate the establishment of technology development as an explicit national purpose.

2. Some Important Definitions

The words "technology development" appear in the title of this chapter. In order to understand the issues that will be raised, we must define "technology development." This is probably best done by constrasting technology development with two scientific or technical activities that are generally better understood; namely, "basic research" and "engineering."

Basic Research

In basic scientific research the purpose is to find why things are the way they are in nature. There is a well-developed methodology relying on experiment and theory to devise a structure of some finite element of the natural world. The emphasis in basic science is always on the word "why." Basic science is mostly an individual enterprise done by a very small number of very highly qualified people. Basic research is carried out and, under certain circumstances, done well in all nations of the world, large and small, and it is encouraged primarily for cultural reasons. There have been (and still are) cultural situations where the quest for new knowledge is not encouraged. However, since the sixteenth century the cultural climate has been favorable toward basic research throughout most of the developed world. Since basic science is carried out by a very small number of people, and since it generally requires only a very small fraction of the resources of the society, it requires no policy decisions in detail, except the very broad one as to whether or not science is to be done at all. Once that decision is taken, what is done in basic research is strictly up to the scientists themselves.

Engineering

In contrast to basic research, engineering is not an open-ended search for new knowledge but a well-defined activity with the purpose of constructing something new that will be useful to the society. The primary question in engineering, therefore, is "how" the end that has been defined should be achieved. The problem in engineering is to optimize the "how." Optimizing in this sense has long included economic questions, and has recently included other aspects as well, especially environmental and other social considerations. Engineering thus tends to be very highly interactive with society, in strong contrast to basic research. The question of building battleships, railways, bridges, houses, and so on, usually turns upon political or economic decisions that are made outside the engineering profession. Engineers then deal with how the political decision is to be implemented in physical terms. Engineering is thus the application of known science to the solution of certain problems; that is, how do you cross a river, how do you communicate at a distance, and so on. A crucial element in engineering is also to estimate how much a proposed project will cost in terms of raw materials, capital, labor, and management, that is, in terms of measurable wealth. Cost is important since the original purpose of the engineering project was to achieve some economic or political end, and in either case the entrepreneurs and the public must know what fraction of their collective wealth will be spent. Finally, engineering is a group activity including designers, builders, and project managers. Successful engineers, thus, must combine technical and management skills in order to meet their goals.

These definitions are quite straightforward and well accepted. The problem that will be dealt with here has its origin in the economic nature of engineering decisions. Usually, in an engineering project, the economics are calculated quite precisely so that the scientific principles that are to be applied in the project must be well understood and well developed. The technical risks, in other words, must be small. This is not usually true in the case of technology development which is the major topic of this chapter.

Technology Development[a]

In applying the results of basic scientific research in engineering projects, a very important process goes on which is outside the two definitions considered so far. This process is called "technology development." In technology development, one takes newly developed scientific principles and brings them to the point where they can be applied in an engineering sense. Technology development differs from basic research in that it does not ask the fundamental question regarding why things are the way they are. In that sense, it is closer to engineering since it seeks to find how new scientific principles can be applied to the solution of certain practical problems. However, the fact that we are dealing with new scientific principles differentiates technology development from engineering in that the economics are not as well known. Thus, if a given technology-development program is undertaken, it is usually done for certain political reasons and cost is not necessarily the dominant issue. Typical examples are the military development programs that are undertaken for the national defense in which cost is a factor but in which national survival is generally the major consideration.

Intellectually, technology development differs from basic research and engineering in important ways. Scientific research is discipline-oriented in that the object is to learn as much as possible about a given scientific "discipline." Where a particular field of scientific study has attracted a sufficiently large group of workers under an established name, these workers tend to form a professional society, start their own specialized publications, and organize departments within the university, leading to recognition of the new discipline by the scholarly community. Sometimes the origin of such a field is through the recognition of a need (the splitting of engineering into electrical engineering, civil engineering, etc., and more recently, systems in engineering, biomedical

---

aTechnology development must be distinguished from "technology transfer" which is the subject of Section 4 ("Technology Transfer"). In the former, one starts with a goal (cure cancer, control nuclear fusion, land a man on the moon); in the latter, one starts with a new scientific development (the transistor, the laser, etc.).

engineering). Sometimes it is the combination of two previously separate disciplines by a brilliant researcher (Niels Bohr—Physics, David Hilbert—Mathematics). Individuals in basic research are rewarded for increasing knowledge in their particular discipline, and it is important to stress again that basic research is almost always a highly individual activity.

Technology development, in contrast to basic research, is interdisciplinary in that a technology-development program tends to involve the combination of several scientific disciplines. Technology development also, therefore, tends to be a group activity rather than an individual enterprise, although there are some important exceptions to this rule when the technology-development process is relatively uncomplicated and inexpensive. In contrast to engineering, the ends of a technology-development program are usually less well defined, since we are dealing here with the application of newly acquired scientific knowledge. For this reason, the economics of the technology-development process are less well understood and it is generally not possible to base the decision for embarking on a new technology-development program on purely economic grounds. If it is done for economic or commercial reasons, then greater risks must be accepted. In contrast to basic research, most technology developments tend to be expensive so that some kind of a policy decision is generally required before the program is undertaken. As a rough rule of thumb for the cost to complete the largest projects, the following figures have been suggested:[3]

Preliminary Analysis	$10,000–100,000
Basic Research	$1,000,000–10,000,000
Technology Development	$100,000,000–1,000,000,000
Engineering and Production	$10,000,000,000–100,000,000,000

Why is it necessary to take pains to define the process of technology developments so carefully? The answer lies in the exponential growth of basic scientific knowledge. This growth in new knowledge, especially in the past few decades, has greatly increased the number of possible choices for new technology developments. In the past, the rate of scientific progress was such that technology developments were generally undertaken as a natural consequence of scientific discovery. Each new scientific discovery was, in due course, developed into new technology and then into engineering projects. This is no longer true today. Since technology development is generally very expensive compared to basic scientific research, choices must be made. We simply do not have enough money to support all the possible technology developments that could be based on current scientific knowledge. For example, should we or should we not develop the technology to let people know the sex of unborn children? Should we or should we not develop the technology of moving earth with nuclear explosives? Should we or should we not develop hypersonic (4,000-15,000 mile-per-hour) passenger-carrying aircraft? All of these things could probably be done if the decision were made to undertake the necessary technology development, since the scientific knowledge on which these developments would be based, already exists. Yet none of these technology-development programs have been undertaken, for various reasons of public policy. Our mechanisms for making choices regarding the initiation of new technology developments are still rudimentary. We have, as we shall shortly see, an established pattern, but it is not at all clear that the pattern we now have is properly geared to the national purpose.

3. Technology Development in the United States

Historical Perspective

The activity that has been defined as technology development has been peculiarly important in the United States. It is safe to assert that for at least half a century now, the United States has been the leading nation in the world in the field of technology development. There are a number of reasons for this circumstance, but before dealing with them it might be worthwhile to list some names of people who have carried out American technology developments so that the impact that these people have had becomes clear:

Robert Fulton and Matthew Calbraith Perry—Steam Navigation
Eli Whitney, Isaac Merrit Singer, and Wallace H. Carrothers—Textile Technology
Eleuthere Irenée Du Pont and his descendents—Chemical Technology
Thomas A. Edison, Nikola Tesla, and Charles P. Steinmetz—Electrical Technology
Wilbur and Orville Wright—Aviation
Alexander Graham Bell—Communications and Aviation
Samuel F.B. Morse, Edwin H. Armstrong, and Lee De Forest—Communications
Ernest O. Lawrence and Hyman Rickover—Nuclear Technology
Walter Reed, William Gorgas, and Jonas E. Salk—Medical Technology
Joshua Humphreys and William Henry Webb—Shipbuilding
George Eastman and Edwin Land—Photographic Technology
Cyrus McCormick—Agricultural Machinery
Robert G. LeTourneau—Earth Moving
Eliphalet Remington and Henry Ford—Manufacturing
Luther Burbank, Henry A. Wallace, Sr., and Henry A. Wallace, Jr.—Crop Technology

This list is not meant to be comprehensive but it illustrates the enormous influence that technology developers have had in this country. None of the people on the list can be considered as a basic scientist. Several were engineers and entrepreneurs but they are generally not remembered for their purely engineering achievements—that is, for their constructions or their designs. What they all have in common is that each one took some recently developed knowledge and produced a new technology around it which made engineering applications possible.

Why does the United States have a unique position in technology development? There is good reason to believe that this circumstance is deeply rooted in our history. That perceptive and articulate observer of early American democracy, Alexis de Tocqueville, entitled one chapter of his famous book (published in 1840) "Why the Americans are More Addicted to Practical than to Theoretical Science." In that chapter he said:

In America the purely practical part of science is admirably understood, and careful attention is paid to the theoretical portion which is immediately requisite to application. On this head the Americans always display a clear, free, original, and inventive power of mind. But hardly anyone in the United States devotes himself to the essentially theoretical and abstract portion of human knowledge. In this respect the Americans carry to excess a tendency that is, I think, discernible, though in a less degree, among all democratic nations.[4]

The following reasons for the unique U.S. position in technology development are plausible and they probably explain the situation described by de Tocqueville.

For most of our history, that is, for the first 150 years of the Republic, the United States depended upon the intellectual capital generated in Europe. Very few Americans became basic researchers during this period. (J.W. Gibbs and possibly Joseph Henry are the only Americans who made really fundamental scientific discoveries before the year 1900.) The problems faced by the young nation demanded that the best young people with a scientific or technical bent devote their energies to things other than basic research. Also, and this is most important, the institutions—that is, well-established universities and scientific academies necessary to nurture work in basic research—were not sufficiently mature during the first century of the nation's existence.

The problems faced by the new nation were peculiarly susceptible to solutions brought about by technology development. For the first 100 years of the Republic, our fundamental national purpose was clear and explicitly stated. It was our "manifest destiny" to extend the sovereignty of the Union across the entire North Atlantic Continent. By the end of the nineteenth century, this objective had, for all practical purposes, been achieved. The problems posed by the "conquest" of the West were unique and were made to order for the application of new technologies. Enormous rivers could be turned into high roads if the proper vehicles and ships were available. Communications had to be established over longer distances than had ever been considered before. New sources of energy had to be found and developed to fuel the new nation. New agricultural methods were needed to feed the rapidly growing population. These problems provided enormous opportunities for technology developers and engineers.

Also, and again this is most important, there were enormous rewards for successful technology developers. The reward system in the new nation was based primarily on achievements rather than on the well-established class structure as in Europe and was, therefore, well suited for the purpose. One practical reason why this reward system encouraged technology development was that the patent law permitted individuals such as those on the above list to become rich.

The vast majority of the people who came to this country were drawn from social classes in Europe that tended to have precisely the qualities necessary to be active and successful in engineering or in technology development. These people were not members of the upper or upper-middle classes of Europe, classes that had a cultural outlook more in tune with that necessary for basic research than for engineering or technology development. Most probably, there were many people among the immigrants who were the more energetic individuals in the relatively underprivileged European social classes. They had strong motivation to improve their conditions in life and were, thus, geared to the goal or project orientation that is characteristic of engineering and technology development. Finally, the immigrants had relatively few intellectual prejudices regarding the application of new techniques to new situations and they were extremely receptive to the educational opportunities in technology that were becoming available to this country at that time.

The physical and political conditions that existed in the early decades of the nation's history were thus very favorable for technology development. Moreover, and this is probably even more significant, the human resources available matched these conditions.

National Defense and Technology Development

Economic arguments are not usually sufficient to justify undertaking a particular technology development. There must be some reason that transcends purely economic considerations, and in the majority of cases that reason has been national security. The most recent examples arising from World War II are all well known to the general public. The jet-powered aircraft that are in wide commercial use today are all descended technically from the jet-powered swept-wing B-47 and B-52 intercontinental bombers that were developed for military purposes in the late 1940s and early 1950s. The IBM 7090, the first of the "second-generation" digital computers, was a modification of the computer developed for the SAGE air-defense system. The boiling-water and pressurized-water nuclear power reactors now being installed by the utility industry in many parts of the nation are direct technical derivatives of the nuclear reactors developed by the navy in the early 1950s for the propulsion of nuclear-powered submarines. A large and profitable industry based upon television had its origin in the development of high-power microwave devices that were used in radar sets during World War II. A host of substitute materials—synthetic rubber and textile fibers are the best examples—were produced when the war shut off the normal channels of supply available to the nation.

The examples cited are only a small sample of the technology development that resulted from conditions existing during World War II. The pattern of technology developments undertaken for reasons of national security is not new—previous military crises in the nation's history led to similar spasms of technical development. The war against Mexico (1846-48) was the first time that the U.S. Navy employed steam-driven warships on a large scale.[5] They were used to support the landings of U.S. forces at Vera Cruz. Technical difficulties were encountered that caused a very high failure rate. For example, the seals in the propeller shafts of steam-driven sloops leaked alarmingly after a few hours of service, so that the warships had to be taken out of action and towed to bases many hundreds of miles away for repairs. Difficulties such as these led to a series of programs in which the U.S. Navy during the 1850s subsidized the construction of commercial steam-driven vessels in order to understand and iron out technical problems encountered by warships during the Mexican War.[6] The rapid advancement of railroad technology undertaken by the Union during the Civil War in order to supply the troops that invaded the South was essential to the rapid expansion of our population westward after the war was concluded. The early development of aviation technology is another good example. Although the early experiments of the Wright brothers were privately financed, their enterprise had its first major growth only after they received a contract to supply an airplane to the U.S. Army Signal Corps in 1908.[7]

The examples listed here are all in a category that might be called "hard" technology; that is, technology dealing with the production of new things or machines. "Soft" technologies, which tend to be concerned with the creation of new services such as public health or education measures, also receive stimulating financial support during great military crises. For example, Dr. Walter Reed (Major, U.S. Army Medical Corps) and his associates discovered the means of transmission of yellow fever and Dr. William C. Gorgas (Major General, U.S. Army Medical Corps) and his collaborators developed the means to wipe out yellow fever, directly as a result of our conquest of Cuba during the Spanish-American War in 1898-99.[8] This technology was essential in the subsequent construction of the Panama Canal, a project that was also undertaken essentially for reasons of national security. The vaccine against yellow fever[9] came much later, the research having been conducted under a grant from the Rockefeller Foundation. Vaccines for the prophylaxis of typhus and typhoid fever were developed by military doctors, as were the synthetic drugs to prevent and cure malaria.[10] A great many public health measures were originally developed for military purposes. The earliest example is perhaps the prevention and cure of scurvy[11] that was developed and tested experimentally by Captain James Cook, RN, during his second exploratory voyage to the South Pacific in 1772-75. Another is the chlorination of drinking water[12] and later examples are the large-scale employment of DDT and penicillin during World War II to combat epidemics caused by the dislocations of war. Finally, the extensive use of blood transfusions, blood banking, and plasmas all were first pioneered by military surgeons dealing with people injured in combat.

The use of national defense as a spur for technology development is natural for a number of important reasons. It has been recognized for many centuries (even millenia) that technical superiority means victory in war. The Vikings, for example, were able to dominate, or at least occupy at will, the coastline of Europe in the eighth, ninth, and tenth centuries because of their early mastery of maritime technology. This condition has been recognized for a long time, and each nation, in its own way, has striven for technical superiority in those areas that it felt to be vital to its own national defense.

National security and national defense are permanent objectives. Thus, it is possible to undertake long-lead-time technology developments if they can be justified on the grounds of national security. It is true that modern nations often have civilian requirements that might be used as a justification for heavy investment in new technology. The "energy crisis" is the most recent example in this country of a situation that will lead to new funding for technology development. The difficulty is that civilian requirements tend to fluctuate more rapidly than the lead-time required for long-term technical developments. For instance, the "energy crisis" was caused in part by the "environmental crisis" that preceded it by a few years; technical developments such as antipollution devices helped to cause a new crisis for which a different set of technical fixes was perceived to be necessary.

The national defense is perceived to be important by the entire society. Even though there have been bitter political divisions caused by certain wars that this nation has fought, there is no accepted general argument against the maintenance of military forces. This circumstance will probably be true as long as the present era of nation-states lasts. For this reason, there are none of the internal arguments that are bound to occur for technology developments that are undertaken for reasons other than those of national defense. In the case of nonmilitary technology developments, it is usually true that some sectors of the society gain and other lose. The disputes arising from these circumstances are often extremely difficult to resolve

The Constitution sanctions federal investment for military purposes since it gives responsibility for national defense exclusively to the federal government. There is, thus, no jurisdictional quarrel about who should do this particular job.

All of these reasons are cogent and have been well understood for many years. It is quite likely that national defense will continue to be a major reason for undertaking federally sponsored technology development in the forseeable future.

Technology Development for Nonmilitary Reasons

There are, of course, reasons other than those connected with the national defense for undertaking new technology developments. Outstanding examples of this are the telephone, the automobile and, most important of all, the development of agricultural technology. Table II-1 shows the federal funding for the conduct of research and development in fiscal year 1975 (July 1, 1974 to June 30, 1975). Next to defense, the most significant investments in technology development are those devoted to aeronautics and space exploration, energy, and health and public welfare. It can be argued that the investment in aeronautics and space is strongly related to national defense and national prestige and should therefore be included in the defense item. Furthermore, about $500 million of the "energy" item is devoted to research and development in the field of nuclear weapons which must also be included in the "defense" item. If this is done, then it can be seen from Table II-1 that about two-thirds of the federal investment in research and development is devoted to things dealing

Table II-1
Federal Spending on the Conduct of Research and Technology Development Fiscal Year 1975*

Item	Amount in Millions of Dollars
Defense	8,833
Aeronautics and Space	3,327
Health, Education and Welfare	2,092
Energy	1,892
Basic Science (National Science Foundation)	619
Agriculture	428
Transportation	368
Interior (Natural Resources)	303
Environmental Protection	287
Commerce (National Bureau of Standards, National Oceanographic and Atmospheric Administration)	
All Others	421
Total	18,781

*FY 1975 estimated obligations from "The Budget of the United States Government" (Special Analyses), February 3, 1975.

with national defense or national prestige and the remainder to other purposes.

It would be a mistake to make a direct connection between the dollar figures in Table II-1 and the priorities of the various items. While defense still has first priority in a general sense, it is also true that developments in defense, space exploration, and certain energy projects require very heavy hardware investments such as large testing facilities, wind tunnels and research reactors. Such facilities are generally not required for research in agricultural and in the health sciences, consequently work of equal or greater importance can be carried out for less money in these fields. It should also be recognized that the figures shown in Table II-1 are essentially the operating expenses and they do not include funds allocated for the construction of new facilities. The figures for new facilities for the fiscal year 1975 are shown in Table II-2. It is significant that investment in energy research and development is the largest item on this list. Since these new facilities will not be available for use for some years to come, heavy investments in energy research and development facilities now indicates a long-term commitment that will raise the spending on conducting energy research and development in future years.

There is also a substantial investment in research and development made by the private sector. Exact figures comparable to those shown in Tables II-1 and II-2 are very difficult to generate since there is a lack of uniformity in the definition of what is meant by research and development among the many hundreds of different enterprises in private industry. The best estimate is that private sector spending in research and development for fiscal year 1975 lies somewhere between $7 and $9 billion so that the total investment in technology development in the United States for that fiscal year is close to $30 billion.

Table II-2

Federal Spending on Facilities for Research and Technology Development Fiscal Year 1975*

Item	Amount in Millions of Dollars
Energy	468
Defense	228
Aeronautics and Space	154
Health, Education and Welfare	47
Transportation	25
Agriculture	16
All Others	63
Total	1,001

*FY 1975 estimated obligations from "The Budget of the United States Government" (Special Analyses), February 3, 1975.

The federal investment now being proposed for energy research and development is shown in Table II-3. The largest single fraction of the funds in this category have been, and still are being, devoted to the development of nuclear power. Originally—that is, approximately twenty-five years ago—these expenditures on nuclear development were justified entirely on military grounds for the development of nuclear weapons and nuclear-powered submarines. After the successful operation of the Shippingport reactor, which was the first demonstration of civilian nuclear power in 1958, an extensive technology-development program in civil nuclear power was undertaken.[13] As a result of these heavy public investments, nuclear power became a commercially attractive alternative to conventional fossil power in most regions of the country in the period between 1965 and 1967. The federal investment was supplemented by substantial private investments, although initially it was not nearly as extensive as the federal investment.

This is a good example of public and private sector collaboration. However, the research and development equipment necessary to bring the technology to commercial fruition (critical facilities, test reactors, and the like) is extremely expensive, so that only the federal government had sufficient resources to concentrate on this particular job. Without federal involvement in this case, nothing would have happened.

Since the "energy crisis" in 1973, there has been a substantial increase in proposed federal energy research and development spending. This is in response to the national objective stated by President Nixon to gain "self-sufficiency" in energy.[14] It will be interesting to see if this objective becomes a permanent feature of national policy or if it will be replaced in a few years by something else. Should it become a permanent feature, then the prospects for eventually

Table II-3
Federal Spending on Research and Technology Development on Energy Fiscal Year 1975*

Item	Amount in Millions of Dollars
Fossil Fuels	208
Nuclear Energy	712
Solar, Geothermal and Advanced Concepts	316
Conservation	16
Safety and Environment	150
Nuclear Weapons	490
Total	1,892

*FY 1975 estimated obligations from "The Budget of the United States Government" (Special Analyses), February 3, 1975.

achieving self-sufficiency, and perhaps even becoming an energy-exporting nation again, are good.

The case of research and development in agriculture also illustrates some important points regarding federal research and development policy. The reasons for federal sponsorship of research and development in agriculture are well founded in our history, going back to the Continental Congress. The Northwest Ordinance of 1787 governed the settlement of the vast tract that now includes the upper tier of middle-western states from Ohio to Minnesota. This measure laid the basis for the various homestead acts that followed, of which the most important, enacted in 1862, provided that veterans of the Civil War could occupy tracts of land (160 acres) and would gain ownership if the land were properly developed. The importance of the Homestead Act of 1862 was primarily due to two contemporaneous events:

1. The provision that all veterans of the Civil War were eligible suddenly made a large pool of people available who would take advantage of the opportunities provided.
2. The rapid development of railway technology during the Civil War made it possible to settle a large number of people in the empty western countryside. The first transcontinental railroad link was completed in 1869.

These circumstances led to the rapid settling and development of the West once the Civil War was concluded.

Another extremely important act was passed in 1862 by that same farsighted Congress.[b] Justin Smith Morrill (representative and senator from Vermont, 1855-98) sponsored the so-called Land-Grant College Act which provided for a large number of new educational institutions in the newly settled territories. In the words of the Act, it was intended to provide for the support "of at least one college (in each state) where the leading object shall be, without excluding other scientific and classical studies and including military tactics, to teach such branches of learning as are related to agriculture and the mechanic arts, in such a manner as the legislatures of the states may respectively prescribe, in order to promote the liberal and practical education of the industrial classes in the several pursuits and professions in life." The Act was subsequently amended (in 1887) to establish "agricultural experiment stations" at each of these institutions. Finally, an extensive system of county agents was organized to disseminate the technology that was created in the new universities. All of this was done as a matter of national policy with heavy federal financial support.

There is little question that the superbly productive agriculture system we have is largely the result of these policies. The agricultural case is perhaps the best example of a technology-development program carried out in the United States for reasons other than national defense. The important point is that it was

---

[b]That Congress also chartered the National Academy of Science.

done consciously as part of a long-term national objective—the "manifest destiny" of the nation to expand westward and to occupy the North American continent.

A partial list of the areas in which technology development in agriculture has been important would include the following:

1. Plant physiology, genetics, etc., with a view in mind toward improving crop yields and disease resistance by better genetic selection.
2. Pesticides, predator development, host removal, and other methods of controlling plant diseases.
3. Fertilizers and soil chemistry.
4. Irrigation and hydrology.
5. Mechanization.

The research and technology-development investments required for useful work in these areas tend to occur in smaller increments than those encountered in the examples of nuclear and aeronautical technology. Thus, private sector investment, especially in mechanization and also in the production of fertilizers, has been an important aspect of agricultural technology development. (This point will be more fully examined in the next section.) Nevertheless, the federal role has been crucial. The U.S. Department of Agriculture runs several large regional research centers and sponsors a large number of research and development projects at universities and in industry. It is very likely that this system of laboratories and development institutions will increase in importance, since critical food shortages are likely to develop in parts of the world in the coming years. The export of agricultural technology developments produced by our system is thus likely to be one of the mainstays of U.S. influence in the future.

In the field of public health, the situation is somewhat different, although, here also, the federal government has made important investments and has established large permanent institutions. The U.S. Public Health Service was founded in 1796 and grew out of various public health activities undertaken by the military establishment.[15] This organization has been enormously influential in creating the high level of public health existing in the United States. The National Institutes of Health grew out of a complex of federally sponsored research and development institutions devoted to various specific health problems. These institutes have an annual budget of over $2 billion, and they constitute one of the most important research and development complexes in the world today. The great pharmaceutical houses in the United States have also had a major impact in nurturing technology applied to health. All of the larger firms have very extensive research laboratories. Every major development in new pharmaceuticals and drugs since the Second World War has been carried out in the United States by the powerful combination of public and private institutions. The creation of practical oral contraceptives in the last decade is perhaps the most recent example of the work that has been done.

In recent years, federal research and development funds have been allocated increasingly to areas where the federal government has regulatory responsibility. Federal agencies to which these responsibilities have been delegated are, for example, the Federal Aviation Administration (aviation safety), The Nuclear Regulatory Commission (radiation safety and reactor safety), the Food and Drug Administration (drugs and medical technology), the Environmental Protection Agency, and so on. These agencies all have modest research and development budgets which help them to remain in contact with the technologies that they are charged with regulating. The constitutional authority for federal regulatory agencies is generally derived from the Interstate Commerce clause of the Constitution. It is well founded in law and tradition, but these activities tend not to be funded as heavily as those technology developments that are based on national defense. The probable cause of this circumstance is that regulatory agencies often find themselves in adversary situations with industries that they are trying to regulate.

In fact, there is sometimes no general public agreement that a specific regulatory activity is even desirable, in contrast to the case of national defense where few deny that some type of defense establishment is required. This situation has the consequence that regulatory agencies, while they have some modest research and development funding, are not very likely to have the influence necessary to command really large new technology-development budgets. Large, long-term technology developments must thus be tied to some consciously stated national policy.

Technology Development in the Private Sector

For good economic and political reasons, private investors have often been slow in promoting new technology. For example, although it was quite generally recognized that steamships were technically feasible well before the middle of the nineteenth century, the capital investments necessary to build steam-driven oceangoing ships that were clearly superior to the then highly evolved sailing ships were large enough to frighten off private capital. The great clipper ships and the even larger fore-and-aft rigged barques that followed them in the latter half of the nineteenth century were extremely efficient and profitable. There was simply no incentive to invest heavily in replacing them rapidly and, thus, it was not until the end of the nineteenth century that steamships finally replaced the commercial sailing fleets (see references 5 and 6).

This experience was repeated after World War II in connection with air transportation when propeller-driven aircraft were replaced by the more efficient jets.[16] The large number of propeller-driven transports used during the war could easily be adapted to civilian service, the major operational problems having been solved during the war. Jet engines were developed during World War II in several nations on both sides, including Italy, Germany, and Great Britain. These engines were based on new developments in materials science and in fluid mechanics. However, after the war was over, private investors were very reluctant to supply the capital necessary for the development of commercial jet transport aircraft, primarily because the operational problems associated with flying large jet aircraft were not well understood. For example, it was believed that the maintenance of jet engines was much more difficult than it finally turned out to be. High fuel consumption was also a problem with the early jet engines. Indeed, there were several economic studies made during that period indicating that jet transports would not be economical, because of high fuel consumption and high maintenance costs among other things. Once enough operating experience was obtained by the U.S. Air Force with B-47's and B-52's, and this experience was gained at public expense, more accurate forecasts could be made. Jet aircraft were finally introduced into commercial service in 1959, twenty years after the jet engines themselves were conceived and developed, and turned out to be immediately highly profitable.

Nothing that has been said is meant to be critical of private investment procedures. It simply illustrates the fact that there are certain important technical developments, especially in those technologies requiring large and expensive research, development, and manufacturing facilities, where private investors are not able to take the large risks generally associated with new technology. The important point that must be recognized is that in the case of difficult and complex "hard" technology developments, there must generally be some politically acceptable reason for making the necessary public investment; otherwise, the development will not occur.

Although the funds devoted by the private sector to technology development are large in total, they are divided among many hundreds of different enterprises. Thus, there is a fragmentation which limits the size of private investments that are possible. Traditionally, those fields in which new technology developments are relatively inexpensive, but which tend to have a large leverage on profitable markets, have been carried out in the private sector. For cases of this kind, a healthy private industry can, and does, afford the relatively small amount of risk capital required to seek out new technologies. Good examples of this are the chemical industry (dyes, fibers, plastics), the drug industry, and the electronics industry. The privately sponsored technology developments in these fields have had a major impact on the American economy and on the quality of life in the country.

Industries have generally been quite willing to invest in new technology because of the large rewards inherent in the exploitation of the new markets created by new products, provided the initial investments are not too large. We have, as a matter of national policy, encouraged private enterprise and, therefore, the private technology-development system rests on a sound foundation. From an economic viewpoint this has been wise, since private industry is generally more capable than the federal government of estimating the purely economic returns that might be generated by the creation of a new technology. Also, private industry is generally much more adept at carrying out the process of "technology transfer." This point is discussed in more detail in Section 4 ("Technology Transfer"). The only limitation is that private capital is more difficult to concentrate in large amounts on a given area than are public funds. Thus, when a really large, new technology development is required, such as, for example, the development of a large, new jet aircraft, then public funds are usually necessary to start the development process.

4. Institutional Considerations

The United States already has a large number of institutions of wide variety devoted to technology development. It is important to understand how these institutions operate and how they must be nurtured to maintain and expand the position we now have in this field. Also required are educational resources (universities) to train the people who carry out technical projects, and an institutional structure (capital market) which permits the concentration of financial resources to achieve particular technical ends.

History of Technology Development Institutions

Institutions devoted to technology development have a relatively long history, ranging back well over five centuries. Although our information is, unfortunately, rather sketchy, it is likely that the first organization in the Western world devoted to the creation and advancement of new technology was founded in 1420 by Prince Henry of Portugal (known as Henry the Navigator). Prince Henry's "laboratory" was located at Sagres near Cape St. Vincent on the southwest tip of Portugal and was specifically devoted to mastering the art and science of navigation. It was multidisciplinary in that Henry collected people with a great many varied skills and talents. Astronomers, mathematicians, cartographers, shipwrights, sailmakers, and coopers were brought in to build the best ocean-going vessels then existing in the world and to develop the means to navigate them as accurately and safely as possible.

Henry also recognized the importance of expanding the intellectual capital that his institute required and, thus, he sponsored the first chair of mathematics at the University of Lisbon. Although it cannot be proven, since reliable historical records are lacking, it is extremely probable that Portugal's dominant position in the world during the fifteenth and sixteenth centuries was due in large measure to the work carried out by Henry and his collaborators at Sagres. When Henry died in 1460, the Sagres group dispersed slowly (Columbus spent some time at Sagres after Henry's death). It is tempting to speculate that, had Sagres been kept up, the decline of Portugal as a major sea power would have been delayed.[17]

The examples set by Prince Henry in the field of navigation was eventually followed by other nations. The most extensive of these early institutions was the complex developed around the Royal Naval Shipyard and the Royal Observatory in Greenwich on the River Thames near London.[18] The observatory was founded in 1675 by Charles II and was an example of the intellectual ferment that followed the restoration of the English monarchy after the rule of Cromwell. The primary practical charter of the observatory was to make astronomical observations of sufficient accuracy to improve substantially the quality of navigation. Following Henry's pattern, the observatory had, from the very beginning, strong relationships with the academic community. Among other things, Sir Isaac Newton served as chairman of the Board of Overseers of the observatory from 1710 until his death in 1727. From 1713 onward, the funds for the observatory were part of the budget of the Master of Ordnance; thus, the military value of the work being done to improve navigation was explicitly recognized. The observatory is today still supported in part by the defense establishment.

In contrast to Prince Henry's institute at Sagres, the Royal Observatory was a permanent establishment. It still exists and is an active research-and-development center. In more recent times the observatory has branched out from purely astronomical work to many other fields of importance to navigation including such things as oceanography, magnetic field surveys, and meteorology. It has also maintained first-class work in observational astronomy, although recently this has not been possible at the original location, which is now urban. There is no question that the existence of the observatory and its surrounding technical institutions contributed in important ways to Great Britain's supremacy at sea.

At about the same time that the Royal Observatory was established, scientific academies were founded in several European countries. The first of these was the Royal Society, which was also established by Charles II in 1662. Although the Royal Observatory was initially independent of the Royal Society, the society quickly established a strong degree of control over the observatory through the Board of Overseers that has already been mentioned. Similar patterns were established in other nations, and the academies played a dominant role in the development institutions that were eventually organized.

Technology Development Centers
in the United States

Before discussing the creation of technology development centers in the United States, it might be well to characterize such enterprises in a simple way:

1. Development laboratories are mission or goal-oriented, not discipline-oriented. All the disciplines necessary to achieve the laboratory's objectives are brought together under one roof.
2. The laboratories are in certain cases quite expensive to operate, and so their missions must support some well-defined, important, and publicly accepted national objective.
3. In order to staff the laboratories adequately, close and continuing relationships with institutions of higher learning are absolutely essential.

In the United States, federal involvement in technology development also began around those technologies oriented toward navigation. In 1799, Congress authorized the establishment of a Naval Shipyard in Washington, D.C.[19] The original purpose of this establishment was to provide a focus for competence in the building of warships and armaments within the federal government. Several arguments were advanced in support of the new Washington Naval Yard. Secretary of the Navy Benjamin Stoddard demonstrated to Congress that private existing shipyards were simply too small for the rapid and efficient building of warships and their ordnance, and in any event were too busy filling orders to spend time and materials on experiments for the navy. Another argument used was that the government could deal more effectively with the contractors who actually built the ships if it had its own competence in that field. This argument is still used to justify federally sponsored research in federal institutions. The Naval Shipyard was also intended as a storage place for ships when they were laid up between wars.

The Naval Shipyard enjoyed the attention of the highest U.S. officials from the beginning. When Thomas Jefferson was inaugurated president in 1801, he took a personal interest in the new shipyard. Jefferson, together with Benjamin Latrobe, the noted architect, designed the drydock that was to be one of the shipyard's central facilities. Congress never appropriated the funds for the project, so that the designs were never executed, although the original drawings for them are still in existence.

The Washington Naval Shipyard has had a long and honored history in the development of American military technology. Robert Fulton spent some time there in the early years of the nineteenth century to initiate the process of converting the U.S. Navy to steam propulsion. During the 1820s the Du Ponts conducted experiments there to test the new explosives they were producing for American naval ordnance; quality control in manufacturing black powder was extremely important for the achievement of better fire control. From 1847 to 1863 the distinguished John Dahlgren was ordnance officer and later commandant of the Naval Shipyard. Dahlgren was the leading figure in the development of naval artillery and ordnance for many years. He was able to combine developments in metallurgy with new high-explosive technology to produce artillery that was greatly superior to what was then in use. Dahlgren's work had a significant impact on the outcome of the Civil War. The Naval Shipyard in Washington, later renamed the U.S. Naval Gun. Factory, was for many years the leading development center for naval ordnance in the country as a result of Dahlgren's work.

The Naval Shipyard in Washington was founded because it was recognized that a strong and modern navy was essential to maintain the independence of the young nation. Each major military crisis encountered by the United States has led to establishment of technical programs or institutions designed to deal with problems that arose during that conflict. For example, the naval actions in the Spanish-American War exposed certain weaknesses, particularly in gunnery and communications, that caused President Theodore Roosevelt to establish a committee chaired by Thomas Edison to look into the problem of providing better technology for the navy. As a result, a Naval Research Establishment was created which culminated in the formal founding of the U.S. Naval Research Laboratory in Washington, D.C., shortly after the end of World War I.[20] The laboratory is still in existence and is one of the most distinguished of the Federal Research and Development Centers.

Although aviation technology first saw the light of day in the United States, the first year of World War I revealed that other nations were far ahead of us in the practical application of this technology. Accordingly, as part of the naval appropriations bill in 1915, a National Advisory Committee for Aeronautics (NACA) was established that had as part of its function the establishment and operation of an Aeronautical Laboratory at Langley Field near Hampton, Virginia. This laboratory, now known as the NASA-Langley Research Center, is still in operation and is still making important technical contributions. Several of the larger military research and development centers, the great arsenals of the U.S. Army, were also established or greatly expanded as a result of problems encountered in World War I.

This process was continued and greatly accelerated during World War II. Two other aeronautical laboratories were established by the National Advisory Committee for Aeronautics (the Lewis Laboratory in Cleveland, Ohio, and the Ames Laboratory near San Francisco, California) to secure supremacy in aerial warfare. A great complex of Nuclear Development Centers was constructed to create the technology that led to the atomic bomb; these include laboratories at Oak Ridge, Tennessee; Los Alamos, New Mexico; Argonne, Illinois; Hanford, Washington; and several other sites. A concentrated effort was made to produce synthetic rubber in large quantities, and the necessary institutions to accomplish this objective were established, mostly at private industrial establishments, but with federal funds. Large technology-development laboratories to bring radar to a usable status were constructed, of which the largest was at MIT. A large laboratory to advance the technology of rocket propulsion was established at Pasadena in collaboration with the California Institute of Technology. This laboratory, the Jet Propulsion Laboratory, is still in existence and has made many important contributions to rocket technology and space exploration. The list of these institutions is much longer, but the examples already mentioned make the point.

Most or all of these establishments were planned or established before the United States actually entered World War II. They were part of a policy urged on the nation by President Franklin Roosevelt to make the United States the "Arsenal of Democracy." Even though public opinion at that time was opposed to U.S. entry into the war, no serious objections were raised to the president's policy, partly because he was proposing something that was within our traditions and consistent with our high technical capabilities. All of the institutions that were created were designed to draw on existing scientific knowledge to accomplish certain practical ends to support the war effort. They were, in a word, truly technology-development centers and not basic-research laboratories.

Finally, it is instructive to consider what happened on the Axis side during the same time. The Germans had, before 1939, actively pursued various military technologies, particularly in the field of aviation. However, once the war began, they severely curtailed their technology development efforts. The leadership anticipated that the war would be a short one, and felt that it made little sense to embark on technological programs having lead times so long that the war would be over before the projects came to fruition. It was only when it was already too late that the Germans resumed full-scale technology development on objectives such as the V-weapons. They managed in a short time to produce practical intermediate-range ballistic missiles, the so-called V-2's. These weapons were very formidable, but they were not decisive because they were employed too late. One wonders what would have happened if the Germans had had V-weapons in quantity prior to the Allied invasion of Europe in June of 1944.

In the last two decades, the cold war with the Soviet Union also spawned a number of new development laboratories. The nuclear weapons research center at Livermore, California, was established to develop warheads for intercontinental ballistic missiles. Research and development facilities at the Redstone Arsenal in Huntsville, Alabama, and at several other locations were greatly expanded to produce the rocket propulsion systems necessary for these missiles. Two large development centers, the Knolls Atomic Power Laboratory in Schenectady, New York, and the Bettis Atomic Power Laboratory in Pittsburgh, Pennsylvania, were established to create the nuclear propulsion systems that would be employed by nuclear-driven submarines. In order to develop the submarine-launched ballistic missiles that would eventually be placed on these ships, the navy relied heavily on the Applied Physics Laboratory of Johns Hopkins University. Finally, the challenge posed by Sputnik in 1957 led to the creation of the National Aeronautics and Space Administration (NASA), an agency charged with the development of the technology to explore space. The core of the new agency was the old National Advisory Committee for Aeronautics and its research laboratories, together with elements of the Naval Research Laboratory and a portion of the Redstone Arsenal in Huntsville.

As befits a diversified society such as ours, there is no particular pattern of organization that fits all of these institutions. Some of them, primarily the research and development centers operated by the military, are staffed by people entirely in the federal service, either military or civilian. Others, the NASA Laboratories among them, are a mixture made up of Civil Service and private contractor employees. Still others are operated entirely by the contractors. The contractors may be universities (Livermore, Los Alamos, Applied Physics Laboratory, Lincoln Laboratory, and Jet Propulsion Laboratory), consortia of universities (Argonne National Laboratory, Brookhaven National Laboratory, National Center for Atmospheric Research), large private industrial concerns (Knolls Atomic Power Laboratory, Bettis Atomic Power Laboratory, Oak Ridge National Laboratory, and Sandia Corporation), or consortia of industries (Hanford Laboratories), or they may be private not-for-profit corporations (Rand Corporation, Aerospace Corporation). What all of these institutions have in common is that they are funded by the federal government and that they have clearly defined missions which they perform in return for continued support.

Many of these laboratories are now working on programs that differ substantially from those that were originally initiated at the laboratories. Thus, these institutions have demonstrated considerable flexibility in adapting to changing national requirements. The laboratories have also developed very strong working relationships with private industry. In many instances, the federal technology-development laboratories actually serve as the conduit through which public funds flow to private industry for various purposes. Many of the large federal development contracts executed through private industry are managed by people residing in the federally funded development centers. It should be mentioned here that the largest private enterprises also maintain technology-development centers that are very similar in function and organization and even in size to some of those sponsored by the federal government. The most famous of these are the Bell Telephone Laboratories in New Jersey. However, there are others that are almost as important. These would include the Experiment Station of the DuPont Corporation in Wilmington, Delaware; the great petrochemical laboratories operated by the large oil companies; the IBM Research Centers; and the great laboratories of the General Electric Corporation in Schenectady, New York. The privately sponsored laboratories tend to be active in technical field that require smaller capital outlays for their facilities than those encountered in the federally sponsored laboratories. The construction of a large wind tunnel or a large nuclear reactor test facility may cost as much as $100 million. Such investments for research and development facilities are generally beyond the capacity of private investors.

A difficult institutional question that must be answered in managing large research and development centers is to devise ways of measuring their productivity. In manufacturing and operational enterprises, this is done by means of well established and accepted economic indicators. Basically, it is a question of counting units produced or services rendered and then putting an appropriate market value on the units or services. In the case of technology development institutions, this method cannot be used. One cannot simply count, say, the number of technical reports issued by the laboratories without also measuring somehow the impact of the work in technology. Nor can one count new inventions, for instance, without also assessing whether they will be useful or profitable. The difficulty is that there is usually a much longer time lag between the recognition that a technical report has impact or that an invention has value than the time lag that exists between the manufacture and sale of a product. Thus, it is a characteristic of technology-development institutions that their productivity can usually be measured only long after the fact—the lead time for a technology development may be as long as ten years.

It is obvious from this argument that simple number counts will not work. Indeed, a single technology development that is really successful can pay for all other technology development programs for many years; DuPont's nylon is a classic example of this. It is essentially for this reason that historical assessments of the value of research institutions are so important. In view of these considerations, some concerted efforts should be made to determine more precisely the output of research-and-development organizations in the near term.

In the past, a small but fixed fraction of our national wealth has been put into the development of new technology. At the present time, the federal expenditures in new technology development (Table II-1) are about $19 billion per year out of a total federal budget of $300 billion. Thus, technology development is roughly 6 percent of the total budget and less than 1.5 percent of the gross national product. This number is obviously the starting point but is not necessarily a good guide. The lower limit of expenditures is obviously zero. An upper limit can be obtained by estimating the number of people in the country who are actually capable of working productively in technology development and multiplying that number by $60,000 per year, a figure generally accepted as being necessary to keep a development scientist or engineer employed and adequately supported. There are obviously several ways to estimate the number of people capable of doing technical development work, but a reasonable upper limit of the cost to keep all these people busy would probably be somewhere around 25 percent of the current federal budget. The main point of this estimate is simply to illustrate that the system is by no means saturated and that technology development activities could be greatly expanded before we even come close to saturation. An expansion from 6 percent to 7 percent (i.e., from $19 billion to $22 billion) could easily be absorbed, and it might have enormous leverage in the nation's technical output. This assertion can only be proved by recourse to past history. There can simply be no question that our productivity has been increased enormously by technological means and it is important (although not within the scope of this chapter) to develop means to relate quantitatively the increase in industrial productivity to prior investments in technology development.

These technology-development institutions taken as a whole constitute an enormous and unique national resource. Nothing like it exists anywhere else in the world (with the possible exception of the Soviet Union). The capital investment in research and development facilities in the laboratories exceeds $10 billion. These institutions employ in total well over 300,000 of the most talented development engineers and scientists in the nation. The technology that has been created over the years in these laboratories pervades our society and the rest of the world as well. Some examples of these developments have already been discussed briefly.

Relationships with Educational Institutions

In the previous section, the establishment of the land-grant colleges in the United States was described and its importance to the development of our highly productive agricultural system was cited. It is obvious that the successful operation of the large technology-development complex that exists in the United States depends in a crucial way on our educational system. If the development centers are not staffed by highly qualified technical people, they are quite useless. Fortunately, the United States possesses the best system of higher education, both public and private, in the world. The tradition of public higher education in this country is an old one which had its beginnings even before the Revolutionary War. Thomas Jefferson thought that his role in public education was important enough that he had the phrase "Father of the University of Virginia" engraved on his tombstone. (The other item that can be read there is: "Author of the Declaration of American Independence and of the Statute of Virginia for Religious Freedom.") Today, the land-grant college system still accounts for the training of about 70 percent of the engineers and applied scientists in the United States.

A close and continuing relationship exists between these universities and most of the technology-development institutions in the country. These relationships can easily be nurtured and expanded, since it is to the mutual benefit of the universities and the development centers to do so. What does require public action is the provision of adequate scholarship funds for qualified students in a wide number of technical areas. It is often said that in the last decade we trained a "surplus" of engineers and technical people because of the great stimulus of the space and defense programs. This is true if the argument is limited to space and defense, because we are spending less than half as much a year on space—$3 billion in 1973 versus more than $6 billion in 1967—and defense research-and-development spending has remained roughly constant in actual dollars (that is, it has decreased in constant dollars) during the last ten years.

Thus, there are fewer jobs in those areas for which the people were originally trained; however, the system had adapted remarkably, and many engineers who originally intended to work on space or defense applications are now gainfully employed elsewhere. There are now many signs in our major universities of a resurgent interest in engineering and science among our young people. Thus, there will probably be no shortage of people interested in engineering and science, but there will be the perennial problem of maintaining the quality of technical education. In maintaining quality, it is essential that the universities be strongly encouraged to establish links with the future employers of the students: the technical industries and the large federal laboratories.

One extraordinary result of the interaction of universities and industries was the establishment in the 1950s and 1960s of certain new commercial enterprises around major universities, started by university professors and based on new and very sophisticated technology. The major example of this occurred around MIT and Harvard, and because many of the factories were sited on Route 128, a circumferential highway around Boston, the growth and development of these enterprises has often been called the "Route 128 Phenomenon." Another similar proliferation developed around Stanford University, and there were smaller developments in many other university towns, including Ann Arbor, Michigan.

Typically, such firms were founded by one to three professors who had been outstanding in research and in interaction with industry and with defense development. It was based initially on some very new and complex technology: optics (Itek); acoustics (Bolt, Beranek and Newman); and especially electronics (Sylvania, Hewlett-Packard). Many such firms prospered, expanded, and diversified, largely on military research and development funding in the early stages, but eventually becoming largely independent, and manufacturing profitable and useful products. The typical firm continued to maintain close ties with its parent university, supporting its research and supplying consulting for its staff and jobs for its graduates. Its founders and backers became wealthy, the community prospered, and the economy of the nation was improved.

Technology Transfer

"Technology transfer," "technology diffusion," and "technological fall-out" are names commonly given to the phenomenon of applying a technology that was originally developed for one purpose to another. While these terms have slightly different meanings ("transfer" implies transfer from the laboratory to a user, "diffusion" to many users; "fall-out" implies application other than that originally intended), we shall use them synonymously. There are no hard-and-fast rules as to how this transfer is best accomplished in a particular case, but we have carried out technology transfers often enough now to make some generally applicable statements.

A common, and generally effective way to accomplish technology transfer is to encourage private industry to do the job. The normal course here is awarding a government contract to a particular firm to accomplish a certain project. The primary project has usually been undertaken for reasons of national security; the company then uses its own experience and expertise to adapt the technology developed for the government to commercial purposes. Classic examples of this are the development by the Boeing Company of large commercial jet transport aircraft and by IBM of the 709 and 7090 digital computers—cases that have already been discussed. There are a great many others, and it is not unreasonable to say that one of the major social functions of private industry is to carry out the process of technology transfer.

Another effective method is to encourage the relocation of people who have participated in the development of military, space, or other federally sponsored technology development to positions in industries or agencies that are commercially-oriented or have responsibilities in the private or civil sectors. A recent example was the appointment of a distinguished engineer who played a leading part in the Apollo project to become chief engineer of the Bay Area Rapid Transit District in California. Thus, the experience acquired in an advanced-technology project is directly applied to the solution of technical problems in rapid transit on the ground.

The least successful way of "transferring" technology from one purpose to another is to have the federal government do it directly. Unfortunately, there seems to be something of a mismatch between the civil economy and the existing federal institutions for many technology developments. This is principally a result of the people within the federal government not having the necessary special skills to effect the transfer. Successful transfer requires that a market for the technological product be available, that the technology is adapted well enough to that market so that accurate cost projections can be made, that the necessary risk capital be accumulated, and that the special organization structure be created to carry the new product successfully to the marketplace. Private enterprise has these necessary skills and is therefore best able to do this job. A disastrous example of federal technology transfer is the "people mover," based on advanced technology, that was partly constructed in Morgantown, West Virginia.

The process of technology transfer is an important one that must be nurtured and encouraged. It is strongly recommended that, in view of our experience in this field, proper incentives be provided for private industry and for individual technical people to encourage the transfer of appropriate new technologies to commercial markets as soon as feasible. In addition, it is important that the federal government, in undertaking a technology-development program, understands thoroughly which part of the development is best done by private industry and which part is best accomplished under federal direction.

5. Opportunities in Technology Development

Introductory Comments

One of the clear threads that has emerged from the studies initiated by the Commission on Critical Choices for Americans is the crucial role of technology development in almost all fields of human endeavor. The working papers developed by the Commission describe opportunities that could be grasped if the necessary technology becomes available. The purpose of this section is to summarize some of these technical opportunities and to outline some possible strategies to take advantage of them. In doing this, we shall attempt to select examples of technology developments that have two important features:

1. The development must be one which can only be carried out if the technological resources of the United States are brought to bear on it. This means that many important things that could be done with smaller resources by other nations will be left out.
2. It must be possible for the United States to carry out the technical development unilaterally, that is, without securing the agreement of other nations or having the development depend on the existence of international agreements.

These criteria are not meant to exclude international collaboration or multinational arrangements. Quite the contrary, it has often been the case that once the United States has initiated a technical development, then international arrangements that are of benefit to all have followed based on that development. The INTELSAT Communications Network is the best recent example. What is important is to select examples where the United States alone can take the initiative to bring about the first steps of a process that may ultimately be exported and result in substantial benefits to the rest of the world.

The following sections describe some technological opportunities that have been selected as a result of an examination of the material prepared by and for the Commission on Critical Choices for Americans in different fields.

Energy

The availability of cheap energy is the foundation of modern civilization. It is probably not an exaggeration to say that the possibilities for human freedom depend directly, up to a point, on the availability of energy. It is obviously a matter of political choice how much energy we elect to provide to society. There is some upper limit beyond which more energy cannot be usefully employed—at least if we restrict ourselves to applications on the surface of the earth. The essential point is that there are no technical problems in securing energy enough to exceed any forseeable requirements. The constraints that force limits on energy availability are financial (lack of sufficient capital to develop known energy resources), political (embargoes by oil and gas producing nations), and environmental considerations. These limitations are extremely important and they constitute the framework within which the choices regarding energy policies will have to be made.

Following the gasoline and fuel shortage in late 1973, President Nixon announced that the United States would embark on a program to become "self-sufficient" in energy. The president also announced a comprehensive technology-development program to achieve that objective, one which if successful might exceed the goal and turn us into an energy-exporting nation. There are some elements of the program that deserve further emphasis since they represent the development of resources that are unique to the United States or the expansion of technologies in which we enjoy a leading position in the world.

The United States possesses well over half the known resources of oil shale in the world.[21] It is estimated that in terms of reserves, the oil that could be extracted from the shale formations would equal the known oil and gas reserves in the Persian Gulf area. One problem in recovering oil from shale is the cost. Another is that adverse environmental effects are caused by the massive amounts of material that must be processed. One barrel of oil—42 gallons—requires the processing of 1.25 to 1.5 tons of material. The shales are located in a region of the country where the availability of water is a problem. If shale is mined and then processed, means must be found to deal with the residues. It is possible that some of the other materials contained in the shale—such as aluminum—might be extracted to help defray expenses for disposal of the tailings. Another technique might be to process the shale underground by first crushing it with explosives (chemical or nuclear) and then heating the crushed material underground to drive out oil and other volatile materials present in the shale. The state of development of the technology to recover oil under these conditions and at this scale is such that the costs cannot be predicted with sufficient accuracy to attract private capital in the near term. Federal partnership with private industry is needed to develop advanced methods of recovering oil from this vast natural reserve.[22]

The United States has a significant fraction (30 percent) of the world's known coal reserves. Most of the unmined coal in the country is located in the western states of Montana, Wyoming, and Colorado. These coal deposits may be thought of as a number of gigantic slabs of material 100 or more feet thick lying underground, tilted in such a way that the northern end of the slab is closer to the surface of the earth than the southern end. Where the slab is closer to the surface, strip-mining techniques can be applied provided that the proper environmental measures are taken. Further south, strip mining will not work; and when the seam is a thousand or more feet below the surface, the economics of recovery are not favorable. It is in these regions that various in situ processes could become important. In situ processing of coal is not a new technology and has been carried out in several different places.[23] What is new is that no one has attempted in situ processing at the depths encountered in Colorado. As in the case of shale, the coal must first be crushed by explosives; it is then burned underground in the presence of steam, yielding a complex mixture of gases, including hydrogen, methane, carbon monoxide, and carbon dioxide. A considerable technology-development program is necessary to process the deep coal in situ. This program must be sponsored to some extent by the federal government since the technical risks are probably still too high for private investment.[24]

The United States has a unique position in nuclear energy production. Although the first commercial pilot-model nuclear power plants were built in Great Britain, we have now built and are building more commercial nuclear plants than anyone else in the world. Large nuclear power reactors are now an important "high-technology" export item for the United States.

Our leading position in the reactor business is largely due to the fact that we have extensive isotope separation and enrichment facilities. These represent an enormous investment by the federal government that was made originally for national defense and is now the mainstay of our nuclear technology. With current reactor technology—that is, thermal-neutron reactors—an important limitation is the very small percentage of the fissile isotope U-235 in natural uranium. This point was recognized long ago, by people working at the University of Chicago Metallurgical Laboratory during World War II, and it was also known that under certain conditions it is possible to "multiply" or "breed" more fissile material from isotopes that originally are not fissile. Isotopes that can be used for breeding fissile materials are called fertile isotopes. If such a breeder reactor can be made to work, then nuclear fuels will become much more "abundant" in the sense that 100 times as much of the uranium, plus enormous supplies of thorium, will become available for use in generating nuclear energy. There are two possible fuel cycles that can be used for breeding, one based on uranium-plutonium and the other based on thorium-uranium. Both of these are being intensively investigated and technology developments for the uranium-plutonium cycle have been under way for a number of years. These efforts should be continued and the work on the thorium-uranium cycle should probably be expanded. The proper development of nuclear-fission reactor technology is absolutely essential if we are to meet the nation's energy requirements in the coming half-century.

Perhaps the most important problem that must be solved for nuclear-fission energy production on a very large scale is how to dispose of the long-lived radioactive waste products that are produced by the reactors. There are a number of promising approaches that have been proposed for a long-term solution of this problem. They should all be investigated and then two or three should be chosen for technology development.[25]

For the long-term future, we have the prospect of controlled thermonuclear energy. If this can be achieved, we will have at our command a clean source of energy with an inexhaustible supply of fuel. Furthermore, there will be less serious problems with respect to the disposal of radioactive waste products. Unfortunately, we do not yet appear to be at the stage where all the scientific principles on which controlled fusion is to be based are fully understood. We may, therefore, not yet be ready to embark on a technology development in this case. Intensive scientific research is needed to uncover the principles upon which the fusion reactor is to be based. Such efforts should be very strongly supported.

A few other things should be done that are peculiarly suited for work in the United States. For example, it is probably feasible to increase the efficiency of electric power plants by the addition of high-temperature topping cycles. Boilers could be made more efficient—and the same is true of much of the other machinery used in energy production. The efficiency of the machines that consume energy should also be improved. First among these is obviously the automobile. There is no question that many steps can—and will—be taken to reduce the energy consumed by automobiles. In the field of housing, much can be done to improve insulation and to stop heat leaks that would save much fuel.

More sophisticated energy-saving techniques await new technology development. For example, much energy is expended in separation processes, of which the largest is the distillation of petroleum. At the present time, much energy is wasted in petroleum refineries because it is not economic to recover it. Such recovery requires trading capital investment for operating costs; since capital is expensive and energy still cheap, such recovery has not been attempted. Other industries, notably sugar refining and water desalination, have taken such steps as insulating stills and using "multiple-effect evaporators" where the vapor from one distillation is used to supply heat to another. Such methods can reduce energy consumption toward the theoretical minimum based on the entropy of separation. However, that minimum is lower at lower temperatures. In the past, low-temperature separations, using enzymes (breweries), solvent extraction (sugar refineries), vacua (freeze-drying), and membranes (certain pharmaceuticals) have been more expensive, and have generally been used only when the products are thermosensitive organic materials. However, research and development on the application of such techniques to petroleum refining is being actively carried on by the laboratories of oil and chemical corporations, and it should be strongly encouraged by the government in anticipation of higher energy costs. Ironically, the United States has no Federal Institute of Oil Research although we have institutions concerned with wood, cotton, carbohydrates, proteins, and fats. Germany, France, and England all have active institutes concerned with petroleum research.

When steps are taken toward improving the energy situation through the regulatory and political processes, they often have unanticipated and disadvantageous effects. We have mentioned the increased energy consumption resulting from the antipollution legislation of the early 1970s. Another example arose from controlling petroleum prices in 1974. To encourage vigorous exploration for new supplies, the price of "new" oil was fixed at about $10 per barrel and "old" oil at $5 per barrel. As a result, capital was directed from secondary recovery efforts, and in some cases recoverable underground petroleum has been thereby abandoned. Great care must be taken in the design and application of regulatory steps to make certain that they have the intended effect.

Food

Ever since the Reverend Malthus made his gloomy calculations at the beginning of the nineteenth century, men have been concerned about a famine that affects the entire world. That this has not happened is in large measure a result of the really remarkable developments in agricultural techniques in the last two centuries. In spite of this circumstance, it is obvious that there is some limit to the amount of food that can be produced. Furthermore, there exist local situations where, for one reason or another, starvation is a fact. In 1974, conditions occurred in the Sahel in Northern Africa that caused death by starvation for many thousands of people. The situation in the Sahel is unique, complex,[26] and not subject to easy solution, but local famine conditions are certain to arise in many other regions in the coming years. For the near term, the only way to deal with these situations is to ship food to the afflicted regions from countries that possess surplus food supplied. For example, roughly 120,000 tons of foodstuffs per month (which is more than the total local food production under normal conditions) were being brought into the Sahel by various international relief organizations during the height of the crisis. (*Newsweek*, August 5, 1974.) This is expensive, but it can be done, provided the situation is a local one.

The long-term problem is more difficult to deal with. Even though extreme conditions such as those existing in the Sahel region are still relatively rare, a large fraction of the world's population suffers from chronic malnutrition. This situation is likely to continue into the foreseeable future given probable population trends and fertilizer shortages. Certain obvious measures must be taken to alleviate this state of affairs, among them being population control and the development of more efficient agricultural methods. Both of these activities have strong technological components, but other considerations are dominant. Effective means of population control exist—the problem is to get people to adopt them. Advanced agricultural methods also exist, and the primary problem is to persuade people that the situation is sufficiently serious so that they should be adopted as rapidly as possible in many parts of the world. With respect to that technology, there is a well-developed network of agricultural research under both public and private sponsorship seeking to find new ways to increase agricultural productivity.

The most conspicuous recent success in this field is the "Green Revolution," led by such people as Norman Borlaug and George Harrar. By applying the principles of genetics they were able to develop strains of corn, wheat, and rice which produced large yields in regions where these crops had not previously been economic. Unfortunately, these high yields depended on large applications of fertilizers which have recently drastically increased in price. Support for such activities should be continued and expanded.

In addition, there are two new technical developments on the horizon that should be accelerated in order to help prevent acute food problems of the kind now being experienced in Africa. During the past two years, the first Earth Resources Technology Satellite has flown and has yielded a large quantity of data. This satellite (now renamed LANDSAT-1) is equipped with cameras that can photograph the Earth's surface with good resolution—200 feet—from an altitude of about 200 miles in several regions of the spectrum. The information received by the cameras is telemetered back to Earth where it is picked up by several different receiving stations. Multispectral images of the kind received from LANDSAT-1 can be used to monitor agricultural production on almost a worldwide basis. The spectral "signatures" of various crops are quite distinctive; that is, rice can be distinguished from wheat, and so on. Furthermore, it is possible to make some statements regarding the status (i.e., maturity) and also the health of the crops from the data provided by LANDSAT-1; early warning on infestations can be provided.

Although very good data regarding the status of crops within the United States are generally available, the same is not true for much of the remainder of the world. For example, LANDSAT-1 photography clearly delineated the problem that exists in the Sahel region. What is even more important, LANDSAT-1 photographs also showed some isolated regions of the Sahel which remained productive in spite of the drought because proper conservation measures were being taken. If information of this kind were available at the right time to anyone who wanted it, it is possible that acute famine situations might be avoided.[27]

It is obvious that accurate crop surveys would be extremely valuable to many of the less well-developed nations to assist their agricultural planning. There are, of course, national sensitivities that must be taken into account if a network of Earth-observation satellites based on LANDSAT-1 technology is to be established. However, a good precedent exists in the case of the INTELSAT communications satellite network, and it is possible that the nations belonging to it could also participate in an Earth-observation network.

An area of research and development that might be crucial to agricultural planning and other activities in the coming years is meteorology. A new generation of high-speed computers, such as the CDC-7600, has recently made it possible to utilize much more accurate theoretical models of the Earth's atmosphere. These models should eventually make possible long-term forecasts of climatological patterns of sufficient accuracy that droughts, periods of heavy rainfall, unusually severe winters, etc., can be predicted prior to their occurrence. A great deal of work needs to be done before this objective can actually be accomplished, both in the computer technology and in the accurate determination of atmospheric wind patterns, temperature profiles, radiant energy balances, and other parameters required as initial inputs to the computer models. The unique position of the United States in advanced computer systems makes this a natural field for the concentration of substantial resources. Several large efforts are indeed already underway (GISS, New York; NCAR, Boulder, Colorado) and work in this area should be expanded.[28]

One final point needs to be made. Several hundred million people, living mostly in tropical zones, are afflicted with a number of diseases such as yaws, hookworm, trachoma, and schistosomiasis. All of these diseases are well understood and could, in principle, be wiped out. All of them are related to or are at least aggravated by malnutrition. To the extent that these diseases are caused by deficiencies in the food production and distribution system, the measures suggested in the previous paragraphs would help.

Raw Materials

While acute shortages of energy and of food have occurred in various parts of the world during the past few years, other fundamental raw materials such as basic metals and fibres have been less seriously affected. The limitations in supply that may exist for some of these items come from political (i.e., embargoes by raw-material suppliers), economic (i.e., lack of capital), environmental, and, in the longer term, technological circumstances. There are a number of critical problems that seem to be amenable to technological solutions if the proper steps are taken now. Generally, these fall into two areas: the development of substitute materials, and the development of means to extract materials from ore bodies that cannot now be exploited economically. The economic problems may arise from the remoteness of the ore body (very deep, in the arctic, on the ocean bottom, perhaps even on the moon) or from the ore being "low-grade." The latter usually means that it is diluted by worthless impurities ("high-grade" gold ore averages about 99.997 percent impurities), but it may mean that the desired material is in an undesirable or refractory chemical state (as in the case of aluminum, which is a common constituent of most rocks).

The United States has long held a leading position in the development of substitute materials for the basic metals and for some other natural commodities such as wood and rubber. Much of this effort has been concentrated in our highly developed plastics industry. Organically-based substitutes have the advantage that their properties can be more readily tailored to the ultimate application than is generally the case with metal-based materials. The major difficulty with plastics is that the current raw materials used to manufacture them are most often derived from petroleum. With the continuing shortage of oil, a high premium should be placed on using other organic raw materials such as coal, wood, and possibly agricultural or aquacultural products, such as sugar beets or algae, to supply the basic organic chemicals needed in the manufacture of plastics.

Also in the longer term, strong efforts should be made to develop substitute plastic materials based on silicon rather than on carbon. Silicon has a chemical versatility somewhat similar to that of carbon, but has no alternative use as fuel because it occurs in nature only in oxidized state. Silicon-based plastics (silicones) exist, but they are more expensive and much less extensively developed than carbon-based materials. A concerted technology-development effort in this area might have very important practical results. Because of the nature of this technology, it is probable that private industry, with the proper federal incentives and help, could carry out the major share of this work.

There are numerous areas of promise for future technological innovation in extractive metallurgy. For example, the pyrometallurgical processes are adaptable to large continuous reactors, providing high production rates and consequently low unit output costs. Hydrometallurgical processes are quite flexible in the desired range of the chemical and physical nature of the end product. Vapor metallurgy permits utilization of a range of temperatures from below $0°$ C to above $1000°$ C and at pressures from a small fraction of atmospheric to several hundred atmospheres. Thus, desired elements in the solid state are selectively converted to new compounds as solids, liquids, or gases, from which pure metals are recovered and the original gaseous extractant recycled.

In the development of low-grade ore bodies, the central difficulty is that much larger volumes of materials must be treated in order to extract the same quantity of finished metal. One means of surmounting the resulting environmental and economic difficulties might be to use nuclear explosives to break up and crush low-grade ore bodies underground and then to employ various chemical methods to leach out the metals. This technology is not one that lends itself to development by private capital, since the risks involved in working out the methods are too large. On the other hand, it is likely that a major change in the economics of low-grade ore extraction could occur should nuclear mining methods prove to be practical. This is an example of the kind of technology development that must be supported initially by the federal government if it is to be done in the near future.

A pioneering effort in the private exploitation of low-grade ores is the Reserve Mining Company's taconite processing plant in Silver Bay on Lake Superior, which has become a cause célèbre.[29] This plant deposits 67,000 tons per day of waste solids into the lake, which are supposed to sink harmlessly. They have not done so entirely as planned, and impurities have thereby been introduced into the water supply of Duluth which may be carcinogenic. As a result of this and other unforeseen pollution effects, Reserve will either have to close the plant or, more probably, spend some hundreds of millions of dollars to develop an alternative depository for the "tailing." While pollution of Lake Superior cannot be tolerated (the total natural supply of solids to this largest fresh-water lake in the world is estimated at 12,000 tons per day), it should be noted that Reserve did obtain government approval before constructing the plant. Private capital, contemplating major new projects, must take cognizance of the fact that the government, having approved a pollution level incident on some such project, reserves the right to establish more stringent pollution controls ex post facto.

Two other approaches to raw-material availability should be seriously pursued. In the near term, the technologies associated with recycling should be intensively developed, probably by private industry (since there are already some very profitable scrap operations), encouraged by government through subsidies, tax rules, and price regulations. In the longer term, we should look into the problem of recovering certain basic metals from sea water. While sea water extraction is never likely to be economical except for a limited number of materials, (it is now our principal source of bromine) this work should be pursued to provide emergency sources of materials if and when the normal supplies are disrupted.

Transportation and Communications

Transportation and communication technologies are closely related. In a highly interdependent world, the economic well being of the human race depends critically on cheap and efficient transportation. Easy communication is equally necessary for the highly sophisticated system of international trade on which we currently rely. Aside from commerce, transportation and communications may be even more important in improving the quality of life. Easy access to other parts of the world is clearly of cultural value and has a broadening effect on those people who can travel.

The introduction of efficient jet transport aircraft has revolutionized world travel patterns. The wide-bodied transport is one of the cheapest conveyances known since it can move large numbers of people for costs that may be as low as a few cents per seat-mile. The use of jet transport aircraft for intercontinental travel has also had significant impact on cargo movement, especially if the cargo is not bulky and if it has high time value. An interesting example of this is the movement of transistors and LSIs (Large Scale Integrated Circuits) from the United States to Taiwan, several thousand miles away, where the transistors and LSIs are assembled into completed electronic devices by cheap labor. Once completed, the circuits are shipped to where they will be used—also by air. Some of the large wide-bodied jets are now being converted to cargo carriers (such as the Boeing 747-C with a gross take-off weight of 750,000 pounds) with special provisions for handling larger items. Studies are being conducted to determine the economic viability of even larger cargo-carrying aircraft with a gross take-off weight of about 3,000,000 pounds. It is too early to tell whether this will actually be done, but if such aircraft are actually built, they will have a significant impact on world trade.

Analogously, supertankers and large container ships have recently become operational in the transportation of heavy cargoes. These have been quite successful, but compared to aircraft they are slow. To get something in between—slower than the aircraft with more payload and faster than the tanker with less payload—nuclear-powered hovercraft have been suggested. These would have speeds in the 100-knot range and would carry payloads up to 10,000 tons. No development of these vehicles has been initiated as yet, but the federal government has carried out some preliminary studies of their economic feasibility.[30] While the project is unlikely to come to fruition, it is cited here as an example of the kind of "wild ideas" that may have to be explored.

Technological developments in the field of communication may be even more important. In a very real sense, the difference between an open and a closed society lies in the control of the communication system, a situation that needs much more detailed examination and understanding.

Two separate issues must be considered when discussing communications. One has to do with the transmission of information and the other with the processing of information. As long as the message is relatively simple, transmission is clearly most important. However, when things become more complex, then some processing is required in order to render the message intelligible to the receiver.

One important technical development in the field of information *transmission* has been the creation of the satellite communication networks. The essential technical point of satellite communications systems is that they make instant, worldwide communications possible at high data rates (TV, two-way voice links, computer-to-computer, etc.). As in so many of the other examples we have discussed, the first communications satellites were developed for military purposes. Starting in 1960, the U.S. Navy put into service a number of communications satellites (Echo, Transit, Early Bird, etc.) that proved to be highly effective. The commercial potential of communications satellites were quickly recognized and a corporation (COMSAT) was formed in 1963 under a charter from, and with partial ownership by, the U.S. government to exploit the commercial potential of communications satellites.[31]

In addition to COMSAT, an international organization (INTELSAT) was established in 1969. There are now ninety nations in the INTELSAT organization that contribute to its support by providing ground receiving stations or—in the case of major powers—technology for new satellites. These satellites make it possible to transmit TV directly from one continent to another—and this has been the major application that is known to the public. What is not as well known is that a significant fraction of the intercontinental telephone traffic now also proceeds via satellite. The most recent communications satellites—the INTELSAT IV series—are large geostationary satellites placed over various points on the equator at an altitude of about 25,000 miles. Each one can carry simultaneously twenty-four TV channels and about 10,000 two-way telephone conversations. With these satellites it will soon be possible, in principle, to direct-dial telephone between any two points on the globe and to hold a two-way conversation at low cost.

The current communications satellites are essentially repeaters; that is, they are low-powered devices intended to operate between two central stations, one of which at any instant transmits to the satellite while the other receives from it. Each central station then has a ground network associated with it that transmits the information between the central station and the individuals using the system. The next generation of communications satellites could carry larger power supplies which would (in principle) make it possible to transmit directly TV signals which originate in one nation to standard TV sets in the homes of people in another nation (perhaps another continent) *without the need* for a central station. Obviously, this possibility raises difficult international questions that touch upon some fundamental issues dealing with national sovereignty and the financing of these systems. Because communications satellites have turned out to be quite profitable, it is likely that the political difficulties inherent in direct-transmission satellites will eventually be overcome and that they will be developed. The United States currently has an overwhelming lead in this technology; it is important that we continue to hold this advantage by developing the power systems necessary for direct-transmission satellites.

The techniques that are associated with information *processing* pose much more difficult and subtle problems. We now have the capability to accumulate, process, store, and retrieve vast quantities of data. For example, the memory bank of a moderately large computer can easily store all the knowledge we have, say, about the civilization of the ancient Greeks. What is, of course, much more important is that we can accumulate all kinds of information about individuals (census data, credit rating, medical records, etc.) and program the computer so that we can retrieve information about people in any combination we want. The same can be said for businesses and other organizations. Obviously, this capability has great advantages but it also poses serious problems, especially in a society that considers the right to privacy as basic. We are just beginning to struggle with this problem. It is obvious that the technological advantages inherent in large-scale data processing equipment should be grasped, but it is equally clear that great care must be taken to do this in such a way that our liberties are not compromised.

Large digital data-processing machines were developed, starting immediately after World War II, for a variety of purposes. With the introduction of transistors in the middle 1950s, and the subsequent development of large-scale integrated circuits, it became feasible to build machines having truly enormous capacity in moderate volumes. In addition, the once costly circuitry is now so cheap that sophisticated hand-held calculators can be manufactured and marketed for a few dollars. The next obvious step in this direction are small "mini computers" for the household that will make it possible to perform many tasks such as bill paying, budget estimating, and purchase planning by having large data banks at the fingertips of the householder. This prospect has some obvious implications for our life-style. The advantages of such systems should be carefully examined, and if found desirable the technology necessary should be brought into being. This field is ripe for private exploitation.

Large-scale information-processing systems have important applications in the organization and conduct of world trade. If possible, we should try to use our mastery of this technology in a conscious way to help our trading position. It is not easy to see how (or whether) this can actually be accomplished, but it is worth investigating.

National Defense

Perhaps the central fact about our present position in relationship to the rest of the world is that we are no longer the world's leading military power. In many military fields the Soviet Union has exceeded us in number of weapons available, and in certain areas their equipment is of higher quality. It is probably not feasible or even desirable to regain the military position we had relative to the world's other nations two decades ago. The social costs of such a step would simply be too large. What we must do instead is to find those few things in which military weakness would be fatal for our survival as a nation and then concentrate our efforts on these. It has already been made abundantly clear in this chapter that new military developments tend to have a heavy technological component. This is still true, and the proposals made here call for several new technical steps that should be taken.

Two fundamental policies will characterize the defense posture of the United States in the next two decades:

1. The United States must maintain a credible deterrent force to prevent an attack by intercontinental ballistic missiles.
2. The United States must help to maintain freedom of the seas.

The first of these policies is aimed at our survival as a nation. The second one is intended to ensure our prosperity by preserving the trade links that we must have. Should we fail to preserve these trade links, then the navy would still be vitally needed to provide adequate defense for our sea frontiers.

Both of these policies will require some investment in new technology developments. Our strategic deterrent force has three major components: the manned bomber force of the Strategic Air Command, the land-based ICBM force, and the nuclear submarines with their submarine-launched ballistic missiles. We are now developing new and more effective bombers (the B-1) and submarine systems (the Trident). The land-based ballistic missile force is becoming increasingly vulnerable to a "first strike" attack as Soviet missile technology improves, particularly with respect to guidance and accuracy. One way to defeat these Soviet advances is to introduce mobility into our land-based ballistic missile systems. In this way, the target position will not be known to the Soviets and thus a larger fraction of the land-based force is likely to survive a "first strike." Several proposals have been made to accomplish this objective, including movable launchers that could be moved using railroad tracks or highways, or airborne launching systems in which the ballistic missiles are launched from large airplanes of the Boeing 747 class.[32] This is not the right place for a discussion of the advantages and disadvantages of these systems. What is important is that a decision will have to be reached in the near future as to which—if either—of these systems to develop, and the necessary steps will have to be taken to implement the decision.

The United States has a long and important naval tradition. From the beginning of the Republic, freedom of the seas (and the freedom to trade that follows) was a central tenet of our foreign policy. Two of our early wars, one against the Barbary pirates in the Mediterranean during the early 1800s and one against Great Britain in 1812-14, were fought over this issue. At the end of World War II, the United States had the most powerful sea force that had ever been created. This force was a combination of sea and air power and was based on the great aircraft carriers that are still the most important naval units in the world's fleets. It is very likely that this combination of air and sea power will continue to be one of the two important parts of naval power—the other one is, of course, that based upon the submarine.

The tactics used by the carrier fleets that characterized our World War II navy were devised before the advent of nuclear weapons. In a naval war fought with tactical nuclear weapons, aircraft carriers as large as those used in World War II would be too vulnerable since they represent a highly concentrated force. In order to disperse the naval airpower represented by the large carriers, it has been proposed that the United States embark on an extensive program to construct a large fleet of much smaller aircraft carriers called "Sea Control Ships."[33] These vessels would be equipped with a series of new aircraft that would have the capability to perform a large variety of missions. There would be helicopters and Lockheed S-3 type aircraft for convoy coverage and antisubmarine patrols. There would be high-performance vertical take-off and landing (VTOL) fighter aircraft in order to establish local air superiority wherever necessary. Finally, there would be light short takeoff and landing (STOL) transports that would be employed to supply a fleet at sea or landing forces when required. The Sea Control Ships are sufficiently small—each would carry only a dozen or so aircraft—that the loss of any one of them would not be a crippling blow. There are a number of technology developments, especially in VTOL and STOL aviation, that must be initiated as rapidly as possible if an effective sea control force of this type is to be brought into existence.

In addition to the major developments outlined above, there are several other things that we should initiate or continue to do. One is to maintain and perhaps expand our worldwide military air-supply system. Currently, this system is based on 80 long-range C-5 aircraft, 250 long-range C-141 aircraft, and a larger number of medium-range C-130 aircraft. In addition to the military air transport fleet, the United States also has at its disposal about 3,000 commercial jet transports that can be, and in some cases have already been, used for various military supply missions. This air supply system was absolutely crucial in the resupply of Israel during the October 1973 war. We must at least maintain this air supply system and in certain areas expand its capabilities.

A more difficult and controversial issue is our status as arsenal for the military storehouse of our friends around the world. It is not certain that friends will remain friends; yet we must make some choices, and then make certain that the people with whom we have vital interests in common have the ability to defend themselves. Generally, our weapons have proved to be effective—particularly in things such as tactical air support of various ground forces. These supporting activities should be continued.

Finally, there is an issue related to the national defense which is very controversial but which needs to be reopened. Even before the shooting down of the U-2 reconnaissance aircraft over the Soviet Union in 1959, President Eisenhower proposed an international "open skies" policy. In essence, the proposal was to declassify all intelligence data acquired on the strategic capabilities of other nations in order to reduce the element of fear present in international relationships. For a number of reasons, this proposal was rejected at the time. However, there are now good reasons for reconsidering the "open skies" proposal. Our society is an open one and we cannot keep things secret in the long term. Our opponents do not have open societies and they can keep secrets. Since we are no longer far in the lead militarily but falling slowly behind, it would be to our advantage to have as much public knowledge as possible about the distribution of strategic weapons in the world. We could unilaterally declassify such data and ask other people to do likewise. Obviously, this suggestion is a controversial one and the step proposed should only be taken after the most careful analysis. However, the question should be reopened and considered.

In all of the technological developments proposed here, we should keep our eyes open for possible civil applications of the developments. The importance of technology transfer has already been mentioned and it is important to make our financial investments in defense serve a double purpose if this can possibly be done.

The Quality of Life

In the last decade, it has become very common among certain influential groups in the United States to equate technology and its effect with a reduction of what is loosely termed "the quality of life." What is usually meant by such critics of technology is that the effects of the mass applications of technology are deleterious. Air pollution, water pollution, and the overcrowding of scenic areas are indeed sometimes caused by the application of technology; but the positive effects of the applications are generally not factored into the equation when these arguments are made.

For example, Herman Kahn has said that criticisms of overcrowding scenic areas are directed at technology by people who already have the improved quality of life that technology brings and against the people who are just getting it. Upper-middle class people with enough leisure time to enjoy the wilderness in its pristine state are upset by the moves to build highways and recreational areas for the masses in "their" wilderness areas. Most of the rest of us, so Kahn argues, are not that fortunate, and we must have the highways and the hotels and the other technological appurtenances that make our weekend trips possible. We cannot afford to take the time for a leisurely approach and are, therefore, relatively unsympathetic to demands that the world be returned to its "natural" state. Similarly, no one wants a petroleum refinery in his neighborhood, but everyone demands the products of such refineries.

In commenting on the "natural" condition of the world more than three centuries ago, Thomas Hobbes asserted that "in a state of nature, . . . the life of man is solitary, poor, nasty, brutish and short."[34] He is clearly correct and we make a fundamental mistake if we believe that our efforts to change the world to our liking are somehow immoral or wrong. The agent of that change is the application of technology, and in a very general sense the quality of life depends largely on our ability to do this intelligently. This statement is almost too broad to be really useful, but it is important to recognize that almost all of the issues dealt with here are related to the application of technology. In order to narrow the discussion, we shall comment on only one extremely important area that bears strongly on the quality of life, namely education.

In the last five years, there have been some important technical developments in education based on two new technologies: television, and computer networks. Both of these technologies are already being applied to some extent in schools throughout the United States. As cheaper and more reliable receivers are developed, television will come into more widespread use, not only in the United States, but in the rest of the world as well. In this respect, the transmission of direct television signals from high-power communications satellite systems might be particularly important in making it possible to reach schools that are geographically dispersed. The computer networks might have an even greater impact than television. Computer terminals with the appropriate graphics equipment are now used in some of the more advanced primary and secondary schools as a teaching aid. They can be used very effectively for certain basic things, such as learning the elementary rules of arithmetic and grammar. They have also been effectively used in the administration of examination to students. Finally, the computer networks can be tied to an archival memory, thus making library resources available to schools that could not normally afford them. Both of the technologies mentioned here are very attractive items for export to other nations who might wish to use them, and such possibilities should be vigorously explored. Because of our uniquely advantageous position in electronics and computer technology, we are in a good position to embark on such a program.

Some Suggested Strategies

In the foregoing sections, a number of technical opportunities that seem to be on the horizon have been discussed. It is not our purpose here to attempt to justify undertaking these developments. Rather, the descriptions are a sample of what might be done. However, there are common methods that might be employed in bringing about some of these developments in the institutional sense and, what is more important, exporting them in such a way that benefits accrue to other countries as well as to the United States.

For many years, the United States has been an exporter of manufactured goods that are the products of our "high" technology. As a particular technology is reduced to better engineering practice we have often lost out to other nations in recent years because of the relatively high manufacturing costs in this country. The most recent case in point is the "export" of our electronics technology to Japan. The transistors, electron guns, luminescent screens, and other devices necessary for the manufacture of television sets were mostly developed in the United States in the 1950s. Once the technology was well in hand, the firms who had mastered it made arrangements with Japanese collaborators to have the manufacturing done in Japan. This procedure has been followed not only in electronics but in certain other fields (textiles, optics, watches) with other countries, as well.

One could argue that procedures of this kind are not to the ultimate advantage of the United States. By "giving away" the technology to other nations, we are creating jobs elsewhere in the world rather than in this country, thus contributing to unemployment. This argument was recently made by George Meany in connection with the "export of jobs" in the aeronautical industry. Moreover, the manufactured goods produced in the foreign countries are resold to us at prices that might adversely affect our balance of trade. This situation is bound to develop; but we can compensate for it *if we continue to develop new technologies* as the older ones are being exported. Such technologies must have a sufficiently large domestic market that a "critical mass" exists, leading to economies of scale and ultimately to profitable export.

The case of the export of aeronautical technology mentioned previously is a good example. If an American airplane manufacturer is approached by a nation with a request to build a factory in that nation, to construct aircraft based on current technology, then we should look with favor on this request provided that the factory is geared to current construction methods. For example, the current methods might be based on aluminum technology; we should then push hard the technology of titanium and modern composite materials that might eventually replace aluminum as the primary structural material in aircraft. If this technology development succeeds, then the first production runs of the next generation of aircraft will be built in the United States with the resultant benefits accruing to us in terms of employment and other economic benefits. Once the new technology is well developed, it can, in turn, be exported and the cycle is repeated.

We have been following the procedure outlined above in our agricultural technology, a point that has already been made, and in the plastics industry, among others. We not only export our agricultural products, but we also export the *techniques* that have made our agricultural system so productive. We have organized projects and we have built laboratories in other countries that have helped in significant ways to raise agricultural productivity in these countries. Similar procedures have been used in other fields as well. American firms have not only exported plastic products, but they have also built factories and laboratories.

6. Summary

Technology Development as a National Purpose

We have attempted to develop strong arguments why the United States should define a national purpose around technology development as a means to reach our national goals. In many ways, we have already used technology development as a primary means for achieving some of them. What is still lacking is the explicit recognition by our political leadership and by the electorate that this is what we have been doing and that it is a natural role for the United States to play in the future.

Our national goals tend to be vague, subjective, sometimes transitory, and rarely unanimous. Things such as "A Better Life for All," and "The Pursuit of Happiness," and "An End to Poverty" are all national objectives of a permanent sort, but they mean different things to different people and are thus highly subjective. The interpretation of what is meant by these things can and should form the substance of recurrent national debates. Other national goals that may be more objective are also more transitory. "The Preservation of the Union," "The Defeat of the Axis," and "Putting a Man on the Moon" are in that category. Such goals are usually adopted as a reaction to some external crisis. Still other goals lack unanimous support. Subjecting the Russians to our will (or the Arabs, or the South Africans); increasing the level of morality (or religion, or rationality); preserving the environment (or the family, or racial purity)—any of these may be the single most important national goal for some individuals and anathema to others. But what every one of the above goals have in common is that technological means are often the most effective way of achieving them. It has not been our purpose to define a set of national objectives. Rather, we have argued that the nation should explicitly choose technology development as a principal means for achieving our ends once they are defined. This is the critical choice that should be laid before the American people.

Deciding Among Technology Developments

A great many reasons have been used to justify technology developments. The federal government has generally used military arguments in favor of certain large-scale projects (even the interstate freeway system was so justified; it is officially called the National System of Interstate and Defense Highways). While the needs of national defense have been an adequate driving force for technology development in the past, it is obvious that other equally compelling reasons should be developed. The international nature of technology makes it natural to ask whether technology development should be an explicit element of our foreign policy.

We have discussed the export of "high technology" to other nations—not just the products of high technology, but the techniques themselves. There is no reason why this cannot be done in such a way that national benefits and advantages accrue to us. An interesting example of this is our collaborative efforts with other nations in space exploration. Since much of our work in space exploration in recent years no longer has a strong military component, this is a natural subject for international collaboration. Indeed, space exploration is an excellent reason for undertaking technology developments. The conditions in space (i.e., the high vacuum, the radiation environment, the enormous distances) and the requirements of the mission (i.e., to measure subtle effects or to attain very high reliability) are such that existing technology is stressed to the very limit and new things are invented as a result. Indeed, the primary reason that the European space organization has entered into an agreement with the United States to collaborate in the development of payloads for the Space Shuttle

Vehicle is that they have recognized the importance of space exploration in developing new things that will later yield large economic benefits for their industry.

The profit motive is important in stimulating technology developments, but private organizations are generally quite limited with respect to the capital they have at their disposal for such enterprises.

In addition to military, foreign-policy, and profit motives, it would be a mistake to ignore purely altruistic motives in developing new technologies. Many of the significant advances in agriculture and public health have been sponsored by the great endowed foundations that were established to administer large fortunes and spend some of the money for the public welfare.

The importance of finding new and better reasons for undertaking new technology developments cannot be exaggerated. If indeed technology development is a national strength, then a purposeful search for new and politically acceptable ways to promote specific programs is essential. An important element of this search is a much better understanding of the direct effects as well as the secondary and perhaps unanticipated effects of the implementation of a new technology. The new field of *technology assessment*, developed and encouraged by Emilio Q. Daddario, is an attempt in this direction, and such efforts should be strongly encouraged. Decisions regarding the priorities of various programs that are proposed will still have to be made, and the more carefully this is done the better. The various reports prepared by and for the Commission on Critical Choices for Americans may be a good guide in helping us to define these priorities more explicitly.

Institutional Arrangements

The United States has a large and sophisticated institutional structure to perform technology development. The federal government's laboratories are operated by mission-oriented agencies: Agriculture, Commerce, Health, Education and Welfare, Energy Research and Development Administration, National Aeronautics and Space Administration, the military services, and others. The essential problem that the federal institutions must face is how to deal with new technologies and with changing missions among the agencies and how to make the laboratories respond to these changes.

At the present time, the response is probably too slow. Bureaucracy, both in Washington and at the laboratories, has sufficient inertia that there is sometimes a considerable lag between the time the technical problem or opportunity is perceived and the time that the appropriate development project is initiated. In more specific terms, the situation can be described as follows: Agency X has a laboratory, the X Development Center, which has done excellent work for Agency X and has played a major role in fulfilling the Agency's missions. As a result of these successes, Agency X is now in a period of relative inactivity and the X Development Center is not as busy as it could be. Agency Y has a problem that could be worked out by people at the X Development Center, but Agency Y has no real means for getting the job done at the other agency's Center. There are very natural jurisdictional barriers between Agency X and Agency Y, and largely because of these the management of Center X is often not willing to go after the work. As a result, nothing happens. It is not only the bureaucracy in Washington that is reluctant to cross jurisdictional lines—the people at the laboratory are often even more conservative in this respect. Even people who are fully aware of the fact in a rapidly changing technological situation tend to be conservative about crossing institutional lines.

Mission-oriented agencies are notoriously anxious to respond to an increase in the importance of their mission, but unwilling to respond to a decrease. Instead of naming a particular federal organization, we may cite the example of the March of Dimes, organized by Franklin D. Roosevelt to defeat poliomyelitis (infantile paralysis). When polio was defeated, the organization did not wither away—it found a new mission and expanded.

Generally speaking, institutional changes at the laboratories occur only after completion of a very complex and sometimes lengthy process of decision-making, which results in the formation of a new agency to perform the newly perceived mission. The formation (in 1958) of the National Aeronautics and Space Administration, which combined the three laboratories of the National Advisory Committee for Aeronautics with elements of the U.S. Naval Research Laboratory and the U.S. Army's Redstone Arsenal, was an example of such a major institutional change. The change was triggered by the "Sputnik crisis" in 1957.[35] The recent legislation that created the Energy Research and Development Administration (ERDA) from certain elements of the Atomic Energy Commission, the Department of the Interior, and several other agencies is another example. This institutional change was triggered by the fuel shortage that occurred in the winter of 1973-1974, although elements of the reorganization have been considered for some years.

These examples illustrate the problem, since both of the institutional changes occurred only *after* a crisis was upon us. It is true, of course, that some of the development laboratories show great initiative in working on technical programs not approved by the managements of the institutions or by the agencies in Washington, and thereby they anticipate the institutional changes that follow. Perhaps the best example of this "bootleg" development of the Jupiter rocket launch vehicle, which was used to put our first satellite, Explorer I, in Earth orbit, was the work done by Wernher Von Braun's group at the Redstone Arsenal. It is an amusing—and also tragic—fact that the commanding general of the Arsenal was relieved of his post when the Army authorities in Washington discovered what Von Braun had done. Another, happier, example of the "bootleg" development was the Sidewinder missile that was created by William

McLean and his collaborators in the early 1950s at the Naval Ordnance Test Station at China Lake, California. While bootlegging sometimes works, it is obvious that somehow initiative of this kind should be encouraged so that it is not necessary to use such methods.

In addition to the federal establishment, there are also the technology development institutions sponsored by private enterprises. A significant fraction of the nation's capability to develop new technologies resides in these establishments. One of the very important functions of the federally operated technology centers is to guide and monitor federally sponsored work in private industry. The links forged between the federal laboratories and private enterprise have been very important in carrying out every major technology development program, from the Manhattan Project which developed the atomic bomb three decades ago to the Space Shuttle Project today. Although these relationships are sometimes criticized, as in "the Military-Industrial Complex," they have proven to be very effective and, under different circumstances, have gained strong public approval. Remember the "Arsenal of Democracy" of World War II. The main advantage in using the federal technology-development laboratories as contract monitors for large projects is that the federal government's competence in technical matters resides in these laboratories.

There are numerous examples of successful technology-development programs that have been managed by the federal laboratories—Apollo is perhaps the primary example. Unfortunately, there have also been some failures. Nevertheless the system works well compared to those existing in other Western nations, and we should continue to improve upon and develop it. The technology developments we are starting now to improve our domestic sources of energy should provide us with ample opportunities to expand and improve the federal-industry relationships that exist.

It is always tempting to invent new bureaucratic arrangements that might improve things, and there have been a number of suggestions regarding the organization of the national research-and-development establishment. One proposal that is periodically advanced is the creation of a cabinet-level Department of Science and Technology to manage all of the technology development in the federal government. This scheme has the advantage of being organizationally clean, and it would highlight the importance of technology development as a national purpose. On the other hand, there are serious drawbacks as well. One is that such a cabinet department would concentrate enormous power over our long-term future (not just our day-to-day present activities) in the hands of one person. The Secretary of Science and Technology would have to be a person of superhuman perception to conduct the office properly. A second and even more important objection is that the concentration of technology development in a single department would create institutional boundaries that might make it even more difficult to respond to new requirements. There would also be a great temptation to regard the enterprise of technology development as an end in itself and to lose sight of the reasons for which the technology is being created (or the opposite—too much emphasis on engineering or on basic research). It is essentially for these reasons that the proposal for such a department has never been adopted.

Unfortunately, other proposals that have been made also have serious flaws, so that any progress that might be made in terms of reorganization is really questionable.

A more useful approach might be to list some of the qualities any bureaucratic structure in technology development should have to facilitate the work. Among these might be:

1. The technology development laboratories (both federal laboratories and those which are privately owned but partially federally funded) must have sufficient freedom and flexibility to carry out genuinely new programs. While a certain amount of "bootleg" work is inevitable, it should never become a way of life.
2. The system should be structured in such a way that there is less reliance on national defense as the justification for technology developments.
3. The organization should strongly encourage better relationships between technology-development laboratories and educational institutions. This is actually rather easy to do, since the functions of the laboratories and the schools are generally complementary. However, it should be more explicitly encouraged than it is at the present time.
4. The technology-development organization should be structured in such a way that agencies having common technology-development programs can use the same technology-development laboratory to achieve their objectives. This would require much closer collaboration between the mission-oriented agencies, and is thus probably a very difficult policy to implement.

Ultimately, the detailed structure of the organization adopted is not too important. What is absolutely essential is that good people be drawn into the nation's technology-development efforts. High-quality people will turn out work of high quality with almost any organizational structure. This has been stated succinctly by H.H. Goode and R.E. Machol who wrote:

The performance of a group of people is a strong function of the capabilities of the individuals and a rather weak function of the way they are organized. That is, good people do a fairly good job under almost any organization and a somewhat better one when the organization is good. Poor talent does a poor job with a bad organization, but it is still a poor job no matter what the organization. Repeated reorganizations are noted in groups of individuals poorly suited to their function, though no amount of good organization will give good performance. The best architectural design fails with poor bricks and mortar. But the pay-off from good organization with good people is worthwhile.[36]

The most important result of adopting technology development as a national purpose would be to draw the best of our young people into the effort.

Technical Education

It has already been pointed out that technology development sponsored by the federal government requires a fairly large number—200,000—of highly trained and qualified people. There are requirements at all levels ranging from the doctorate (Ph.D., Sc.D., and the Doctor of Engineering) to the craftsman (i.e., technician). Paradoxically, we have done somewhat better in providing educational opportunities and incentives for people who wish to study for advanced degrees than for those who desire to pursue careers as craftsmen. All technology developments depend ultimately on the existence of a dedicated and competent group of craftsmen. We must provide appropriate incentives so that more qualified people enter careers as craftsmen. It is important to recognize that financial incentives alone are not sufficient; it is also absolutely essential that craftsmen be accorded the proper prestige if we expect good people to engage in this work.

The United States has an excellent educational system that is already geared to providing the people required for carrying out many technology developments. The great public and private universities are clearly capable of providing the scientists and engineers. In recent years, the rapidly growing two-year community-college system has taken a leading role in providing educational opportunities for people who wish to enter careers as craftsmen. A large number of excellent programs have been developed for this purpose by many two-year colleges. However, there are still not enough highly-qualified people going through these programs.

In several instances, joint programs between an industrial enterprise or a federal laboratory and local junior college district have been initiated to make the paraprofessional curricula more attractive. In such arrangements, the industrial plant or laboratory generally provides equipment and facilities that are not available to the junior college. In this way, the programs become much more interesting to many of the students, since they will be able to gain some work experience and also see first hand what rewards accrue to people who become first-class craftsmen. It is recommended that appropriate incentives—perhaps in the form of grants-in-aid—be made available to those junior college districts that undertake to enter into collaborative arrangements of the kind that have been described.[37]

At the professional level, the institutional structure is also satisfactory. The quality of scientific and technical education could probably be improved if students were exposed somewhat earlier to people who actually work as professional technologists. As in the case of the junior colleges, the most effective way to accomplish this end is for the colleges and universities to make arrangements with local industrial and research establishments that will make it possible for students to have strong interactions with the "real world" long before they finish their formal educations.

A particularly effective method with which universities can build this kind of a relationship with industry is to make some part-time faculty appointments available to people who work on technology development in industry or in the federal government. By providing the appropriate incentives both to industry and to the colleges and universities, such faculty appointments could be encouraged by the federal government. Unfortunately the universities tend to be somewhat snobbish about technology development, awarding higher prestige to theoreticians and experimentalists in basic research.

The changes suggested here in the educational institutions are not original nor are they difficult to carry out. This is consistent with the assertion made in Section 1 that the educational institutions required to expand and promote more technology development in the country are already in existence.

7. Concluding Comments

Herman Kahn has said that when our descendants, a few centuries from now, look back on our time, they will recognize this decade as the inflection point in the curve that traces the expansion and growth of the human race. The population of the world may double or even triple, but at some point in the next century population growth must virtually cease. In this chapter, we have sought to define a role for the United States in a world which, during the next two decades, will still be growing rapidly, but where some limits are beginning to be perceived. To accommodate this growth, a vigorous technological program is vitally necessary—precisely because the most rapidly growing portions of the human race have expectations that must be met if peace is to be preserved. These expectations all depend strongly on the existence of physical goods and services that require new technologies to bring them into being. It is a natural, honorable, and above all, a credible role for the United States to act as the primary agent to create the required technologies. Some specific proposals to accomplish this end have been made in this chapter.

One final comment is necessary regarding the nature of growth and expansion. It is obviously true that our planet is finite and that there must therefore be a limit to the expansion of human life on Earth. However, it is important to remember that the human imagination has no such limits. When our descendants, five hundred years from now, look back on this time, they will indeed conclude that this is the era in which the limits of the Earth's capability to support the race were perceived. However, I strongly suspect that they will also have overcome these limits and that they will look upon our time from as yet unimagined perspectives.

We are already beginning to perceive the outlines of the technology that will make it possible for the human race to occupy and live on other planets of the solar system. There is no reason why both Mars and Venus could not be made habitable and colonized during the next two centuries. After that, it is likely that other bodies in the solar system could be made habitable, and beyond that are horizons still too dim to be clearly delineated. It is important to keep these possibilities in mind as we go about our day-to-day business. For better or for worse, it is not in our nature to be satisfied with a static and confining world. It is our destiny to seek, to explore, and to prevail.

Notes

1. George Washington's Farewell Address, September 19, 1976.

2. John Edwards et al., "Evaluation of Tussock Moth Damage Using U-2 and Low-Altitude Air Photos," Symposium on Application of Satellite and Aircraft Remote Sensing of Natural Resources in the Pacific Northwest, sponsored by the Department of Natural Resources, State of Washington, Tumwater, Washington, May 2, 1974.

3. Harold Hornby, NASA-Ames Research Center, Private Communication.

4. Alexis de Tocqueville, *Democracy in America* (New York: A. Knopf, 1945), originally published in 1840.

5. Samuel Eliot Morison, *Old Bruin, Commodore Matthew C. Perry* (Boston: Little, Brown Inc., 1967).

6. Alexander Laing, *Seafaring America* (New York: American Heritage, McGraw-Hill Book Co., 1974).

7. U.S. Army Signal Corps, Specification No. 486, December 23, 1907.

8. John Harvey Powell, *Yellow Fever* (University of Pennsylvania Press, 1949).

9. Max Theiler, "Yellow Fever," in Thomas M. Rivers and Frank L. Horsfall (eds.), *Viral and Rickettsial Infections of Man* (Philadelphia: Lippincott, 1959).

10. Mark F. Boyd (ed.), "Malanology" (1949) and Sir Gordon Covell et al., "Chemotherapy of Malaria" (1955), World Health Organization.

11. James Cook, *Voyages of Discovery*, edited by John Barrow (New York: E.P. Dutton and Co., 1961).

12. American Water Works Association, *Water Quality and Treatment*, Second Edition (New York: The Association, 1950).

13. Glenn J. Seaborg and William R. Corliss, *Man and Atom*, (New York: E.P. Dutton and Co., 1971).

14. President Nixon's Speech on National Energy Problems, November 7, 1973.

15. G.L. Muller and D.E. Dawes, *Introduction to Medical Science* (Philadelphia: W.B. Saunders Co., 1944).

16. "Research and Development Contributions to Aviation Progress," (RADCAP), Volumes I and II, Joint DOD-NASA-DOT Study, August 1972.

17. C. Raymond Beazley, *Prince Henry the Navigator* (New York and London: G.P. Putnam and Sons, 1911).

18. P.S. Laurie, "The Board of Visitors of the Royal Observatory," Quarterly Bulletin, Royal Astronomical Society, April 1971.

19. Taylor Peck, "From Round-Shot to Rockets," United States Naval Institute, Annapolis, Maryland (1949).

20. George S. Bryan, *Edison, The Man and His Work* (New York: A.A. Knopf, 1926).

21. Mineral Facts and Problems, U.S. Department of Interior, Bulletin 650, 1970 and "Oil Shale—A Huge Resource of Low-Grade Fuel," *Science* 184 (June 21, 1974): 143.

22. Sam H. Schurr, "Energy Research Needs," (PB-207516), Resources for the Future, Inc., Washington, D.C., October 1971.

23. D.R. Stephens, "In-Situ Coal Gasification," Lawrence Livermore Laboratory Report, UCRL-75494 (1974); R.N. Pitin, "Certain Problems Involved in the Reduction of Losses of Blast and Gas in Underground Gasification of Brown Coal from Moscow Area" in "Underground Processing of Fuels," translation TT-63-11063 (1963), pp. 109-118.

24. G.H. Higgins, "A New Concept for In-Situ Coal Gasification," Lawrence Livermore Laboratory, Report UCRL-31217 (1972).

25. K.J. Schneider and A.M. Platt (eds.), "Advanced Waste Management Studies, High-Level Radioactive Waste Disposal Alternatives," U.S. AEC Report BNWL-1900, Battelle, Pacific Northwest Laboratory, Richland, Washington, May 1974.

26. Nicholas Wade, "Sahelian Drought: No Victory for Western Aid," *Science* 185 (July 19, 1974): 234.

27. Ibid.

28. R. Jastrow and M. Halem, "Simulation Studies and the First GARP Global Experiment," *American Meteorological Society Bulletin* 54 (January 1973).

29. Luther J. Carter, "Pollution and Public Health: Taconite Case Poses Major Test," *Science* 186 (October 4, 1974): 31.

30. Frank E. Rom, "Airbreathing Nuclear Propulsion—A New Look," NASA-Lewis Research Center, TMX-2425, December 1971; and Frank E. Rom and Charles L. Masser, "Nuclear Powered Air-Cushion Vehicles for Trans-Oceanic Commerce," NASA-Lewis Research Center, TMX-2293, May 1971.

31. Leonard Jaffe, *Communications in Space* (New York: Holt, Rinehart and Winston, Inc., 1966).

32. See, for example, *Aviation Week and Space Technology* 100, 5 (February 4, 1974): 15.

33. Stephen T. De La Mater, "The Role of the Carrier in the Control of the Sea," *U.S. Naval Institute Proceedings* 98 (May 1972): 110.

34. Thomas Hobbes, *Leviathan*, Part I, Chapter 13.

35. Robert L. Rosholt, "An Administrative History of NASA, 1958-1963," NASA-SP 4101 (1966).

36. Harry M. Goode and Robert E. Machol, *Systems Engineering* (New York: McGraw-Hill Book Co., 1957), p. 514.

37. Foothill Junior College District Cooperative Program, NASA-AMES Research Center (1974).

III Military Aspects of Change, National Security, and Peace

John S. Foster, Jr.

1. Introduction

The debate over defense spending continues. Who has more military power, the United States or the Soviet Union? How important is military power, particularly strategic nuclear power, in international affairs? How much is enough? Does the United States have too much or too little? How much nuclear power does it take to deter nuclear war? Why cannot the United States and the Soviet Union agree to a reduced level of armaments? These provocative and important questions deserve an answer, but viable answers are hard to find, with or without the impassioned rhetoric of today.

In contemporary America, there are those who question the utility of military power in international affairs and firmly believe the United States is

It has been a great privilege to participate in the work of the Commission on Critical Choices for Americans. I especially thank those members of Panel V, Change, National Security and Peace, whose many constructive and illuminating comments and suggestions I have endeavored to incorporate into this report.

My thanks to Paul Nitze, former deputy secretary of defense and a member of the Strategic Arms Limitations negotiating team; Everett Pyatt of the Office of the Secretary of Defense; Dr. Edward Teller of the Stanford University Hoover Institution on War, Revolution and Peace; Dr. Herbert York of the University of California at San Diego; Dr. Hans Mark, director of the NASA Ames Research Center; and Dr. George Bing of the Lawrence Livermore Laboratory whose contributions proved invaluable in the writing of this report.

My special thanks to Robert D. Colvin whose insights, suggestions, and dedication have made this report possible.

spending too much on military programs. There are others who believe that military power is useful for protecting the United States, but that, with all our problems, a $20 to $30 billion cut in defense spending is in order. Others feel that present levels of defense spending are about right and all we can afford. And there are those who feel that the United States is in peril of rapidly becoming a second-class power, if, in fact, we are not one already; they say we must make much larger defense efforts.

To complicate the debate, some people charge that U.S. military power is being greatly undersold to justify even larger defense budgets. Others argue that the true state of U.S. defenses is not being admitted because to do so would weaken the U.S. position in negotiations with the Soviet Union and in other important concerns around the world. With such a diversity of strongly held opinions and motives, it is small wonder that most Americans are left wondering just what the situation really is.

The underlying assumptions in this report are threefold. First, the purpose of international political, economic, and military power is to deter war, not wage it. Second, that nuclear weapons are a reality that will not go away and we must continue to live with that reality. Third, that the leadership of the major military powers will behave rationally and act in their own national interests.

The Soviet Union is currently the only other major power with worldwide military capabilities and, therefore, this report focuses primarily on the trends in the military balance between the United States and the USSR. Because the focus is on the military balance, there are several things the report does not do. There is no attempt to analyze the major political, economic or social trends abroad in the world today. Nor is the current balance in military capabilities assessed in detail. There is no grand design for a new military force structure for the United States nor complete recommendations for new weapons systems. These are matters of detail that are under continuous and intensive study within the U.S. government and elsewhere. Important as these matters may be, they are difficult and highly controversial issues. Instead, this report attempts another approach to assessing the military balance that is hopefully less controversial and more useful. Unfortunately, the military balance is not a static thing. It is constantly evolving and is the cumulative effect of thousands of decisions and programs. The totality of these actions results in visible trends that show where we have been and where we may be going. Illumination of the trends over decades can be informative and help us to decide if where we are going is, in fact, the direction we want to take.

This report has been prepared to help American citizens understand the trends and clarify the issues so that they can make the critical choices regarding U.S. military preparedness that are rightfully theirs to make. The report attempts to bridge the gap of currently polarized opinion and bring the trends in military balance into sharper focus. To do this, the report summarizes several of the major features of today's international environment; then it examines the trends in military balance and the problems the present trends might cause for the United States. It offers some alternative national choices on the military posture for national security and suggests some basic objectives for national military policy.

Today's International Environment

Military power is not an end in itself; it both influences and is influenced by the world around it. Before addressing the trends in the military balance, it is useful to consider some of the more salient features in today's international environment.

Rapid and accelerating change in the political, economic, social, and military forces of the world is one of the most striking features of this era. The forces of change are powerful, complex, contradictory, and threatening. They affect the domestic and international affairs of nations. No one seems to be immune from the effects; everyone has a stake in the outcome. In the past, Americans have by and large adapted very well to changes, not only as individuals, but as a nation. We tamed a continent, transformed an agricultural society into an advanced industrial society, led the world's technological revolution, and along the way became the world's most powerful nation. This willingness to accept change and the ability to manage change are hallmarks in the American tradition that began with our own Revolution. Yet, these American attributes are being sorely tested in today's world.

A second major feature in today's international environment is the growth of economic interdependence. It would seem that, as economic interdependence grows and intensifies, it would portend greater international cooperation. However, other political and economic forces such as nationalism, local political interests, and economic shortages of certain energy and raw material resources could limit the degree of cooperation. In fact, these forces could tempt nations to export their economic problems to others or to engage in destructive competition for available energy, raw materials and markets. Probably the greatest threat to world peace and the national security of the United States today is a potential economic collapse of the advanced industrial nations and the worldwide political upheavals and realignments that could ensue from such a collapse.

The third major feature to consider is the evolving relationship between the Soviet Union and the United States. Although the two superpowers are still deeply divided by their differing values, social systems, and philosophies, they have intensified a process of negotiation and accommodation that is popularly referred to as détente. However, despite some apparent lessening of tensions under détente, the two nuclear superpowers are still locked in a relationship in which each regards the other as a dangerous adversary. This situation is not surprising given their widely differing perceptions and objectives for détente.

For the Soviet Union, the main foreign policy preoccupation is and probably will remain China. For many reasons, including disputes over territory, ideology, and leadership in the Communist movement, the mending of the Sino-Soviet split seems unlikely in the near future. Concern over China, the possibility of China and the United States acting in collusion against the USSR, and Soviet needs for Western technology appear to be principal driving forces behind the Soviet policy of détente. Although the Soviets are likely to continue with this policy, they will also continue to define and implement détente within the constraints of a relationship that they perceive as basically adversary.

For the United States, détente is a process of developing strategies for coping with the rise of Soviet power. In principle, the rise of Soviet power is neither inevitable nor inexorable, although the drive for power has been a dominant preoccupation of the leaders of the Soviet Union for over fifty years. They make no apologies for their efforts, seem to suffer no guilt feelings, and publicly take great pride in every added increment of power. This internal drive of the Soviets is likely to continue and there is little that the United States can do about it. What the United States can do is constrain the uses to which the Soviets put their power and limit the influence which their power provides. There are serious weaknesses and vulnerabilities in the Soviet system that limit their capabilities to use their power and influence. For the United States, hopefully, détente will continue to be a means of exploiting these Soviet vulnerabilities and weaknesses and to limit the capabilities of the Soviet Union to use its power and influence in situations and ways that could be detrimental to U.S. interests.

The development of a new set of relationships between the United States and the Soviet Union is greatly complicated by the emergence of new centers of economic and political power. The superpowers cannot devise their policies with only each other in mind. They must consider the impact on others and the ability of other power centers to influence and initiate actions which may or may not be in the individual or mutual interest of the United States or the USSR.

This latter point is nowhere better demonstrated than by the situation in the Middle East. Despite what the major powers may have wanted, the war of October 1973 occurred. This event, resulting in part from the unresolved conflict between the Arabs and the Israelis, forced the superpowers to face a major confrontation over conflicting interests. The use of oil as a weapon became a reality; the subsequent increase in oil prices strained the Western alliances and the economies of both the underdeveloped and the advanced industrial nations: worldwide inflation skyrocketed, and the massive transfer of funds to the oil-producing countries upset the Western monetary system. Whatever goals the superpowers may have set for themselves in regard to the Middle East prior to October 1973, it is obvious that each had to reassess its goals in light of events and other interests.

In attempting to accommodate each other's interest on a broad range of subjects, the United States and the USSR have found that competing interests in an area neither controls, and economic difficulties caused by third parties, which affect each country differently, are a source of friction and suspicion. In the long run, the ability of the United States to influence the events triggered by the Middle East War in a manner that is favorable to its interests will depend on its economic and military potential, its relationship with the USSR, and on the strength of its ties with other countries with similar interests.

The interdependence of economic, national security, and foreign policies is one of the most important features of our time. National security, in its broadest sense, is based on economic, political, and military strength. The United States must insure that each of these elements of national security has the requisite strength to prevent any nation, or group of nations, from achieving a degree of power that would allow them to unduly influence our affairs.

Foresight in setting goals and policies toward these ends is an obvious necessity. Yet, as Americans, we have often tended to drift too deeply into crises before we react, while, at the same time, we take great pride in our ability to react strongly and decisively to events, even at great cost. Amid today's rapidly changing world environment, political instabilities, economic interdependence, awesome weapons, and advancing military technology this apparent need to await a crisis before acting might in itself create the conditions for disaster. Instead, we must set the goals and initiate long-term policies now.

2. The Trends in Military Balance

For the next ten years, only the Soviet Union has the potential for aspiring to a position of power from which the affairs of the United States and other regions of the world can be dominated. Therefore, the USSR remains the principal threat to the national security of the United States. For this reason, and the fact that the Soviet Union is now the only other major military power, this report focuses primarily on the trends and balance in military power between the United States and the USSR.

Military power may be measured in several ways. A nation's total military potential is a combination of standing forces, reserves, other available man-power, industrial capacity, resources, economic power, political cohesiveness, and the willingness if need be to use the attributes of power. Although these characteristics explain the superpower status of the United States, the Soviet Union, and the emerging power of the Peoples Republic of China, they do not measure actual military capability. For the purposes of assessing military capabilities, it is more appropriate to use measures such as the quantity and quality of strategic nuclear forces, naval forces, land and air forces, technology, and budgetary support. It is these components that add up to total military capabilities and even more importantly to the ability to deter war. This section will discuss the past and future trends in each of these components and their impact on the military balance by 1985.

Strategic Nuclear Balance

In the past ten years, the relative balance in nuclear delivery capabilities between the United States and the Soviet Union has undergone fundamental and major changes. Starting from a position of gross inferiority, the Soviet Union has moved to a position of at least rough parity in strategic nuclear capability. In numbers of strategic nuclear delivery vehicles (missiles and aircraft), in lifting power (which determines the weight of deliverable warheads), and in total megatonnage or raw power in nuclear explosives, the Soviet Union has surpassed the United States. The United States still retains the advantage in numbers of deliverable nuclear warheads, in flexibility of targeting and, from a technological point of view, in missile accuracy.

The nuclear balance between the Soviet Union and the United States has two important dimensions. One is quantity and the other is quality. Trends in the relative strengths of the two countries on the quantitative side of the nuclear balance are shown in Figures III-1 through III-6. As the figures show, the momentum in the build-up of strategic nuclear forces presently lies with the Soviet Union. The figures also show the raw nuclear power available to the United States and the USSR, giving added urgency to the serious questions of how to effect a reduction in nuclear armaments. The SALT Agreements are an essential first step in controlling the quantitative aspects of the nuclear balance—especially SALT II, which would put a numerical ceiling on total numbers of nuclear delivery vehicles for both the United States and the Soviet Union. United States and Soviet discussions on strategic arms also serve a useful educational purpose by involving the political leaders of both countries intimately in the rationale for the development of nuclear weapons, their deployment and force levels.

The trends in the qualitative aspects of the nuclear balance have been less affected by the SALT Agreements mainly because a full resolution of the complex issues raised by qualitative changes requires a better understanding by both sides of the other's essential national needs and a degree of confidence in the opposing nation that neither the United States nor the Soviet Union has been prepared to give. This lack of agreement is understandable for several reasons. Qualitative changes go hand-in-hand with advancing technological developments which are difficult to monitor, control or guard against cheating. Also, quality goes to the heart of deterrence. It can determine the vulnerability of strategic forces to attack and the retaliatory capability of each country. An important question is whether qualitative weaknesses are developing which might induce instability, weaken deterrence and limit the possibilities for future negotiations on nuclear arms reductions.

It generally takes eight to twelve years under normal conditions to develop, produce, and deploy major new weapons systems in sufficient numbers to significantly affect the nuclear balance and alter the trends. The decisions made in the recent past or that will be made in the near future will dictate the relative nuclear balance in 1985. The current nuclear weapons programs and the presently existing nuclear forces of the major nuclear powers are therefore of critical importance to the strategic nuclear balance in 1985, to the ongoing negotiations over Strategic Arms Limitations and to U.S. national security planning into the next decade.

The Soviet Strategic Nuclear Program.[1] In assessing the Soviet program, it is well to keep in mind that because of the secretive nature of their society and governmental system, the Soviet government is less than candid in spelling out its objectives and activities. The Soviets are the first to point out that they consider secrecy an essential element of their security. Thus, analysis of their motives, intentions, and activities is at best an uncertain business. Assessment of their weapons capability, though difficult, is easier.

Historically, the Soviet leaders have placed highest priority on their national security and have made extraordinary efforts to increase their military power, especially since World War II and the Cuban missile crisis. Whatever its reasons, the Soviet Union has developed a powerful strategic nuclear offensive force consisting of Intercontinental Ballistic Missiles (ICBM), Submarine Launched Ballistic Missiles (SLBM), and bombers, as well as defensive forces that include the world's most extensive air defense, Anti-Ballistic Missiles (ABM), civil defense, and command and control programs. In spite of the incomplete nature of the available information, it is quite clear that the Soviets are still not content with their present capabilities and are engaged in massive development programs to improve further the quality of their strategic nuclear weapons systems.

1. The Soviets have been developing and testing *four* new Intercontinental Ballistic Missiles (ICBM) that exhibit improvements in launching, guidance and reentry techniques. The new missiles are more powerful, flexible, and less vulnerable to attack than the present ones they may replace. After a series of tests, the Soviet Union has placed three of these missiles into production and deployment commenced in mid-1975. They will probably produce the fourth missile which could be mobile and capable of being deployed outside of the present missile fields. The United States has stated that it would consider the deployment of operational landmobile ICBM launchers during the period of the Interim Agreement as inconsistent with the objectives of that agreement; however, the Soviet Union did not concur in that statement.

2. This modernization of the Soviet missile forces will increase the payload of their missiles and permit them to introduce Multiple Independently Targeted Reentry Vehicles (MIRVs) into their strategic systems. When deployed, MIRVs will greatly increase the number of nuclear warheads, significantly increase Soviet ability to attack U.S. ICBM forces, increase the number of targets of all kinds that can be hit, and increase the assurance that the targets will be destroyed (see Figure III-3).

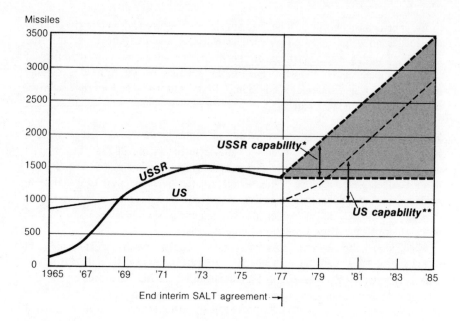

Missiles

End interim SALT agreement →|

*1977—Soviet Union could increase deployment of ICMBs at a rate of 250 per year based on 1967-71 deployment rate. Four missiles have been developed (SS-16/SS-17/SS-18/SS-19) and three have been placed in production in 1975.
**1977—United States could increase deployment of ICBMs at a rate of 250 per year with present facilities for building Minuteman III missiles. Newer ICBMs could follow after several years.

Source: For the period 1965-1975, *United States Military Posture for FY 1976*. For the period 1975-1985, author's estimates on limits.

Figure III-1. United States and USSR Intercontinental Ballistic Missiles.

3. Construction and modification of missile silos is continuing with emphasis on further hardening of these silos to make them even harder to destroy if subjected to a missile attack.

4. The Submarine Launched Ballistic Missile (SLBM) force is rapidly being modernized. Although only introduced in 1968, production of the Yankee Class submarine (which is equivalent to the U.S. Polaris Submarine and its 1500-mile missile) has given way to the Delta Class which is equipped with 4800-mile missiles. These missiles have a range equivalent of the U.S. Trident missile which will be operational in the early 1980s. The first Delta Class submarines went to sea in early 1973. By mid-1975 there were at least twenty-five others launched or under construction. The range of the missile in these submarines is sufficient to reach most of the United States even if the submarines are in Soviet ports or territorial waters.

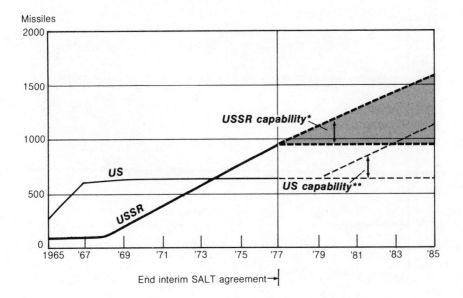

*1977—Soviets can produce at least six DELTA class ballistic missile submarines per year, each with a minimum of twelve missiles. DELTAs are presently under construction; the first unit went to sea in 1973. The take-off point assumes the Soviets build to the 950 SLBM allowed in the interim agreement by retiring older SS7/8 ICMB. Otherwise, take-off point would be from 740 SLBM as allowed in the interim agreement.

**1977—United States could increase its SLBM force starting in 1979 when the first TRIDENT submarine becomes operational. Under present conditions it could then build TRIDENT submarines at a rate of three per year, each equipped with twenty-four missiles.

Source: For the period 1965-1975, *United States Military Posture for FY 1976.* For the period 1975-1985, author's estimates on limits.

Figure III-2. United States and USSR Submarine Launched Ballistic Missiles.

5. The Soviets have developed and are producing a supersonic, variable-geometry wing bomber called the Backfire. This aircraft is one of the most modern in the world. It is over twice as large as the U.S. FB-111, but slightly smaller than the U.S. B-1. It has considerably less nuclear delivery capability than that projected for the B-1 but it is capable of flying some 6200 miles without refueling (see Figure III-4).

6. Although limited by treaty to one Anti-Ballistic Missile (ABM) site, the Soviet Union is conducting an active research program in ballistic missile defenses. It has new rapidly deployable ABM systems under development.

7. The USSR maintains the largest air defense system in the world (see Figure

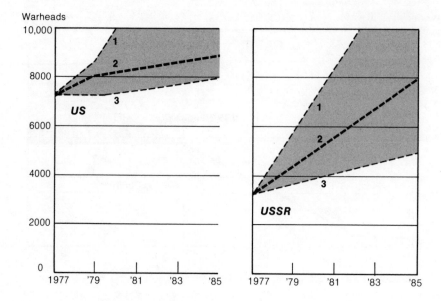

1. MAXIMUM LINE represents the present force level plus adding the maximum number of missiles with MIRVs.
2. MIDDLE LINE represents for the United States the replacement of Minuteman II with Minuteman III and for the USSR replacing present missile force with new missiles with MIRVs.
3. MINIMUM LINE represents the present missile force with the United States adding TRIDENT submarines and the USSR continuing to add MIRVs to the SS-11 force.

Source: Estimates of projections developed by author.

Figure III-3. United States and USSR Missile Warheads.

III-7) and is continuing to improve its air defense by adding new surface-to-air missile systems and supersonic interceptor aircraft. As technology advances, the capabilities of some air defense systems and ABM systems could coalesce, thus leading to an air defense system that would have substantial ABM capabilities.

8. Potentially more important than any of the above military systems is the Soviet civil defense program. The central feature of this program is its comprehensive dispersal-evacuation plan which would evacuate or disperse Soviet population from urban centers in about 72 hours and could limit Soviet casualties to fewer than ten million people, about 5 percent of the population, in the event of nuclear war. The emphasis placed on civil defense by the Soviet

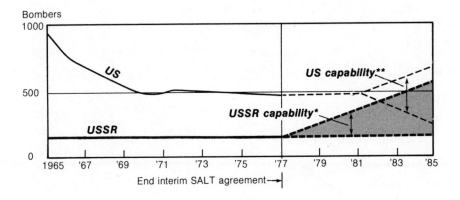

*1977—Soviet Union could increase production of its BACKFIRE aircraft which entered service in 1974 and is currently in production. A rate of fifty aircraft per year (equivalent to U.S. production rate) is assumed.
**1977—U.S. development ⌐ the B-1 would allow for production to fifty aircraft per year starting in the late 1970s with replacement of the B-52 starting in 1979.

Source: For the period 1965-1975, *United States Military Posture for FY 1976.* For the period 1975-1985, author's estimates on limits.

Figure III-4. United States and USSR Intercontinental Bombers.

government is illustrated by the publishing of more than sixty million copies of a civil defense booklet, mandatory civil defense training at all levels of schooling, adult education classes, realistic emergency exercises, and a major network of shelters for employees of critical industries.[2]

The United States Program. The U.S. strategic weapons program, which reached its numerical peak in nuclear delivery vehicles about 1965, has concentrated on qualitative improvements in recent years. This basic change from quantity to quality has permitted the reduction of real annual expenditures on strategic nuclear programs by almost two-thirds in the last ten years. Strategic nuclear forces now account for less than 10 percent of the total defense budget.

The objective of the present U.S. program is to provide a hedge against (1) uncertainty with regard to the Soviet Union's intentions caused by its vigorous strategic nuclear program; (2) uncertainty about the outcome of the ongoing Strategic Arms Limitation negotiations; and (3) technological surprises that could reduce the effectiveness of U.S. nuclear forces as a deterrent to a major war.

The major features of the U.S. program are as follows:

1. About three-fourths of the United States land and submarine-based missiles will be equipped with MIRVs, completing a program begun in the late 1960s. The U.S. MIRV program was designed primarily to penetrate the anti-ballistic

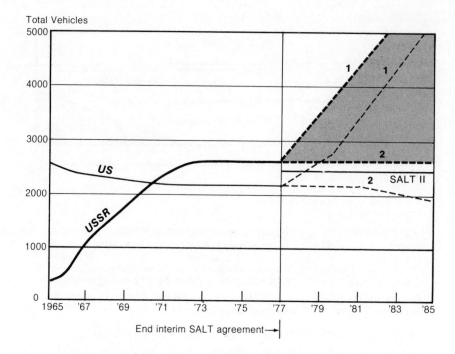

1. Lines represent maximum production additions to the force levels.
2. Lines represent continuation of present levels with United States retiring
   B-52's starting in 1980.

Source: For the period 1965-1975, *United States Military Posture for FY 1976.*
For the period 1975-1985, author's estimates on limits.

Figure III-5. United States and USSR Strategic Offensive Delivery
Vehicles (ICBM, SLBM, Intercontinental Bombers).

missile defense system being deployed in the Soviet Union. The concept was to
deploy multiple reentry vehicles so that the United States would be able to
saturate the Soviet defenses, thereby assuring that most of our retaliatory forces
would penetrate the Soviet defenses. Following the ABM treaty, this program
was continued as a hedge against Soviet ABM development activity and also
because MIRV permits more efficient targeting. The larger numbers of smaller
warheads, while delivering less total yield or explosive power, would provide
superior target coverage and flexibility and reduce collateral damage. At the
present time, the MIRV capability continues to offer our best hedge against
production of the rapidly deployable Soviet ABM systems now in development.

2. The land-based Minuteman III, with up to three MIRV warheads, replaced
the older, single warhead Minuteman I in July 1975. The Minuteman III
production line will be kept open to provide operational flight test missiles and

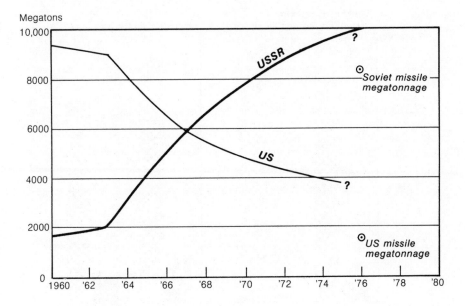

Source: Estimates developed by the author.

Figure III-6. Strategic Offensive Megatonnage, U.S. v. USSR (Bombers and Missiles).

to replace the single warhead Minuteman II force should future events prove this necessary.

3. Programs to improve the accuracy, nuclear explosive power and the number of warheads that can be carried by Minuteman III are continuing.

4. A modest program of developing advanced technologies for a new ICBM with alternate basing modes, for example, aircraft launched or land-mobile, will continue.

5. Poseidon missiles with up to ten MIRV warheads will replace the older Polaris missiles in thirty-one submarines by 1977. Plans for the Trident submarine and missile program call for producing ten submarines by the early 1980s as replacements for the ten oldest Polaris submarines, which will not be equipped with the Poseidon missiles. The Trident missile will have a range in excess of 4500 miles, about double that of Poseidon.

6. Development of the B-1 bomber will continue with an option for future production. If a decision to produce B-1's were made in 1976, B-52 retirements could begin by the early 1980s. To maintain the present bomber force level into the 1980s, there is a program to modify the older B-52 bombers to prolong their usefulness.

7. As a hedge against improved Soviet air defenses, research and development

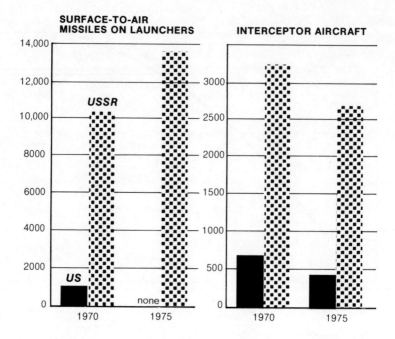

Source: *United States Military Posture for FY 1976.*

Figure III-7. United States and USSR Strategic Defensive Forces.

is proceeding on long-range cruise type missiles that could be launched from aircraft and submarines. These missiles would penetrate enemy territory at high speeds and very low altitudes.

8. The program for strategic defense forces included the completion of the one Safeguard site allowed by treaty. This site, with 100 interceptor missiles, was designed to provide some protection for the 150 missiles of the Minuteman missile wing at Grand Forks, North Dakota. However, the Safeguard site is now being deactivated and effort related to future capability to defend against ballistic missiles is focused primarily on advanced design and the construction of test units, not on the production of a new system.

9. The United States Civil Defense program has emphasized shelters in major cities and not dispersal or evacuation plans. There is a very modest program of preliminary contingency planning being undertaken to designate high risk areas, develop plans for relocation of the population in a crisis, and to expand the present shelter survey to assess the ability of existing shelters to protect against all the effects of a nuclear attack such as radiation, blast and fire.

The People's Republic of China (PRC) Nuclear Program. Information on the Chinese strategic nuclear program, its objectives, and intentions, is much more sketchy and difficult to obtain than information about the Soviet Union. There is considerable evidence, however, that the PRC is creating a major nuclear force. Although information is limited, we have considerable assurance about certain features of the PRC program.

1. The PRC is installing capability to conduct tests and produce weapons comparable to those of the United States or the Soviet Union. The PRC record of nuclear testing indicates more progress in weapons design per test than that of any other nation.

2. At the present time, the PRC has more nuclear delivery vehicles than either France or Great Britain.

3. The pace of the PRC nuclear program suggests limitations in their technology and in the availability of technically qualified personnel. Economic constraints do not appear to be a factor since the program has only required about 2 percent of the PRC's Gross National Product as estimated for 1964; their GNP has grown 60 percent in the past decade.

4. The PRC has four different land-based missile programs underway. Of these, both a medium-range ballistic missile and an intermediate-range ballistic missile have been developed, produced and deployed. Also, a limited-range inter-continental ballistic missile (ICBM) has been tested and may be produced in the near future. A full range ICBM is being developed but has not been test-flown.

5. None of the existing missile or aircraft delivery systems are capable of reaching the United States although, they can reach most of Asia and the Soviet Union east of the Ural Mountains.

Critical Problems in the Strategic Nuclear Balance

By 1985, whether or not there is an extended SALT I or a new SALT II Agreement, within presently understood guidelines, the Soviet Union, if both sides carry out present programs, will exceed the United States in every significant measure of nuclear deterrent and war-fighting capability: in total raw destructive power, in survivability of strategic forces against enemy attack, in penetration of enemy defenses and resulting damage.

In the event that a SALT II Treaty is executed, some aspects of the quantitative side of the nuclear balance should be stabilized, but as noted earlier, the qualitative balance will still require close attention. Given these trends, the principal question facing the United States is whether it will have sufficient capability to deter the Soviet Union in 1985 and beyond.

Deterrence, as viewed by the United States, is the combination of retaliatory forces and a state of mind which assures an aggressor that, no matter what the temptation, the prize is not worth the price. It involves his calculation of risks and benefits. Admittedly, determining what constitutes deterrence is like determining what constitutes beauty: It is all in the eye of the beholder. For reasons just this basic, the calculus of what constitutes nuclear deterrence is more than just a question of how much is enough. Also, it requires rationality of national leaders, perceptions of power and opportunity, survivability of strategic nuclear forces to retaliate if attacked, and ability of the surviving nuclear forces to penetrate enemy defenses and inflict unacceptable levels of damage to the aggressor.

The first of these can be enhanced considerably by discussions and negotiations between national leadership. The latter three aspects are more a function of quality than quantity. The present U.S. and Soviet strategic weapons development and deployment programs have major implications on the qualitative aspects of the future nuclear balance and, hence, are directly related to the future quality of the U.S. nuclear deterrent capability. The following paragraphs discuss some of the difficulties facing the United States in an effort to maintain strategic deterrence.

The present U.S. nuclear deterrent capability is the result of the technology and decisions of a decade ago. At that time, the United States had a clear lead in missile and nuclear technology as a result of the broad and intensive research and development program of the late 1950s and early 1960s. But the trends clearly indicate that the momentum in strategic nuclear weapons programs is now held by the Soviet Union. As noted earlier it takes about ten years to develop and deploy new systems in sufficient quantity to be effective in redressing the strategic balance. Unless the United States takes further steps to assure continued qualitative improvements, it will not be able to maintain a high quality deterrent force in the face of Soviet improvements. Also, the appearance of a future imbalance caused by the Soviet momentum and qualitative improvements, could, even before an imbalance was achieved, detract from the creditability of the U.S. deterrent forces.

The United States has sought to maintain qualitative characteristics in its nuclear forces of such a nature that, if the Soviet Union should contemplate an optimum attack to reduce the U.S. retaliatory strike to a minimum, the United States would still be able to inflict a level of damage on the USSR that they would judge to be unacceptable. The Soviet Union's strategic nuclear program is moving in a direction and developing capabilities that could pose a major threat to present U.S. strategic nuclear forces and the USSR is thereby threatening the future quality of the U.S. deterrent.

Because the U.S. land-based Minuteman ICBM force is located in fixed silos, each missile is targetable by Soviet ICBMs. In the past, the Soviet missiles have carried high-yield warheads, but we did not believe they had the required accuracy nor numbers of warheads to attack U.S. missile silos effectively. Through the new missiles equipped with MIRVs, now being deployed, the Soviet Union could have by 1985 an arsenal of more than 9,000 high yield warheads, equaling the United States in number of warheads, but greatly exceeding it in explosive power. With the combination of numbers, improved accuracy, and high yields that characterizes the Soviet program, a force of about 400-600 ICBMs (about one-fourth to one-half of their ICBMs) could pose a major threat to the survivability of the 1,000 U.S. Minutemen. If the Soviets chose to make such an attack, the United States could expect to have as little as a few tens of ICBMs remaining for a retaliatory attack. The United States has no comparable capability against the USSR with our present or planned missile forces and the current debate in the United States concerns the question of whether or not we should attain such a capability.

One solution would be for the United States to launch its missiles against Soviet military targets upon receiving unequivocal warning of an enemy attack. This strategy has been rejected by the United States for the last two decades as too "trigger-happy." Instead, the United States has developed, and to date has maintained, the capability to ride out even the worst attack and still be able to retaliate and cause unacceptable damage to the Soviet Union. If the United States is to keep this capability in the face of improving Soviet capabilities, it will have to reduce the vulnerability of some of its land-based missiles by providing them with adequate active defense or remove their targetability by some form of mobility.

A second concern is that our bombers are increasingly vulnerable to attack by Soviet SLBMs launched from 50 to 200 miles off our own coast. The short time from the first detection of a Soviet missile launch until the aircraft can be at a safe distance from nuclear explosions requires that the bombers be based inland and that crews be constantly near the alert aircraft. Assuming that we can assure adequate warning and safely launch the alert bomber force, there is growing concern over the improving Soviet air intercept and air defense capabilities. The combination of these two concerns casts doubt over the future retaliatory capability of present U.S. bomber forces. To some, these problems are best solved by eliminating the bomber. This solution has been rejected in the past because such an action would enormously simplify the enemy's calculations and reduce our flexibility to maintain deterrence as vulnerabilities arise in the other strategic forces. Thus, the United States must find the solutions through continuing programs to improve the capability of its bomber forces.

During more than a decade of worrying about measures to offset this or that potential vulnerability of our Minuteman or bomber forces we gained some reassurance by observing—"There's always Polaris." Currently, the least vulnerable of all U.S. strategic forces is the Polaris/Poseidon submarines.

Because the Polaris/Poseidon submarines can operate very reliably and submerged for long periods it has been extremely difficult for an enemy to be able to acquire and follow any significant fraction of these ships at sea. Some years ago, the Soviet Union apparently recognized the need to redress this situation and established an extremely aggressive antisubmarine program that in many respects has developed programs that are unique with the Soviet Union.

There are some worrisome aspects of these Soviet activities that could degrade the survivability of our Polaris force at sea. As these were recognized in the past, the U.S. Navy took steps to remove them or limit their consequences. The ability to recognize Soviet capabilities, and to deal with them effectively, deteriorates steadily as Soviet efforts in antisubmarine warfare increase compared to those of the United States. A consequence of Soviet antisubmarine efforts is that the United States cannot be sure that the present Polaris force will remain invulnerable in the next decade. To redress the trends and increase the assurance that Polaris will remain invulnerable will require that U.S. anti-submarine efforts be expanded and the quality of U.S. strategic submarines be continually improved.

Through detailed consideration of the characteristics and limitations of the forces on each side and implementation of measures to assure the continued effectiveness of our forces, it does seem possible to maintain U.S. strategic deterrence. Such measures do require that any agreements made in SALT II provide for the flexibility to implement the necessary changes. This requirement flies in the face of some efforts to constrain the growing Soviet strategic power. There is the serious political consideration that the presence of considerably larger Soviet forces would, in a confrontation, require that the United States back down, even though we would possess the capability to extract a penalty far in excess of any advantage to be gained by either side. To negotiate comprehensive limits to the growth of Soviet strategic forces might also require that we give up something. In the face of this dilemma, we might agree to give up some flexibility, or agree to levels for U.S. forces below the levels of the Soviets. In resolving this dilemma, the first priority is to assure that we possess the resolve and flexibility to maintain deterrence and second to give up what we can spare to limit the growing Soviet strategic power.

Presently, the United States and the Soviet Union have more than enough nuclear power to provide deterrence. Although the Soviets enjoy a numerical advantage in some delivery vehicles and throw weight, U.S. technology has provided offsetting advantages in numbers of warheads and accuracy. The problem is that the relative balance in nuclear power is changing, primarily because the Soviet Union is developing the technology that once gave the United States offsetting advantages. As technology continues to advance in both nations, the view of the United States has been that it is in the interests of the United States and the Soviet Union to deploy their nuclear forces so that they do not invite attack and to insure that new developments on each side do not exploit the vulnerabilities of existing forces. We continue to try to persuade the Soviet Union to exercise restraint in developing new capabilities that jeopardize U.S. deterrent forces.

However, since there is limited assurance that such efforts will be sufficient, we must make every effort to minimize the potential future vulnerabilities of our nuclear forces. In this regard, at present force levels, numbers are not as important as quality. As quality goes up, numbers can, and often do, go down.

Improvements in quality that make nuclear forces invulnerable in their bases or operating areas and in their ability to penetrate enemy territory are much more important from a technical military viewpoint as a deterrent than sheer numbers.

Soviet civil defense planning and capabilities are markedly superior to those of the United States. Soviet emphasis on civil defense and evacuation and shelter plans might reduce their casualties in a nuclear war to fewer than 10 million. The potential U.S. casualties might be 70-120 million under a comparable attack if the present fallout-oriented shelter plans are not supplemented with dispersal and evacuation plans.

This disparity in potential casualties could place tremendous coercive pressure on the United States in any major confrontation with the Soviet Union. This critical assymetry between the United States and the Soviet Union could only be overcome if the citizens of the United States could be persuaded that such preparations are essential to deterrence, as well as survival, of a nuclear war. There is an even greater disparity in potential casualties between the Soviet Union and Western Europe and Japan in the event of a nuclear exchange because of the high population density and lack of dispersal room in Western Europe and Japan. The allied will to resist in future confrontations with the Soviet Union might well be weakened or even broken by such considerations.

If the qualitative improvements in Soviet strategic nuclear capability and its growing total power is perceived by the United States and the rest of the world as leading to Soviet "superiority," the consequence might be an entirely new international situation. Such perceived superiority could provide the Soviet Union with new opportunities, increased freedom of action and added power in confrontation situations. It could result in definite erosion of U.S. power. It could cause our allies to fear the loss of the nuclear shield with subsequent pressure on economic and political alignments. It could also increase the possibility of nuclear proliferation as our allies resisted these pressures on their own. It could severely constrain U.S. freedom of action in pursuit of its own interests.

Hopefully, this would not mean that the United States must necessarily match the Soviet Union in raw nuclear power, which we could do simply by producing more weapons. It does mean that the United States must at least insure that it has no major Achilles heels that are exploitable by the Soviet Union and have the flexibility to redress such situations in a timely manner should they arise. The United States must maintain a high quality deterrent so that our allies and others will not doubt our ability to deter a nuclear war and, should the political pressures rise, our ability to acquire the forces necessary to remove them.

Naval Balance

The United States and its allies have a vital stake in the naval balance in war and peace. Free movement on the oceans is essential to the well-being, perhaps the survival, of our countries. The events of World War II and the battles of the Atlantic and Pacific remind us of the importance of controlling the seas—to lose the battle at sea was to lose the war.

In times of peace, the oceans are the world's economic lifelines. To be denied their use could spell disaster. The advanced industrial nations and the rest of the world are so inextricably bound economically that our way of life, our standards of living, the welfare of our nations are dependent upon our ability to use the oceans for trade and commerce. Americans, especially, should be mindful of the fact that the protection of the British Navy and recently that of our own has allowed the United States to grow and prosper for 200 years.

The magnitude of economic interdependence and oceanic dependence can be demonstrated by a few basic statistics. The United States, Western Europe, and Japan's share of world trade amounted to $520 billion in 1972 and accounted for 60 percent of the world's total. World trade has expanded from $266 billion in 1960 to more than $950 billion in 1972 and is growing at more than 10 percent per year.

This volume of trade is likely to increase even further by 1985. There are more than 5.5 million American jobs involved in producing and transporting goods for trade. The United States imports, in whole or in part, 68 out of 71 critical raw materials for an industrial economy. Forty percent of our requirements for crude oil and petroleum products are imported, more than 70 percent by sea.

Our allies, the Western Europeans and Japanese, are even more dependent on overseas resources. Western Europe imports 75 percent of its oil; Japan more than 95 percent. At least 99 percent of all U.S. imports and exports, by weight, go by sea. On any given day, there are more than 5,000 ships—not including the 500 ships of the Soviet Union or its allies—plying the ocean trade routes. Two thousand of these are in the Mediterranean and the North Atlantic alone.

In contrast to the interdependence of the United States with the rest of the world, the Soviet Union is almost self-sufficient in energy and raw materials resources. Trade plays a very small part in the daily economic lives of Soviet citizens. Even though the Soviet Union is not dependent on the use of the oceans for its survival, the oceans are a major source of food for the Soviets their maritime fleet is a means for earning hard currencies. The Soviet Union also uses the oceans to project its power around the world. They observe openly tha naval policy is foreign policy and that naval forces play important political roles

There are three distinct trends giving credence to Soviet intentions of usin their navy as a means of increasing their worldwide political power:

1. Major emphasis on quality improvements in their ships.
2. Development of new classes of major surface combatants that are capable ⟨ open ocean operations.
3. Increasing deployments of major combatant ships to distant seas, includi

surge deployments in times of crisis and major worldwide naval exercises such as OKEAN (Ocean) 1970 and 1975.

The Soviets have already shown a willingness to use their naval forces for political and other objectives. For example, in March 1969, the Soviets sent three missile equipped ships to persuade Ghana to release two Soviet fishing vessels and their Soviet crews which had been impounded several months earlier by the Ghanians. This show of force succeeded where strong diplomatic protests and economic sanctions had failed. During the October 1973 war in the Middle East, the Soviets assembled more than ninety ships in the Mediterranean compared to about fifty for the United States.

Soviet Naval Program. In addition to their efforts to overtake the United States in strategic nuclear power and to maintain their continuing predominance in ground forces, the Soviets have embarked on a program of expanding their naval power. That naval power now threatens the United States' supremacy at sea.

The Soviet Union has historically maintained a large navy in terms of numbers of ships, but, by and large, it was a coastal defense navy and it was considered ineffective by Western standards. All that has changed. Since 1962, the Soviet Union has made major qualitative improvements in its naval forces and has put to sea nine new classes of surface warships. They have built more than 900 ships in this period (see Figure III-8), of which 92 are "major surface" combatants and over one-half are missile equipped. The Soviet Union has been maintaining its surface fleet at about constant numbers by replacing older ships with new ones on a one-for-one basis.

Figure III-9 shows the comparative and projected numerical strengths of the Soviet and United States navies in major surface combatant ships.

The Soviets also have built several hundred missile patrol boats. The power of these small ships was amply demonstrated in 1967 by the sinking of an Israeli destroyer by the Egyptians and in 1972 by the sinking of a Pakistani destroyer by the Indians. In each case, the vessels were sunk by missiles fired from Soviet-supplied Komar missile patrol boats. During the October 1973 War, the Israelis completely destroyed the Syrian naval forces with Gabriel missiles fired from their SAAR class patrol boats.

In addition to the increase in global naval striking power of their surface navy, the Soviets maintain a modern submarine force that is larger than that of all the other industrial nations combined. Submarines, especially those with nuclear power, are the most deadly of all naval weapons and to date the least vulnerable to attack. While slowly decreasing in total numbers during recent years, the Soviet submarine force is greatly increasing its quality. There are more than seventy nuclear powered cruise missile and torpedo attack submarines in the Soviet submarine force. The cruise missiles are similar to those on their surface ships; in their newer submarines they can be fired while the submarine is

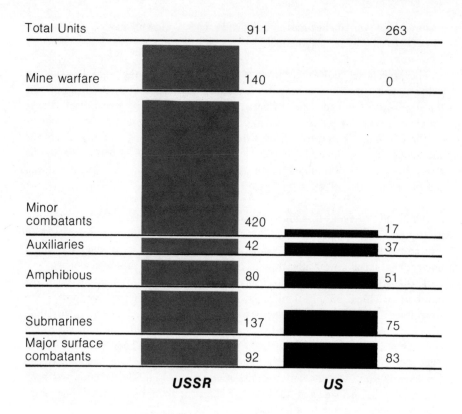

	USSR	US
Total Units	911	263
Mine warfare	140	0
Minor combatants	420	17
Auxiliaries	42	37
Amphibious	80	51
Submarines	137	75
Major surface combatants	92	83

Source: Department of Defense.

Figure III-8. USSR v. U.S. Naval Ship Construction, 1962-1972.

submerged. The decline in Soviet attack submarine numbers may be ending. The Soviet Union is constructing between four and six nuclear attack submarines each year and has started construction of a new class of conventionally powered submarine after a hiatus of five years. This could be sufficient new construction to reverse the recent downward trend in submarines (see Figure III-10).

The upward trend in Soviet navy overseas deployment is paced by the shipbuilding and modernization program outlined above. There has been almost a tenfold increase in the number of ship days the Soviets have spent away from home waters since 1965. A "ship day" is one day for a navy ship at sea away from the local exercise area. Thus, 18,000 ship days means an average of almost fifty ships at sea every day of the year. In total ship days for the Atlantic and Indian Oceans and the Mediterranean, the Soviet Union presently maintains better than a three to two advantage over the United States. In the Pacific Ocean the United States exceeds the Soviet Union in ship days by about five to one. These trends in overseas naval deployments are illustrated in Figure III-11.

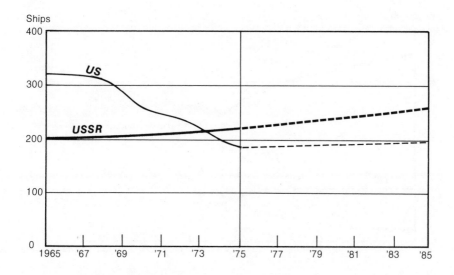

Source: For the period 1965-1975, *United States Military Posture for FY 1976.*
For the period 1975-1985, author's estimates.

Figure III-9. Major Combat Surface Ships.

To support these operations and increased deployments, the Soviet Union has continued to expand its overseas basing and use of facilities in Cuba and Somalia. In addition, it is using ports in Egypt, India, the Andaman Islands in the Indian Ocean, and Aden in the Arabian Sea for refueling the fleet on distant deployments. The Soviet attempts to influence the outcome of events in Portugal and Angola would appear to fit a long-term pattern attempting to gain influence and possible control in areas that allow them direct access and operating bases at strategic locations along or across the world's major trade routes.

Admiral Gorshkov, the commander in chief of the Soviet navy, spelled out very clearly the meaning of all this in 1968 when he said: ". . . The flag of the Soviet Navy flies over the oceans of the world. Sooner or later the United States will have to understand it no longer has mastery of the seas."[3] If these present trends continue, Admiral Gorshkov's boast will be reality long before 1985.

U.S. Naval Program. The United States has made major improvements in the quality of its naval forces, especially in the areas of nuclear submarines, antisubmarine warfare and carrier forces. The United States has introduced eight new classes of warships and built 260 naval ships of all types since 1962. Admittedly, these gains had to be made at the expense of a 50 percent reduction in the size of the fleet since 1969. With fewer than 500 ships, the U.S. Navy is smaller than at any time since before Pearl Harbor. This reduction reflects the

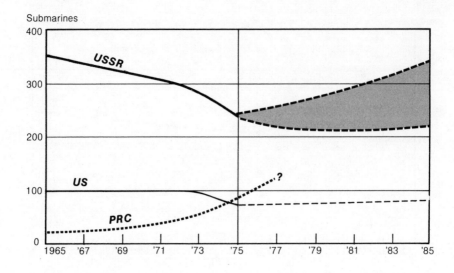

Source: For the period 1965-1975, *United States Military Posture for FY 1976*.
For the period 1975-1985, author's estimates.

Figure III-10. Attack Submarines.

retirement of overage ships faster than new ones are built, the higher costs of replacement ships, and the need to reduce operating expenses by cutting ships in order to provide funds for new ships. As a result, in numbers of major surface combatant ships, the United States and the Soviet Union are now about equal (see Figure III-9).

The United States has concentrated its efforts primarily on carrier, submarine and antisubmarine forces. The aircraft carrier, which is a uniquely complete weapons system, is the backbone of the fleet. It provides the advantage of being able to operate tactical aircraft from a base that is always sovereign U.S. territory. It has the mobility which allows it to be sent almost anywhere in the world in a week's time. It brings with it a diverse range of capabilities that are unduplicated in any other weapons system. A carrier and its aircraft can, for example, fight a sustained battle, evacuate refugees or just by its presence show the seriousness of U.S. interests or intent. And when a carrier is no longer required in one area, it can be withdrawn for use in other areas in response to other events. Along with the continued emphasis on aircraft carriers, the United States has introduced nuclear powered carriers and other major surface combatant ships. This has allowed the development of nuclear powered strike groups with even greater range, speed and fire power.

The United States has also pursued programs to improve its other naval forces.

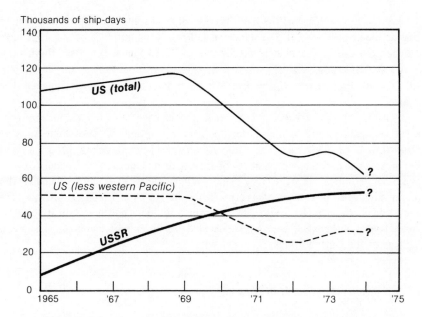

Source: Adapted from *Understanding Soviet Naval Developments*, Office of the Chief of Naval Operations, Department of the Navy, April 1975.

Figure III-11. Trends in U.S./USSR Naval Operations (Ship days out-of-area).

The United States program in submarine and antisubmarine warfare, although not as intensive as those of the Soviet Union, have continued to provide qualitative superiority for the United States in submarines and some aspects of antisubmarine technology. This in turn has helped to reduce the vulnerability of U.S. submarine forces to Soviet antisubmarine forces.

The United States has held an unquestioned edge in capital ships and can still put on an impressive display of naval power. In a prolonged engagement however, these forces could be subject to attrition by the more numerous, though smaller, Soviet ships. To alter this situation, the United States is attempting to reduce the size and cost of its surface combatants so that it can have more ships with more fire power and capabilities, while also retaining the advantages inherent in maintaining a force of capital ships. Improvements in armament and fire power for surface ships are now on the way. The United States is beginning to equip its ships with the Harpoon surface-to-surface anti-ship missile to offset an edge in fire power held by the Soviets for the last fifteen years. The United States has also begun the construction of smaller, moderately priced, destroyer-type ships equipped with these new weapons.

Reduction in the age of the fleet has also been accomplished, but the problem has not been fully solved. Dramatic reductions in the numbers of old ships have reduced the age of the fleet to an average of 12-13 years. However, the United States still has more than fifty destroyer-type ships more than twenty years old. In contrast, the Soviet Union has less than twenty-five approaching twenty years.

In summary, the trends in U.S. naval forces have been toward an improvement in quality and a major decline in the number of ships. The present Department of Defense plans call for a naval shipbuilding program that (1) provides for increasing numbers of missile armed ships; (2) provides for new types of combat ships; (3) replaces overage destroyers; and (4) halts the downward trend in surface combatant forces by 1975. If funds are provided for these plans, the United States can modernize its navy and maintain its present force levels. Otherwise, the gap in naval capabilities will widen to the disadvantage of the United States.

Critical Problems in the Naval Balance

The naval balance is the second area in which a radical shift in the relative military balance is occurring. From a position of unquestioned supremacy, the U.S. navy has slipped to a position where the Soviet Union can now challenge U.S. supremacy at sea. If present trends were to continue, the numerical comparison of the United States and Soviet navies in 1985 would continue to favor the Soviet Union: 240 to 200 in major surface combatants; 140 to 90 in nuclear attack and cruise missile submarines; 160-200 to 0 in non-nuclear attack submarines, and 62 to 41 in ballistic missile submarines. The implications of losing our naval superiority are clear and the resulting problems are profound.

One of the basic premises of our defense strategy has been control of the seas so that Western Europe and Japan are assured they will be resupplied and reinforced in the event of war. Soviet naval superiority would critically undermine the basis of Western strategy while furthering their own. One of the main currents of Soviet strategic doctrine has been to expand areas of naval operations to provide for defense against attacks on the Soviet Union from the sea. In recent years this doctrine has resulted in the stationing of powerful fleets in the Norwegian Sea/North Atlantic Ocean, the Mediterranean Sea, and in the Northwest Pacific Ocean. These areas are all of major importance to the U.S. and its allies. Should the Soviets combine their strategic doctrine with naval superiority, then all of Northern Europe, the countries bordering the eastern Mediterranean Sea, Japan and Korea will, in effect, be behind what the Soviets already consider to be their own front lines.

Given their great strategic nuclear strength, expanding Soviet naval capabilities would allow them to exploit situations throughout the world in ways that have not been available to them in the past. Until the recent expansion in naval capabilities, the Soviet Union was limited in its ability to project its military power to its immediate border areas—for example, Hungary and Czechoslovakia. By 1985, with present trends, the Soviet Union will have powerful, mobile and visible naval forces to use for political purposes worldwide and possibly in support of military intervention in areas far from their immediate borders. The political vulnerability of U.S. and allied interests will increase markedly as Soviet naval forces are used increasingly to respond to crisis situations. Declining U.S. and allied naval power will make the exercise of political power and active intervention all the more feasible for the Soviet Union. The United States used its nuclear and naval superiority to force the Soviet Union to back down in Cuba; in 1985 the tables could be turned against us.

In the interim, the perception of power can be as important as its future reality. Power affects political alignments and naval power is traditionally one of the important elements of visible usable power. Thus, the Soviets can now use the momentum of their increasing naval capabilities for political persuasion and even outright coercion to affect political and economic realignments. Naval power increases Soviet ability to do this in land and sea areas once too remote for them to bring power to bear. In both reality and in the perception of other countries, U.S. power to prevent such coercion is dwindling.

Two critical vulnerabilities of the industrial world are its dependence on friendly trading partners as sources of raw materials and its dependence on the oceans for trade and commerce. Vulnerability invites exploitation. The Soviet Union, with its ever-increasing nuclear and naval capabilities, is developing the ability to exploit this situation. The loss of assurance of freedom to use the oceans as avenues of trade and commerce could cause economic disaster for much of the world. The disruption of the distribution of raw materials and energy resources through coercion of the suppliers by the Soviet Union would place the survival of the industrial nations in jeopardy. To protect its own interests, the United States must be able to deter actions that would reduce the assurance of free use of the oceans for trade, or that would disrupt the flow of materials. The United States must be able to do this without having to resort to a nuclear confrontation.

Land and Air Forces Balance

The military balance in Europe—between the United States and NATO and the Soviet Union and the Warsaw Pact—is of primary importance to the United States and is a major consideration in the force structure of U.S. land and air forces. The security and integrity of Western Europe is second only to the security of the United States itself.

There are many obstacles to maintaining a balance of military forces in

Europe. Principally they revolve around the fundamental differences in the relationship of the two superpowers to their European allies. The Soviet Union enforces an iron grip on Eastern Europe, which it maintains in its own interests. The Soviets station major military units there, not only for their own defense but to insure their control of the area. There appears to be little chance that the efforts of the Soviet Union to dominate all phases of the economic, political, and military affairs of Eastern Europe will change fundamentally in the near future.

The United States and Western Europe, on the other hand, have a more loosely constructed political alliance founded upon mutual interests. Although the United States may be the dominant power, the U.S. presence in Western Europe is dependent on the consent of the countries concerned.

Throughout NATO's history there have been enormous strains besetting the alliance over economic, political and military affairs. Yet, there is no indication that the United States wants, or would attempt, to impose itself on Western Europe as the Soviets have done in Eastern Europe. In fact, it is the possible fragmentation of the alliance over political and economic issues that is cause for the most concern and raises the greatest obstacles to maintaining the military balance in Europe.

Because the superpowers play such important roles in the balance of military power in Europe, it is important to review the trends in their land and air forces, as well as the trends in the overall NATO/Warsaw Pact forces.

The Soviet Program. There has been a continual increase in Soviet land and air forces manpower for over the last decade. The reason for this appears to be associated with the buildup of forces on the eastern borders of the Soviet Union. In the past five years, they have increased the number of divisions facing China from twenty-one to forty-five, with concurrent increases in supporting air defense and tactical air forces. These long-term manpower changes are shown in Figure III-12.

Since 1967, the Soviets also have increased the number of their divisions in Eastern Europe from twenty-six to thirty-one, primarily as a result of their invasion of Czechoslovakia in 1968. However, these forces came from those already available in the USSR. Soviet manpower in Eastern Europe has stabilized in recent years at about 450,000 men.

During the past decade, the Soviet Union has made major advances in weaponry and, in addition, has produced enormous quantities of new armaments. The Soviets have had a continuing program to reequip their ground forces in Europe with new tanks, armored personnel carriers, antitank and antiaircraft missiles, and improved artillery and rocket launchers. For their air forces, they have a program of replacing older aircraft with new and increased numbers of high performance fighter and bomber aircraft. The magnitude of these efforts is apparent. The Soviet Union has added at least 2,500 tanks to its forces in

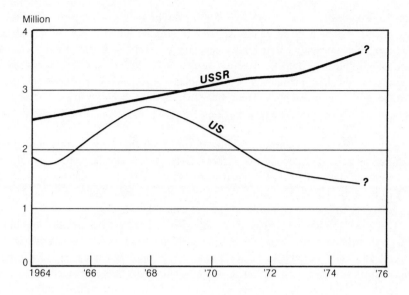

Source: Adapted from *Annual Defense Department Report FY 1976 and FY 197T*.

Figure III-12. Land and Air Forces Manpower.

Europe since 1971 and increased the inventory of its tactical air forces by 1,000 aircraft. At the same time, it has provided almost 4,000 tanks, 2,000 armored personnel carriers, approximately 3,000 pieces of large artillery, and over 1,000 aircraft to countries in the Middle East since 1967. The Soviet Union is maintaining and, in some areas actually expanding, its enormous production capacity for high quality land and air weapons system.

The U.S. Program. The United States has made major improvements in the quality of its weapons systems during the past decade, largely as a consequence of combat needs for Southeast Asia. In the development of equipment for land and air forces, U.S. technology is generally still superior to that of any nation. U.S. tactical aircraft, tanks, and antitank systems, which would play a major role in a NATO war, are qualitatively superior to those of the Soviet Union. The present U.S. program calls for continued emphasis on improving the combat capability of its land and air forces with new weapons, such as precision guided missiles, laser guided bombs and artillery shells, battlefield air defense systems and improved tanks, helicopters, and attack aircraft.

U.S. production capacity for high quality aircraft is still superior to that of the Soviet Union. This is not true for production of other types of military equipment. The U.S. production capacity for tanks, for example, is only about 500 per year, compared to a Soviet capacity of over 5,000 per year. There are plans to double U.S. tank production in the next few years, but these plans are contingent on the availability of new plants to make the necessary armor castings and tank assemblies. There presently is only one foundry in the United States that can turn out the large castings necessary for tanks, and it can produce only about 70 of these per month.

Even with new production, tank output will be considerably less than required to meet the needs of U.S. forces, our allies, and other countries such as Israel, which have relied on U.S.-made armaments. The present tank inventory of 9,000 is well below the level of 13,500 the United States desires and is considerably below the Soviet inventory of over 40,000.

There are numerous reasons for the declining defense production base. Environmental, health, and safety requirements have had serious impacts on certain defense products. For example, rules on handling toxic chemicals forced production of elements essential to some missile fuels to be stopped for several months for environmental considerations. Some manufacturers, rather than comply with new safety or environmental regulations, closed down their facilities. Other manufacturers simply do not want defense contracts. They argue these are not profitable, that return on investment is too low, and government regulations are too cumbersome to bother with. Recently, one major U.S. company refused to maintain a bomb production facility in a layaway status; thus, the reserve capacity to produce 60,000 bombs per month was lost. The cumulative effect of this declining production base is to increase the time it takes to produce weapons and also to increase their cost. In some cases, it has led, at least temporarily, to the inability to acquire elements essential to weapons production.

With the exception of the Vietnam buildup, the trend in U.S. land and air forces manpower has been one of continuing decline since the Korean War. This reduction in manpower has also reflected a change in overseas deployments. U.S. forces deployed in Europe have been reduced from a high of over 400,000 in 1962 to less than 300,000 in 1974. Troops stationed in other overseas areas, such as Korea, also have been reduced. As a result, the number of U.S. bases overseas has been reduced from approximately 2,400 to less than 1,800 since 1964. Of these remaining bases only 315 could be classified as major bases and more than 75 percent are associated with our forces assigned to NATO. These reductions in manpower also reflect a decrease in combat units. In the decade since 1964, land and air forces reductions include: manned fighter interceptor squadrons from 40 to 6; tactical fighter/attack squadrons from 113 to 94; army divisions from 16 to 14, and troopships, cargoships and tankers from 101 to 40.

NATO/Warsaw Pact. There has been a long debate over the relative military power of NATO and the Warsaw Pact. The Western consensus is that there is a relative balance of power at the present time despite major differences in force structures. The Warsaw Pact forces are designed for high speed offensive operations built around their highly mobile tank forces. NATO forces are primarily structured for defensive operations and are designed to hold their ground against offensive forces.

Figure III-13 shows the present ratio in manpower and weapons of the U.S./USSR and NATO/Warsaw Pact forces. The Soviet Union provides 60 percent of the Warsaw Pact force of 1.1 million men. The United States contributes about 30 percent of the 900,000 men in NATO's defense force.

Warsaw Pact. The principal trends in the military forces of the Warsaw Pact have been: improving combat capabilities; increasing Soviet control of the Pact military forces; improving logistic capabilities, and standardizing weapons systems.

NATO. The NATO countries have never tried to match the Warsaw Pact in numbers of men or equipment. Instead, they have adopted a defensive strategy

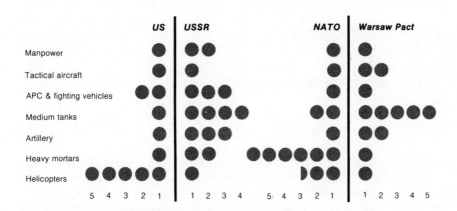

Source: Department of Defense.

Figure III-13. Ground/Air Forces Ratios.

and rely on superior technology and the superior quality of arms to offset any numerical inferiority. The trends in NATO military forces generally reflect a continuing improvement in the quality of its weapons and combat capability. There are other trends, however, that detract from the positive trends in improved combat capability.

The very success of NATO in reducing the threat of Soviet moves toward Western Europe has created a trend—in the absence of a perceived overt threat—toward reduced public support for maintenance of a balance of power in Europe. Also, the concern for individual security and what is sometimes viewed to be a likely drift toward the political left is resulting in less emphasis on national security interests.

The diminishing political cohesion in the alliance and the absence of an effective political structure has had a debilitating effect on the decision processes that support military preparedness and provide decisive wartime command and control of military forces.

Inflation, the expensive and wasteful duplication of maintaining national armament production facilities, also advanced technology weapons, have all combined to cause major increases in the costs of new weapons and slowed the modernization of NATO forces considerably. This has occurred in spite of the fact that most European members of NATO have raised their defense budgets faster than the rate of inflation in the past few years.

NATO has very little standardization in its major weapons systems, such as tanks, aircraft, missiles and troop mobility vehicles. As a result, there is an enormous multiplicity of spare parts and repair items required to keep forces in combat. This is further complicated by the fact that each nation is responsible for its own logistic support, including re-supply of forces in combat. This diversity in weapons systems and multiple logistics requirements severely limits the flexible employment of combat forces and increases the costs of maintaining these forces in peace and war. There has been little progress in correcting this problem and the prognosis is for more of the same.

Critical Problems in Land and Air Forces

There is today a rather general reluctance among many elements in the United States to support an overseas presence with land and air forces. The argument is not about the desirability of defending Western Europe or Japan, which is generally accepted as necessary, but about how best to provide for that defense. The basic choices are to retain sizable forces overseas or to withdraw forces and develop a rapid redeployment capability. Our allies, especially in Western Europe, have generally favored our overseas deployments—and that deterrent has worked. But these deployments also have posed a serious dilemma for our allies—while the presence of U.S. forces overseas is felt to be essential to their security, these forces can be a serious political liability. This state of affairs has resulted in several unresolved problems for the United States and its allies.

Preserving viable alliances will be an increasingly difficult problem, yet, the need for mutual defense alliances will remain undiminished. Neither the United States, nor any grouping of nations which excludes the United States, has any hope of maintaining a satisfactory balance of land and air forces by itself relative to the numbers of either the Soviet Union or the People's Republic of China. But alliances of sovereign states are difficult to maintain at high levels of effectiveness and unified purpose, given the ambiguous threats, issues of fair-sharing of costs and responsibilities and the dissensions over economic and political matters that sometimes occur among allies. A continuation of political and economic crises affecting members of the NATO alliance could lead to further fragmentation and to the collapse of the military structure upon which its defense rests.

The strength and cohesion of the NATO alliance is critically dependent on the strength and steadfastness of its dominant member. In setting their own courses, the other members will continue to look at the United States for any signs of weakness or withdrawal. Thus, the first priority in strengthening the NATO alliance is to improve the strength—political, economic, and military—of the United States.

To an increasing degree, U.S. forces and bases overseas are becoming politically constrained in how they are used, especially when the host nations find themselves at odds with the objectives of the United States. This became increasingly true of Japan during the Vietnam War and of Western Europe in relation to U.S. actions in the Middle East and the eastern Mediterranean. Thus, in the Middle East War of 1973 and again during the Cyprus affair of 1974, our European allies denied U.S. forces the use of bases and facilities to support our operations. U.S. attempts to transfer equipment stored in Europe to the Middle East met with serious political protest by our allies. The use of bases in Asia is becoming ever more constrained as evidenced by the heated reaction of Thailand to the use of bases in their country by U.S. forces for the rescue of the steamship *Mayaguez* during May 1975.

Given the political constraints on U.S. forces deployed overseas and the constraints on their use of bases and facilities for other than mutual defense, there is a serious question of what type of forces the United States should maintain. A slowly evolving trend in U.S. forces toward greater mobility and striking power with less dependence on overseas bases is now apparent. This does not satisfy the NATO allies or Japan, who consider it less effective. They desire a strong U.S. presence as a deterrent to Soviet/Chinese actions.

The trend toward reductions in forces overseas and reliance on rapid redeployment, particularly in defense of NATO, could have a serious impact on the initial defensive capability in Western Europe. In times of crisis, the movement of military forces is a signal of significance. For this reason, during a crisis, movement of forces may heighten tensions and may thus be judged inappropriate. Yet, failure to do so may result in serious disadvantages if hostilities begin. In such a situation, the potential conflict of interests between political and military requirements is apparent; reinforcement may be politically undesirable but failure to reinforce could spell military disaster.

Regardless of how redeployable U.S. forces may be in the event of hostilities in Europe, the Soviet Union is 3,000 miles closer. In addition, the Soviets would be moving war material over relatively secure territory, which they control. The United States would have to cross the Atlantic Ocean. Control of this sea lane could be effectively contested by the Soviet Union.

Technological Balance

Advancing technology is a basic ingredient to advanced industrial societies. It has been the American genius for developing new technology that has led to our position of undisputed leadership in the development and application of technology. No nation has yet matched the total scope of American technological excellence. The technological superiority of the United States, in particular, and the Western nations, in general, has presented a challenge to the Soviet Union. In typical Soviet fashion, they have set out to do something about it. In the 1950s, the Soviet government established as a national goal the attainment of world leadership in science and technology. They backed this commitment in manpower and money.

The magnitude of the Soviet effort to overcome the U.S. scientific and technological lead is shown in Figure III-14. This compares total numbers of scientists and engineers in research and development, both military and civil, for the Soviet Union and the United States. In contrast to the United States, a much larger fraction of all Soviet scientists work in military research and development. Although it is difficult to get agreement on the definition of the terms scientist and engineer, the Soviet Union at present appears to have perhaps 30 percent more people in the general category of scientist or engineer. More important, however, is the rate at which talented individuals are becoming available for the technical manpower pool. The Soviet Union graduates 70 percent more people in the scientific and engineering fields per year than the U.S. and again the gap is growing.

Some might argue that quantity is not important because the quality of Soviet technical education is inferior to that of the United States. In many areas this is true, but no one argues that the best in the Soviet Union are not the equal to the best anywhere. With the emphasis placed upon this type of education, and their increasing exposure to Western technological thought and educational systems, the trend in the Soviet Union is toward increasingly higher-quality graduates.

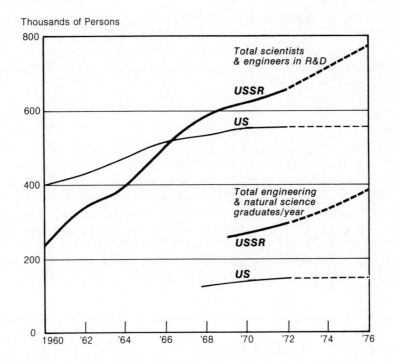

Source: Department of Defense.

Figure III-14. U.S./USSR Natural Scientists and Engineers (Graduates and in R&D).

An important difference between the United States and the Soviet Union is in the allocation of scientific and engineering effort. The Soviets have dedicated their best efforts and people to military, space, and a few other selected fields of research and development. The fruits of this effort are reflected in the quality of their missiles, aircraft, and ships. It is interesting to note that in the Soviet Union the national R&D budget ratio between military/space and civilian expenditures favors the military and space efforts by 70:30. In the United States, the total national expenditures on R&D split roughly 70:30 in favor of the civilian sector of the economy.

Because technology plays such a critical role in maintaining military superiority, trends in the application of technology to military uses are of particular interest. Soviet secrecy makes it difficult to gauge their present technological strength. However, observation of the weapons systems developed by the Soviet Union makes it possible to know the state of their technology development as it existed four or five years earlier. From this, we can draw inferences for the future. Probably the most important indicator of Soviet emphasis on military

R&D is the fact that from 1960 to 1974 their expenditures for R&D doubled, going from 15 percent to 30 percent of the defense budget.[4] In comparison, the U.S. effort has declined from 15 percent to less than 10 percent of defense expenditures. Figure III-15 portrays this trend graphically and shows the dollar equivalent of the 1974 R&D effort.

Critical Problems in the Technological Balance

The trend of proven Soviet military technological capability and their expanding effort is of paramount concern for the decades ahead. If current U.S. and Soviet relative trends in military R&D resource allocations continue, the United States has little reason to assume that it will continue to retain military technological superiority. In two of the most critical determinants of technological strength—talented manpower and money—the Soviet Union is expending considerably more effort than the United States. The determination of the Soviet Union to

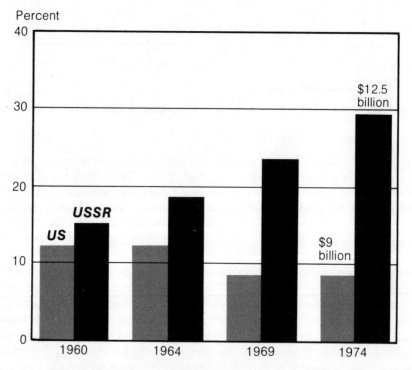

Source: Estimates developed by the author.

Figure III-15. Military R&D as Percentage of Defense Budget.

surpass the United States in technological capabilities is a matter of great national commitment and pride for them. This disparity in effort and determination could lead to Soviet technological superiority in most military weapons systems by 1985.

Soviet R&D advances in the strategic nuclear warfare areas are now apparent in new systems nearing production. Four new strategic missiles, which were first observed in 1972, must have been in R&D in the mid-1960s. U.S. research and development efforts in the areas of strategic warfare, especially in the areas of new ICBM technology and antiballistic missile technology, lag behind that of the Soviet Union. The Soviet Union has chosen to undertake a number of developments and tests which the United States desires, but has judged to be too expensive. With the Soviet Union doubling R&D expenditures since 1960, we can only speculate about what surprises they might have for the United States by 1985. Thus, avoidance of technological surprise that could upset the military balance is becoming a major problem.

The present trends in U.S. expenditures for technological R&D for application to naval, land, and air forces, if allowed to continue, would squander the U.S. technological lead. While they were developing four new strategic missiles, the Soviets were also making substantial technological improvements in ship missile systems, in the military applications of lasers, in battlefield air defense and antiballistic missile systems, in submarine quietness and submarine missiles, in antisubmarine systems, and in ground and air force equipment. The Soviets have already surpassed the United States in some specific areas, such as command/control and communications, in the military applications of laser technology, air defense of the battlefield and in antiship missiles.

Countering technological developments can be a long process during which time uncertainties and risks increase. As noted earlier, reacting to new weapons systems that are technological surprises can take eight to twelve years before an equivalent capability or effective counter systems can be developed and deployed. The most efficient way to reduce this time lag is to have the technology available and be ready to exploit it when needed. Illustrative of this point is the ABM-MIRV interaction. The Soviets were ahead in deploying an ABM system, but the United States was able to quickly counter this deployment with the MIRV.

The declining U.S. military research and development effort, both in budget percentage and constant dollar terms, cannot support the level of new research necessary to insure continued military technological superiority. Although the civilian technological capability of the United States is a great resource upon which to draw, only a small percentage of this technology is immediately usable. This is not the answer, therefore, to sustaining a military technology base that knows what is technologically possible in weapons systems and which is prepared to make rapid counter moves to an adversary's technological developments.

Finally, the United States will have to devote more effort to motivating students to careers in the sciences, to assisting in training new scientists and engineers, and to supporting research and development in technology related to military needs.

Comparative Funding of Soviet Union/United States Defense Programs

Comparison of defense expenditures between the United States and the Soviet Union is difficult and necessarily imprecise because the Soviet Union considers its defense budget to be a state secret. There are also no completely satisfactory methods of converting the value of Russian rubles to U.S. dollars. Therefore, it should be recognized that all Soviet figures in the following discussion are best estimates based upon testimony given before congressional committees, upon academic studies, and unclassified intelligence sources.

There are two principal trends in defense expenditures that are of major significance. The first is the amount actually being spent by the Soviet Union and the United States on defense programs. The second is the relative impact of that spending on the economies of the two countries. With regard to actual defense expenditures, Figure III-16 shows the trends in constant 1973 dollars. Until about 1970, defense outlays by the United States exceeded those of the Soviet Union, but since 1971 the Soviet Union has exceeded the United States in defense spending. As of about 1974, the Soviet Union was outspending the United States by approximately 30 percent in military research and development; by 25 percent in procurement of new weapons; by 20 percent in nonnuclear military forces, and by 60 percent in strategic nuclear weapons systems. As Figure III-16 shows, measured in constant dollar terms, Soviet expenditures have been increasing steadily, whereas U.S. expenditures are declining and are presently lower than the pre-Vietnam level of 1964.

The ability to produce military equipment and to maintain large military forces is partly a function of a nation's economic strength. The Soviet Union is second only to the United States in economic power, with an estimated gross national product equivalent to $660 billion—slightly more than half that of the United States. The trends in GNP growth and, hence, the overall ability of the United States and the Soviet Union to increase military capabilities, are shown in Figure III-17.

Gross national product measures only ability to acquire military capabilities; it does not provide clues to intent nor the degree of economic impact such acquisition might have on a nation. For this, it is necessary to know how much of the GNP is spent on military capability. For the United States the percentage of GNP spent on national defense (Figure III-18) shows a general decline since the Korean War high of about 13 percent to the present level of 6 percent. This

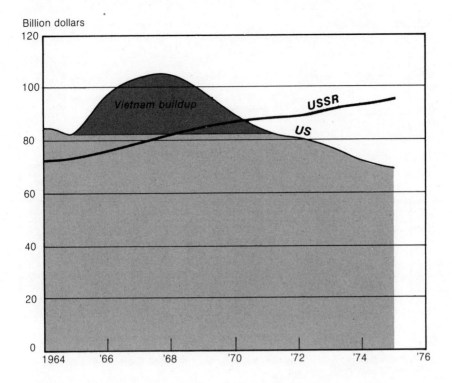

Source: *Annual Defense Department Report FY 1976 and FY 197T.*

Figure III-16. Soviet/United States Defense Expenditures (1973 dollars).

trend in expenditures for military capabilities indicates a relative lessening of the economic burden of defense.

Determining the percentage of GNP used by the Soviet Union for acquiring its military capability is much more complicated than is the case with the United States. For one thing, Western estimates on the ruble value of the Soviet GNP vary as much as 40 percent. For another, estimates of the percentage of GNP allocated for defense by the Soviet Union vary from as little as 6 percent to over 15 percent. The only certainty is that the published defense budget of the Soviet Union bears little relation to their actual expenditures of resources for military capability. These uncertainties make it virtually impossible to measure the economic impact of increasing military capability on the Soviet economy. What we do have, however, is observable Soviet performance in acquiring military capabilities. Based on the actual production of military equipment, their obviously improved military capabilities, the observable growth of the Soviet GNP, and a growth rate for military expenditures that is less than the rate of

Billions of 1972 dollars

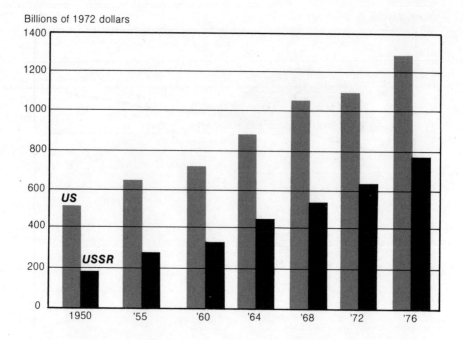

Source: *Allocation of Resources in the Soviet Union and China*, Joint Congressional Economic Committee.

Figure III-17. U.S.-USSR Gross National Product.

growth of the GNP, it is apparent that the Soviet Union is capable of sustaining, or even accelerating, the present rate of growth in defense expenditures.

Critical Problems in National Security Funding

From the charts it is apparent that the Soviet Union has had a steadily rising defense budget for many years. This rise can be explained from their point of view as reflecting the need of the Soviet Union to meet the requirements of the international situation. It is interesting to note, however, that each increment of power that is added as a result of international tensions such as Hungary, Cuba, Czechoslovakia, and China is retained. There are very few dips in the upward trend of Soviet defense spending to reflect the easing of tensions.

In contrast, the overall trend in U.S. defense expenditures is a decline, but this decline is masked by the large peaks in spending caused by the involvements in Korea and Vietnam. Thus, there are large variations in the level of U.S. defense spending that reflect the ebb and flow of world events, but the overall trend is down.

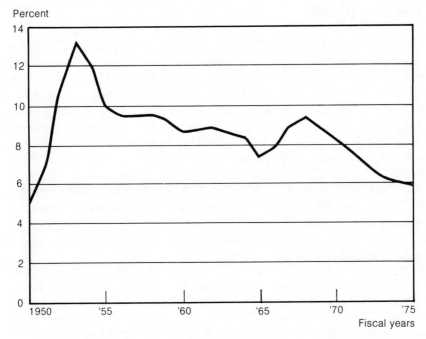

Source: *The United States Budget in Brief, Fiscal Year 1975.*

Figure III-18. Defense Outlays as a Percentage of GNP.

The most critical problem for the United States is the persistence of a 2 to 3 percent increase per year in Soviet defense expenditures and the potential disparity in real military power this can produce. By 1985, if the Soviets continue to expand their effort by 2 to 3 percent per year, and the United States continues to reduce its effort by 2 or 3 percent per year, the result will be a 45-70 percent differential in defense effort. If such divergent trends persist there would be no way for the United States to maintain a military balance with the Soviet Union.

The allocation of money among defense and social programs is also a critical problem for the United States and the other advanced industrial nations. In free and democratic societies these can be extraordinary painful decisions which are dependent on a public consensus for approval. In times of peace, the tendency has been to support defense grudgingly and to opt for social programs until a military crisis actually occurs. For the Soviet Union and the People's Republic of China, the allocation decisions are also difficult, but they do not require a public consensus. Thus, in their case, the ratio of defense expenditures to social expenditures can be what the leadership desires it to be. And they have historically given military expenditures priority.

3. Alternative Choices

The preceding sections have described the trends in the military balance but the question remains as to what the American people will *choose to do* about these trends. This section presents some alternative choices that seem to cover the spectrum of current debate in the United States. The selection of choices is intended to indicate a range of choices and not to define a particular choice in detail. There are some choices at the extremes which have not been included because they are judged to be unrealistic in today's world. One such choice would be to regain "absolute military superiority" over the Soviet Union. Another would be for the United States to renounce its role as a major world power and withdraw to "Fortress America." Within these limits it seems possible that some combination of the choices presented could become consciously, or unconsciously, the American choice.

Reduced U.S. Commitments

A reduction in U.S. commitments is viewed by many as a means to reduce the chances of U.S. involvement in foreign wars and the means to permit reductions in the costs of maintaining military forces. The United States has defense commitments with over forty nations, several of which entail major expenditures of manpower and money in peacetime and would require even more should there be a war. The past and present U.S. defense expenditures have principally been for military forces to cover our major commitments of providing the nuclear shield, participation in the NATO Alliance, protection of Japan, and our own defense. Military forces for use in meeting our other commitments such as the Southeast Asia Treaty Organization (SEATO); the Rio Pact; and the Australia, New Zealand, United States (ANZUS) Treaty have been included in those required by the major commitments. For example, the U.S. Sixth Fleet in the Mediterranean is a major naval force maintained to meet our commitments to NATO but it has also met our requirements for forces to support our commitments to peace in the Middle East. Therefore, a reduction in commitments per se would not necessarily reduce U.S. defense expenditures.

A reduction in the major U.S. commitments to NATO and Japan would, however, have a dramatic impact on U.S. defense spending. Assuming that the United States was to maintain its strategic nuclear deterrent and provide a sizable Navy to maintain freedom of the seas, it would still be possible to reduce defense spending by $20 to $30 billion per year by making major reductions in the size of the U.S. Army and Air Force. In terms of dollars saved, this would represent 7 to 10 percent of the present federal budget. However, there are other considerations besides reducing costs. If the United States should unilaterally set about to reduce its major commitments to any significant degree, the following consequences could be expected.

The United States would be making a major departure from its mutual defense strategy of the past thirty years. This strategy was necessitated by the failures and weaknesses of the appeasement and isolation strategies of earlier decades and the resultant hard lessons of World War II. With a strategy of mutual defense, the United States and its allies have not only recovered from the ravages of World War II, but have prospered enormously and lived in relative peace for three decades. A unilateral reduction by the United States of its commitments to the mutual security of one or another of its major allies would be accompanied by repercussions in political, economic and military affairs throughout the world.

In cutting its share of the responsibility for mutual defense, the United States would be increasing the defense burden of its allies and possibly contributing to the proliferation of nuclear weapons. With the removal of the U.S. nuclear shield and withdrawal of its other military forces from forward deployment areas, our allies would be faced with two undesirable alternatives—either to increase drastically their defense expenditures, including the development of nuclear armaments, or to accept their vulnerability to domination by the overwhelming military power of the Soviet Union.

The economic repercussions of a major change in U.S. defense strategy would impact seriously on our allies. They might well have to realign their budgets to increase defense spending—if they chose to expand their military programs. These would be difficult decisions to make with large internal disruptions. Under these circumstances, cooperation by the allies with the United States in economic affairs would be more difficult at best. Since our allies as a group are a major force in the world's economic affairs, the forced reallocation of their economic resources that our actions could cause might also disrupt the workings of the world economic system.

The political consequences of such a major change in United States defense strategy would be enormous. All the governments of our allies would be under tremendous pressure to redress the hardships caused by the U.S. action. These types of pressures are not conducive to the cooperative diplomacy that is necessary for the advanced nations to confront the myriad problems facing the world or to furthering United States interests.

The savings attributed to a reduction in our principal commitments might be illusory. The basis of the mutual defense strategy has been the deterrence of war. Should the United States withdraw the protection of its nuclear power and our allies were unable or unwilling to provide their own, then the chances of war would increase. If our former allies were to be attacked and the United States were once again to come to their aid, it might well cost many times more to re-arm than the amounts saved. To this must also be added the cost in destruction and human suffering that a major war would bring. Just as preventive medicine is less expensive than treating the illness, deterrence is a less costly alternative than war.

Continue Present Trends

The year-to-year trends in U.S. military power seem to be dominated primarily by fiscal considerations. Basically, in terms of constant dollars, defense spending has been declining.

Defense spending is divided into three principal areas: manpower, operating expenses, and new weapons. As costs rise faster than the budget, one or all of these areas must be reduced. Since 1969 the United States has been solving the problem by cutting manpower and operating expenses, first, by reducing the number of men in uniform and civilian support personnel and second, by retiring older ships, planes, and equipment. The third area, weapons procurement, has now become the principal area for reductions.

If we chose to allow present trends to continue, Americans would be accepting the following conditions by 1985.

The United States's principal competitor and adversary, the Soviet Union would have military superiority:

a. The Soviet Union would have clear strategic nuclear superiority in the quantitative and qualitative measures of nuclear power.
b. Control of the seas would pass to the Soviet Union.
c. Land and air forces would be barely adequate for the initial defense of Europe. The United States could not resupply Europe in the face of Soviet control of the sea lanes. There would be only a limited U.S. capability for using land and air forces in other areas of the world.
d. Technological superiority in armaments would be conceded to the Soviet Union.

In addition to becoming the number two military power, continuation of the trends presents the danger of the United States becoming a second class military power. The United States would forfeit its ability to use military power effectively should it be necessary. There would be increased pressure to use nuclear weapons in the absence of conventional power. In a changing and volatile world, military power will still be necessary to influence the outcome of events that are vital to United States interests and those of its friends and allies.

There should be a strong correlation between our interests, commitments and foreign policy on the one hand and the size and capabilities of our military forces on the other. A continuing reduction in military capability would inevitably force the United States into redefining its responsibilities toward the rest of the world. As one of the world's two most powerful nations, the United States cannot easily escape the burdens power imposes and any redefinition of its responsibilities for the mutual security of its friends and allies will have enormous consequences for friend and foe alike. A major restructuring of the whole international order and alliance system, as we now know it, would ensue from a continuation of the present trends. Americans, if this is our choice, will have to recognize that initiating such changes through our own unilateral actions would not necessarily guarantee a new order that is favorable to the United States and its interests.

Negotiate to Reduce Defense Requirements

One of the most appealing ways to reduce defense requirements is through negotiation with our adversaries. Successful negotiations would mean agreements that would (1) provide equal security to the parties involved; (2) be verifiable; and (3) prevent the acquisition of important advantages that could not be quickly countered should one side or the other break the agreement.

To negotiate such agreements is a difficult and tedious undertaking. In areas such as strategic nuclear weapons, even though there are some similarities in the actual missile forces, there are complicating factors such as geography, allies, and short-range delivery systems that have made negotiating a successful agreement a long and torturous process. This is equally true in the Mutual and Balanced Force Reductions (MBFR) negotiations between NATO and the Warsaw Pact. In this case, there are even larger disparities to be overcome: Warsaw Pact advantages in manpower, tanks, and air defenses; NATO advantages in aircraft and antitank systems; Warsaw Pact advantages in reserve force mobilization and short reinforcement distances; NATO vulnerability at sea; and the long distances from the United States for reinforcement and resupply.

Negotiating a naval balance may be still more difficult. Although there have been agreements in the past, they did not provide stability. There are, however, further complicating factors in the present situation, which were not part of the negotiating scene in the 1920s and 1930s. In earlier decades, there was symmetry in both naval missions and types of ships in the various navies. Today, even though there are only four or five major navies, there are major asymmetries in the power of the negotiating nations, in the missions of the various navies and in the types of ships they possess. The difficulty in negotiating naval limits with these asymmetries is compounded, as it is in other armament negotiations, by the adversary relationship of the political/social/economic systems involved.

The foregoing difficulties by no means indicate that negotiations are fruitless. Despite the difficulties and mixed results of past treaties, the potential benefits from negotiations are so large as to merit their full support. In choosing to follow the path of negotiation, Americans should realize that:

1. Negotiations are a long-term proposition. They require patience, fortitude and relative stability in the areas being negotiated. If one side or the other can achieve its objectives simply by waiting for changes they see occurring, there is no basis for negitiations except to given an illusion of progress.

2. The basis for successful negotiations is reasonable equality of strength. The loss of equality eliminates the incentive for successful negotiations. Thus, the continued erosion of United States power would erode our ability to reach satisfactory agreements with the Soviet Union.

Retain a Military Balance

To retain the military balance would require the present downward trends in U.S. military capabilities to be reversed. This would involve improvements in the quality of some types of weapons for both nuclear and conventional armaments and in some cases, especially in conventional forces, it would require increases in the quantity as well. On the assumption that there is a relative balance in military power now, a program to maintain the balance would require an increase in defense expenditures of at least 3 percent per year in real purchasing power. This annual growth rate would: meet the requirements for technological change to adjust to changing world situations; increase combat capability and effectiveness through technology; allow for additions to the forces levels in conventional forces, and permit the rising standards of living in the United States to be provided to the members of the armed forces.

However, in a period of worldwide economic upheaval and difficult economic problems at home, there is very legitimate concern over whether we can afford these additional outlays for national security. There is no simple answer. There are, however, some basic considerations that can add perspective and shed some light on the subject.

The United States has by far the most powerful economy in the world. Its closest competitor, the Soviet Union, ranks a distant second, as illustrated in Figure III-17. Only the most pessimistic projections of economic collapse could conceivably alter this situation to any significant degree.

The growth of the U.S. economy and the expansion of federal revenues that has accompanied it are shown in Figure III-19. This growth in GNP also has increased the funds available to State and local governments so that the net public spending in the United States (Figure III-20) has shown a dramatic increase in the past twenty years. Spending on defense programs, however, has remained relatively constant and has not matched the growth in other programs. The social and economic programs depicted in Figure III-20 include all governmental activity from local jurisdictions paving roads, building schools, and providing local services, to major federal programs for social welfare, education, agriculture, etc.

As a result of the growth in the national economy and public spending, all the basic economic measures that characterize the economic impact of defense spending on the national economy show a continuing decline.

a. *GNP:* The defense share of the GNP has declined from 10 percent to 6 percent in the last twenty years (Figure III-18) and is at the lowest point since 1950.

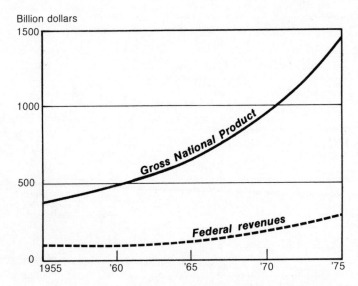

Source: Data derived from U.S. Bureau of the Census, *Statistical Abstract of the United States: 1973.*

Figure III-19. GNP/Federal Revenues.

b. *Labor Force:* From a Korean War high of 14 percent, defense related employment has declined to about 5 percent of the national labor force.
c. *Goods and Services:* The defense share of the total goods and services produced by the private sector of the U.S. economy is about 3 percent as compared to over 6 percent in the early 1960s.
d. *Research and Development:* From a high of over 50 percent in the 1950s, the defense related R&D effort has declined to about 25 percent of the total national R&D effort.

The expansion of the U.S. economy and public spending has been accompanied by a major shift in priorities of federal spending. As illustrated in Figure III-21 the trends are well established with the cross-over point occurring around 1971.

There are other considerations in the question of whether the United States can afford a continued high level of national security. For example:

1. Americans have one of the most affluent societies in the history of mankind. As their affluence and economic well-being grows, Americans have an even greater stake in insuring the continued security of their economy and their physical well-being. The insurance on this security should be carried in an adequate amount, especially when the major potential adversary appears to be relentlessly trying to gain quantitative and qualitative arms superiority.

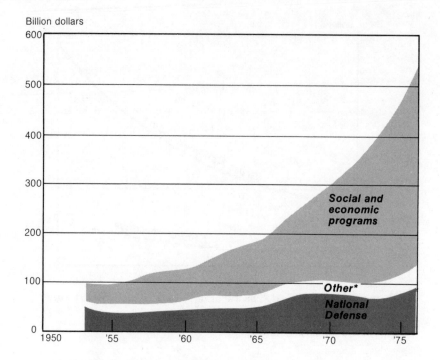

Billion dollars

*VA, debt interest, space, international programs.

Source: Department of Defense.

Figure III-20. Net U.S. Public Spending (Federal/State/Local).

2. Money spent on national security is not a net loss. It provides national security insurance. It also provides employment for over four million Americans directly and secondarily, to an additional 1.5 million persons employed in defense-related industries. These wages and investments in defense materials all provide economic stimulus to the overall economy. Some would claim the same economic benefits would accrue by spending the same money for other socially desirable programs. This, in theory, is true. The difference, of course, is that these other programs do not provide for the military requirements of national security.

3. There are illusory economies in reducing defense spending. Money spent on deterrence is wasted if it greatly exceeds what is required for deterrence. On the other hand, spending money for defense that is short of what is really needed to deter war actually can invite an aggressor to attack. This, of course, would be a tragedy, and it would also be a great waste. The difference in spending levels between adequate and too little is probably a few percent of the gross national product.

4. Figures III-20 and III-21 show that the United States has been supporting

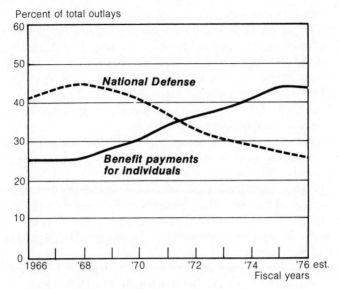

Source: *United States Budget in Brief, Fiscal Year 1976.*

Figure III-21. Changing Priorities.

government programs that the vast majority of its citizens consider to be necessary and desirable to improve the general welfare of the people. However, these charts also show that at this stage, the costs of these programs are expanding at such a rate that even major cuts in defense spending would make available only a minor amount of the total additional revenues that are needed each year. Revenues of the required magnitude can only be obtained, as they have been in the past, from increased national wealth.

The United States has been a superpower for so long that most Americans seldom consider what it would mean if we were no longer the "biggest kid on the block." Because of our strength, Americans have had the luxury of living the past thirty years in relative security and with a large measure of control over our destiny. If, however, Americans allow the military power of the Soviet Union to surpass that of the United States then we should be prepared to play in a whole new ballgame, with new rules and new umpires. The price that Americans would have to pay for our failure to accept the leadership challenge would be measured in political, economic, and military costs that would go far beyond dollars and cents.

For the first time in its 200-year history, the United States would lack the power to pursue its vital interests without fear of coercion and free from blackmail. Even in the nuclear age, our preponderance of strategic nuclear power has provided us this freedom. If the Soviets obtain a perceived position of strategic nuclear superiority, the foundation of Western security—the U.S. nuclear shield—would be eroded. Inevitably, as a result of this erosion, the political cohesion of the advanced industrial nations would crumble. Both Western Europe and Japan, faced with Soviet dominance, could be subject to overpowering political coercion, if not outright domination. The lessons of two world wars have made it abundantly clear that the United States would be in the most extreme jeopardy if the power and peoples of all Europe and Asia were under the control of a single adversary.

With smaller and less capable forces, the United States would have to accept increasing limitations on its ability to influence events and provide help to its allies and friends. The use of military forces to control or influence events, as was done in the Cuban Missile Crisis of 1962 or the Middle East War of 1973, would be a thing of the past. The rapid provision of war materials to allies and friends in trouble would be curtailed or denied. The ability to deter coercive use of force by the Soviet Union, or even lesser powers, would be drastically altered from the present situation.

U.S. foreign policy and diplomacy would have to proceed from a position of relative weakness after years of relative strength. The United States dominated the Middle East negotiations of 1973-74-75. With lessening U.S. influence, the Soviet Union would be able to assume that position. There is no assurance they would be as respectful of our interests as we have been of theirs and others' in such events.

The economic welfare of the advanced industrial nations is based on the goodwill and cooperation of the owners of the world's natural resources. A decline in the power of the Western nations in relation to the Soviet Union could presage an era where the producers of raw materials would for reasons of their own security make realignments in their political and economic relations. Whether this realignment would be detrimental to the advanced industrial nations would depend on how the Soviet Union exercised its power—but the options would be with the Soviet Union. Smaller nations, recognizing the shift in power, could exploit the situation to the detriment of advanced nations by calling on the Soviet Union for support in economic blackmail and/or actual embargo of vital commodities.

Clearly, the United States would be the number two naval power and would be perceived as such by its allies and other nations. Europe could be isolated in the event of war. Freedom of access, in peace or war, to the world's oceans would be in serious jeopardy inasmuch as the Soviet navy would be able to dominate the Mediterranean Sea, the Indian Ocean, the Western Pacific Ocean, the Norwegian, Sea and most of the North Atlantic Ocean.

There are also benefits inherent in defense expenditures which could accrue to the United States. These benefits are not directly amenable to dollars and cents calculations, but nonetheless they are of great value to Americans.

Negotiating Power. In negotiations, be they economic, political or military, it is always desirable to negotiate from strength rather than weakness. Military power, in addition to its deterrent capabilities, is useful in the negotiating process. Military alerts, decisions to build new weapons, deployment of military forces, and obvious military capability are means of bringing pressure to bear in certain negotiating situations where force could be, or has been, applied by the United States's adversaries.

Diplomatic Influence. As military power decreases relative to one's adversaries, so does the ability to exert diplomatic influence. The Soviet Union and, to some extent, the People's Republic of China, are perceived as superpowers and are increasingly capable of exerting their diplomatic influence, not because they are economic giants, but because they are major military powers. Conversely, Western Europe and Japan have considerably less diplomatic influence despite their relative economic power. Not that all diplomacy needs a military presence, but in those instances such as the Middle East War of October 1973, the existence of military power was essential to the control of events and the continuing success of U.S. diplomacy.

A Hedge Against Future Uncertainties. The past forty years have seen surprises and some near-disasters for the United States. Many of the major events were not anticipated—the rapid rise of Hitler and the subsequent onset of World War II, Pearl Harbor, the Korean War, the Berlin Blockade, Soviet intervention in Hungary and Czechoslovakia, the Cuban Missile Crisis, and the Middle East War of 1973. These were major surprises. Readily available military power will provide some assurance, despite the uncertainties of the future, that those who would challenge U.S. interests militarily, would be sure in the knowledge that the United States would be able to defend those interests, if need be, with military power.

Deterrence of Economic Disruption. Military power can provide deterrence against the use of force to interfere with the processes of trade or commerce which are essential to the economic well-being of the United States, its allies and the rest of the world.

4. Desirable and Realistic Objectives

If America is to achieve its goal of maintaining its national security, it should have as a guide desirable and realistic objectives to help formulate the requirements for its military forces. The following objectives, relating to the military requirements of national security are suggested by the preceding sections as being both desirable and realistic. The United States must be determined:

1. To maintain the strategic nuclear balance in order to:
   a. Deter attacks against the United States and its allies.
   b. Provide a continuing incentive to the Soviet Union to negotiate nuclear arms reductions in good faith, to assure it can gain no advantage by abrogating any nuclear arms treaty and to protect against any attempt by the Soviet Union at gaining nuclear superiority in the event that negotiations for limitation and/or reductions fail.
   c. Deter the Soviet Union or the PRC from exploiting their nuclear power to the detriment of the United States or its allies.
   d. Assure that there is no factual political or military basis for the world to conclude that the United States is inferior to the USSR in strategic nuclear power with the consequent loss of political influence and erosion of alliance relationships.
2. To maintain the naval balance with forces of such quality and quantity that we can:
   a. Deter Soviet exploitation of the dependence of the United States and its allies on free access to the world's oceans for trade, commerce and mutual security.
   b. Support U.S. diplomatic efforts by providing the reality as well as the perception of U.S. power and influence, especially in areas of the world where the only feasible United States military presence and capability is that provided by naval forces.
   c. Provide the necessary counter-intervention forces so that Soviet naval power is not used to limit U.S. ability to influence events and also to prevent political or economic blackmail of the United States, its allies, and others upon whom this country depends for friendly relations.
3. To maintain land and air forces that are:
   a. Sufficient in numbers, quality of weapons and supplies so that the United States can meet its responsibilities, in conjunction with its allies, for the continued security of Western Europe.
   b. Rapidly deployable and highly mobile for use in support of U.S. foreign policy and interests.
   c. Technologically superior to U.S. adversaries as a partial counterweight to numerical inferiority.
4. To maintain technological superiority for the United States in order to:
   a. Provide superiority for our armed forces in both their deterrent and fighting capabilities.
   b. Reduce the likelihood of our being placed in jeopardy by technological surprises from our adversaries.
   c. Minimize the cost of our needed military capability.
5. To maintain our national security without unnecessary sacrifice to other important national objectives.

In order to achieve these objectives, the United States will have to maintain a relative military balance with the Soviet Union. Also there must be no major or general disparity between our declared objectives and our capability to achieve them. These considerations will require a positive U.S. program that addresses and seeks to rectify those aspects of the trends that cause critical problems for the United States. The essence of these programs should be as follows.

Strategic Forces

The principal objective would be the maintenance of a strong nuclear deterrent force with the capability to deny to the Soviet Union a war-winning capability. Regardless of the outcome of the Strategic Arms Limitation Talks (SALT), reaching this objective will require modernization of existing U.S. strategic forces. This requires not only that we maintain such a capability but that we take every opportunity to demonstrate that we will not allow this capability to be denied.

At present the Soviets are deploying at least two new ICBMs which seem designed with capabilities to knock out our Minuteman force. We should initiate a strong program to develop a mobile ICBM capability that is not targetable by Soviet missiles.

The Soviets are conducting very aggressive developments and operations designed to be able to find and, if necessary, destroy our Polaris submarines at sea. We believe they do not have this capability today. But, because through intensive effort they could acquire both, we must initiate much more aggressive basic research and development efforts as well as new operations at sea to be sure we are always at least one step ahead and that their efforts are totally frustrated.

Today, Soviet ballistic missile submarines patrol off our coasts and could attack our bomber bases within minutes. We must acquire a fully integrated ballistic missile early warning capability and a strategic bomber/crew posture to assure the Soviets as well as ourselves that our alert bombers will be launched safely and penetrate to their targets. The introduction of the B-1 bomber and a long-range cruise missile will significantly increase our ability to penetrate Soviet defenses.

Naval Forces

To maintain a reasonable naval balance with the Soviet Union will require that the downward trend in U.S. naval forces be reversed. This will entail a naval construction program of about thirty-five to forty ships per year or about 8 percent of the fleet per year. This will hold the average age of ships in the fleet to about twelve to thirteen years and would overcome the Soviet Union's numerical advantage in major surface combatants in about ten years. It would not overcome the major numerical disparity in submarines presently held by the

Soviet Union. This construction program, in addition to providing for replacement and additions to the present types of ships, should also include:
production of new types of support ships that are capable of operating smaller
contingents of aircraft; production of advanced technology ships, such as the
surface effect ships that ride on a cushion of air; design and production of new
high speed and less vulnerable replenishment ships for support of the fleet—submarine supertankers are a possibility; development of mid-ocean aircraft refueling capabilities to support urgent resupply of friends when enroute bases are not
available; and development of other high technology weapons such as Vertical
Take Off and Landing Aircraft. The naval construction program need not
emphasize nuclear power for all surface ships nor increase the percentage of large
capital ships. Rather, the emphasis should be on larger numbers of heavily armed
small and medium-sized ships.

A naval construction program of this type would be in the direction necessary
to provide the United States with sufficient naval power to meet its worldwide
responsibilities for its own security and commitments to its allies. This assumes,
of course, that the Soviet shipbuilding plans remain consistent with their present
performance and that present overseas bases and facilities remain available for
use by the United States. Should such bases be withdrawn, as they were in the
Middle East War of 1973, and we are forced to support the fleet from bases in
the United States, then the numbers become inadequate for worldwide deployments of the present scale. If the Soviet Union increases the size of its navy, then
the numerical gap would widen and the naval balance could not be maintained
without an expanded effort by the United States.

Land and Air Forces

The total size of the U.S. land and tactical air forces would remain at about their
present numbers. There would be marked improvements, however, in combat
capabilities and in inventories of combat equipment. There would be a
continuing commitment of these forces to NATO, including the stationing of
sizable forces in Europe. The remaining forces based primarily in the United
States, would be structured to increase their mobility for rapid reinforcement of
Europe and to make them more effective for use in crisis situations. Increased
quantities of ammunition and spare parts would be stocked. This would improve
the sustained combat power of our forces and provide a ready pool of supplies
to assist our friends in times of crisis.

Technology

Whatever the outcome of the strategic arms negotiations, the United States must
maintain an active technological development program in strategic warfare areas

and, equally important, an active program supporting new technology in naval, land, and air force weapons systems. To reverse the trends in military technology development, to match the efforts of the Soviet Union and to guard against Soviet secrecy in military technology will require a major change in the trends of present programs. It is impossible to close any gap overnight, but the United States should be able to match the Soviets efforts by 1980. To do this will require expansion of the U.S. military R&D program effort by about 10 percent per year for at least five years and programs to enhance the numbers of entrants into scientific and technical schooling.

Improved Efficiency and Reduction of Waste

A continuing program of cost reduction and improved efficiency is required if the necessary military capabilities are to be provided within the means available. This will require that the emphasis in new weapons purchases be placed on developing less expensive equipment that is capable of doing the job. Bigger is not necessarily better, but it is normally more expensive. The trend toward smaller and less expensive fighter and attack aircraft must be applied to other weapons and support systems as well. Elimination of waste will also require the reduction and closing of marginally useful bases and facilities and the termination of programs that have outlived their military but not their political usefulness. More efficient use of manpower, both military and civilian, will be required and the burgeoning ratio of manpower to military equipment must be reversed.

5. Conclusion

After every war there comes a desire to cut defense spending and to reorient this country's goals toward the social welfare of our citizens. The end of United States involvement in the Vietnam War and the apparent lessening of the tensions of the cold war have led once again to cries for reduced defense spending—which means less defense. The arguments for and against defense spending have recently become so polarized that the real facts and potential outcomes of our choices have become obscured. Neither those who claim that defense spending is a waste of money needed for social programs nor those who claim that social spending is weakening national defense are correct. Nothing can be so conducive to the welfare of our citizens as a strong, secure national defense.

The fact is that for a very minimal percentage of our gross national product, somewhere in the neighborhood of 6 percent, the United States can provide for our national security, while, at the same time, expanding our social and economic programs. In thirty years since World War II, the United States has spent about $1.5 trillion on national security, while we have spent almost the same amount in just the last four years on social, economic, and other governmental programs. This type of performance, despite present temporary economic difficulties, would indicate that our ability over the long term to pay for national security, plus social and economic progress, is indeed well within our nation's capability.

Whether the United States *will* provide for our national security is another matter. In the recent talk about national priorities, socioeconomic and defense needs have been typecast into roles of competitors for available resources. And for several years, percentage-wise at least, this day-to-day setting of priorities has led us to reduce defense spending and to accelerate social programs. But the idea that national defense is being achieved at the cost of social programs is not borne out historically. While defense spending has remained relatively constant, expenditures for social programs have grown by more than 400 percent in the past two decades. In fact, in view of the present trends in the military balance between the United States and the Soviet Union, it is a great disservice to the national interest to maintain that defense detracts from social progress. Also, it is unrealistic for the American people to select a policy of reducing military expenditures and yet expect to retain the military balance, maintain national security, and somehow sleep safely at night.

The critical choices before the American people, simply put, are either to reverse the present losing trend or risk another Pearl Harbor or Korea—or to await some lesser crisis that will galvanize us into restoring the balance—or to fall so far behind Soviet military might that it will not matter much what we do one way or the other. We can lose the capacity to deter the application of Soviet political and military strength in war or short of war—or we can roll up our sleeves and get on with the job of protecting the blessings of freedom. We might even get on better with the Russians—who have always showed a healthy respect for healthy strength and a contempt for people who let things slide.

Notes

1. Information on the nuclear, naval, and land and air programs of the United States, the Soviet Union, and the People's Republic of China are derived from the following sources:

James R. Schlesinger, *Annual Defense Department Report FY 1975*, Report of the Secretary of Defense to the Congress (Washington, D.C., U.S. Government Printing Office, March 4, 1974).

Thomas H. Moorer, Admiral, USN, *United States Military Posture for FY 1975*, Statement by the Chairman of the Joint Chiefs of Staff before the

Defense Appropriations Subcommittee of the House Committee on Appropriations, Washington, D.C., February 26, 1974.

James R. Schlesinger, *Annual Defense Department Report FY 1976 and 197T*, Report of the Secretary of Defense to the Congress, February 5, 1975.

George S. Brown, General, USAF, *United States Military Posture for FY 1976*, Statement by the Chairman of the Joint Chiefs of Staff before the Senate Armed Services Committee, Washington, D.C.

2. C.V. Chester and E.P. Wigner, "Comparative Status of U.S. and Soviet Civil Defense Programs," Unpublished Paper, August 29, 1973. Reprinted with permission. See also, Eugene P. Wigner, "The Myth of 'Assured Destruction'," *Survive, An American Journal of Civil Defense* 4 (July-August 1970). Reprinted with permission.

3. Attributed to Sergei G. Gorshkov, Commander in Chief of the Soviet Navy, by Admiral Elmo R. Zumwalt, Jr., in concluding comments in Admiral Gorshkov's book, *Red Star Rising at Sea* (Annapolis, United States Naval Institute 1974). Reprinted with permission.

4. *Allocation of Resources in the Soviet Union and China*, Hearing before the Subcommittee on Priorities and Economy in Government of the Joint Economic Committee, April 12, 1974.

Index

Index

About the Authors

DR. EDWARD TELLER, distinguished nuclear physicist, is a senior research fellow at the Stanford University Hoover Institution on War, Revolution and Peace. He is professor emeritus at the University of California. Dr. Teller participated in starting the Lawrence Livermore Laboratory in 1952 and served as its director from 1958 to 1960. He is the author of *The Legacy of Hiroshima, The Reluctant Revolutionary* and numerous technical papers.

DR. HANS MARK is director of the NASA Ames Research Center and consulting professor of engineering at Stanford University. He is a former director of the Department of Nuclear Engineering at the University of California at Berkeley and was division leader in experimental physics at the Lawrence Livermore Laboratory. He is the co-author (with N.T. Olson) of *Experiments in Modern Physics* and editor (with S. Fernbach) of *Properties of Matter Under Unusual Conditions.*

DR. JOHN S. FOSTER, JR., is vice president of Energy Research and Development for TRW, Inc. He is a former director of Defense Research and Engineering, Department of Defense; he served on the Air Force and Army Scientific Advisory Panels and was a panel consultant to the President's Science Advisory Committee. He is a former director of the Lawrence Livermore Laboratory and associate director of the University of California at Berkeley. Dr. Foster is a member of the President's Foreign Intelligence Advisory Board.